D1134651

A HISTORY
OF OTTOMAN
LIBRARIES

Ottoman and Turkish Studies
Series Editor
Hakan T. Karateke (University of Chicago)

Other Titles in this Series

Uncoupling Language and Religion: An Exploration into the Margins of Turkish Literature
Laurent Mignon

Excavating Memory: Bilge Karasu's Istanbul and Walter Benjamin's Berlin
Ülker Gökberk

The Ottoman Twilight in the Arab Lands: Turkish Memoirs and Testimonies of the Great War
Selim Deringil

Disliking Others: Loathing, Hostility, and Distrust in Premodern Ottoman Lands
Edited by Hakan T. Karateke, H. Erdem Çıpa and Helga Anetshofer

Waiting for Müteferrika: Glimpses of Ottoman Print Culture
Orlin Sabev

Investigating Turkey: Detective Fiction and Turkish Nationalism, 1928–1945
David Mason

For more information on this series, please visit:
academicstudiespress.com/ottomanandturkishstudies

A HISTORY
OF OTTOMAN
LIBRARIES

İsmail E. Erünsal

BOSTON
2022

Library of Congress Cataloging-in-Publication Data

Names: Erünsal, İsmail E., author.
Title: A history of Ottoman libraries / İsmail E. Erünsal.
Other titles: Ottoman and Turkish studies.
Description: Boston : Academic Studies Press, 2022. | Series: Ottoman and Turkish studies | Includes bibliographical references.
Identifiers: LCCN 2022012103 (print) | LCCN 2022012104 (ebook) | ISBN 9781644698624 (hardback) | ISBN 9781644698631 (adobe pdf) | ISBN 9781644698648 (epub)
Subjects: LCSH: Libraries--Turkey--History. | Library science--Turkey--History.
Classification: LCC Z845.T9 E775 2022 (print) | LCC Z845.T9 (ebook) | DDC 027.0561--dc23/eng/20220412
LC record available at https://lccn.loc.gov/2022012103
LC ebook record available at https://lccn.loc.gov/2022012104

Book design by Lapiz Digital Services.
Cover design by Ivan Grave.

Academic Studies Press
1577 Beacon St.
Brookline, MA 02446, USA
press@academicstudiespress.com
www.academicstudiespress.com

To Dr. Christopher Ferrard

Contents

Acknowledgments

I would like to thank the editors of *Libri* for allowing me to use material that I previously published in those journals. I am also indebted to the staff of the Directorate of Endowments, the Ottoman Archives, the Archives of Court Registers, the Topkapı Palace Archives, and to the librarians of the Süleymaniye Library, the İSAM Library, and the Edinburgh University Library.

I am indebted to my colleague Bilgin Aydın at the Department of Information and Records Management at Marmara University for locating some of the documents in the Ottoman Archives. I would also acknowledge my indebtedness to the late Professor Hakkı Dursun Yıldız. He has been a constant support to me in my academic career and it was he who encouraged me to take the post in the Department of Librarianship at Istanbul University. Without his support, this book would never have been written. I am also grateful to Zeynep Kandur for proofreading the text and offering many valuable suggestions and to Lyzbeth Erduran for her contributions.

Thanks also go to Dr. Christopher Ferrard, to whom this work is also dedicated, for his help in writing the English version of this book and his invaluable advice on making much that was familiar to a Turkish readership more accessible to an English-speaking readership. Without his encouragement and patience, this book would never have been completed. I remain responsible for any errors or failings that the book may have.

İsmail E. Erünsal

Illustrations

Note on Transcription and Dates

The letters of the modern Turkish alphabet are pronounced *approximately* the same as their English equivalents, with the following exceptions:

Letter	English pronunciation
c	*j* as in *jam*
ç	*ch* as in *church*
ğ	lengthens the preceding vowel so that *Ağa* is pronounced a-a
ı	like the *a* in *serial* or the *io* in *cushion*
j	like the *s* as in *measure*
ö	like the German ö
ş	like *sh* in *shop*
ü	like the German ü

Place names are given in the modern form in the country where they are now. Hence, the Ottoman town of Üsküb in today's Macedonia is given as Skopje and the classical city Adrianople is given as Edirne. The exception to this rule is in the case of towns and cities that have an English name, as in Cairo, Mecca, Damascus, or Athens.

I have given all dates according to the Gregorian calendar, except when quoting a source when the Islamic date is given, but I have added the Gregorian equivalent in parentheses afterwards. In the footnotes, books that were published in the nineteenth and early twentieth century bear the Hijri (Islamic) date, which I have left as it is an essential part of the reference. However, to save confusion I have added H to these dates. The reader should be aware that 1250H, for example, is 1834 AD, 1300H is 1883 and 1330H is 1912. In the mid-nineteenth century, a new solar calendar (known as Rumi), based on the Julian calendar but with the Islamic years, was introduced. Towards the end of the Ottoman Empire, it became increasingly common to find the Rumi rather than the Hijri year as the date of publication. It is often not clear whether the year is Hijri or Rumi, unless the month is given. I have therefore presumed all these dates to be Hijri unless a Rumi month is given, in which case I have indicated the year by adding "R"—for example, 1325R.

Preface

As early as the end of the nineteenth century, scholars had entertained the idea of writing histories of Ottoman libraries, but these early attempts did not come to fruition.[1] In the early Republican period (1923–1938), scholars such as Selim Nüzhet Gerçek took a keen interest in the Ottoman library and, although some newspaper articles were written, no serious study of the subject emerged. This gap in Ottoman cultural history may well have gone unnoticed had it not been for the opening of departments of librarianship in Turkish universities in the 1950s. It quickly came to light that there was very little written about Ottoman libraries and certainly no comprehensive study of the subject.

In 1977, after returning to Turkey from Scotland with a PhD in Ottoman literature, I found myself appointed to teach Ottoman language and culture in the Department of Librarianship at Istanbul University. Naturally, I looked for

---

1 Serkis Orpelyan and Abdülzâde Mehmed Tahir had planned a six-volume history of Ottoman sciences entitled *Mahzen-i Ulum*, of which the sixth volume was to be devoted to the history of Ottoman libraries. Only the first volume of this work was published (İstanbul: A. Asaduryan Şirket-i Mürettibiye Matbaası, 1308H). Another scholar, Mahmud Cevad İbnü'ş-Şeyh Nâfi, planned a two-volume history of Turkish educational institutions entitled *Maarif-i Umumiye Nezareti, Tarihçe-i Teşkilatı ve İcraatı* (İstanbul: Matbaa-i Amire, 1338H), of which the second volume was to be devoted to the history of Istanbul libraries. This second volume never appeared.

materials to allow me to teach the history of Ottoman libraries. It was then that I discovered this huge gap in the history of Ottoman institutions. I also noticed that works in English dealing with libraries throughout the world avoided the subject of Ottoman libraries, for the very good reason that there was virtually nothing written about it in Western languages.

Looking through the materials available to me, I noted that the only useful materials were some articles by the late Süheyl Ünver and Müjgan Cunbur. Neither of these scholars studied Ottoman libraries per se, but as they came across documents dealing with libraries, especially foundation deeds or records, they made these materials available to scholars in a number of articles. Although I do not always share the opinions at which they arrived, we should be grateful for their contribution to this field of study.

In the complete absence of secondary sources on the subject, the decision regarding how to go about the task of writing the history of Ottoman libraries was made for me: I would have to look almost exclusively at primary sources, and most of these would be archival materials. Since almost all educational institutions in the period I wished to deal with began as religious foundations, there had to be written foundation deeds. If I could find these, I would be able to make a start on the task I had given myself. When I searched for these deeds in the Archives of the Directorate of Endowments (Vakıflar Genel Müdürlüğü Arşivi-VGMA.), the Ottoman Archives (Başbakanlık Osmanlı Arşivi-BOA), the Archives of Court Registers in Istanbul, Ankara and Bursa (Şer'i Siciller Arşivi-ŞS), the Topkapı Palace Archives (Topkapı Sarayı Arşivi-TSA), and in some libraries, I was able to trace almost four hundred foundation deeds.[2] However, it was clear that while there was much useful material in these deeds they represented the wishes of the various founders and, as noted by Ömer Lûtfi Barkan, were prescriptive and did not reflect how the libraries operated in reality.[3]

To discover how the libraries functioned, I had to search through various account books in the archives, starting with salary accounts and registers of appointments, and then proceeded to the account books and general correspondence. Unfortunately, the materials on libraries were scattered amongst all the other materials in the archives, and the only way to find it was to

---

2 Much of information to emerge from these deeds was repetitive and I have therefore only cited or quoted from the more interesting ones or from deeds that supported an argument.

3 Ömer Lütfi Barkan, "Süleymaniye Camii ve İmareti Tesislerine ait Bir Yıllık Bir Muhasebe Bilançosu 993/994 (1585/1586)," VD 9 (1971): 109-110. Ömer Lütfi Barkan, "Edirne ve Civarındaki Bazı İmaret Te'sislerinin Yıllık Muhasebe Bilançoları," Belgeler 1, no. 2 (1965): 237-239; See also Maya Shatzmiller, "Islamic Institutions and Property Rights: The Case of the Public Waqf," JESHO 44, no. 1 (2001): 48.

sift through the documents looking for small nuggets of information. This task took me over thirty years, by the end of which I had gone through some 250,000 documents.[4]

I looked at other materials as well as the archival sources. On reading the official Ottoman chronicles, I discovered that they invariably seemed to have taken little interest in libraries, and the few instances where they mention the existence of a library would be, for example, on an occasion when the sultan attended an official opening. Travel works were far more promising, because foreign travellers were at pains to describe things of interest they came across on their travels. However, with rare exceptions, such as Toderini and Ubicini, these travellers either stated the obvious or, worse still, were misinformed by their guides. Unless they had something useful to contribute, I have not mentioned these travel works in the notes.

This book is therefore, by necessity, based on archival material which is piecemeal in its nature and scattered throughout the archives. I have tried to organize it to the best of my ability, but if in parts it comes across to the reader as a list of archival entries it is precisely because that is what the book is based on. For this I ask for the reader's indulgence. Throughout my research, I attempted to discover what patterns could be discerned in the development of the Ottoman library network, and in this I hope I can claim some success. I hope too that I have laid to rest some mistaken notions that have held sway among scholars due mainly to the complete lack of serious study on the subject.

This work is divided into two sections. First, I survey the discernible phases through which the history of Ottoman libraries developed. With the earliest libraries, those founded in the fifteenth and sixteenth centuries, I have gone into considerable detail as I believe that given their relative rarity, they may be of interest to the reader. Towards the end of the Ottoman Empire, however, libraries had become relatively commonplace, and I have tended to note their foundation and give only information which makes them unusual. The latter part of the book deals with the various functions of the Ottoman library, such as lending, staffing, budgeting, cataloguing, and so forth, to which I have appended a small chapter on archival materials referring to the architecture and furnishing of the library building. I have written a short introduction intended for the reader who is unfamiliar with the Ottoman college system and the nature of the Islamic book.

---

4 The text of the most interesting of these documents has been published in a two-volume anthology: İsmail E. Erünsal, *Kütüphanecilikle İlgili Metinler ve Belgeler*, 2 vols. (İstanbul: Edebiyat Fakültesi Matbaası, 1982-1990) and in "Tanzimat Sonrası Türk Kütüphaneciliği ile İlgili Belgeler," *The Journal of Ottoman Studies* 31 (2008): 229-339.

Throughout the text I have given the foundation dates of libraries or their foundation deeds whenever they are known. The date following the name of a founder refers to the date of the foundation deed and not to the death of the founder, unless the date is preceded by the letter "d." The dates following the sultans' names are the dates of their reigns. Ottoman personal names and technical terms appear in their modern Turkish form.

I imagined when writing this book that my readership would be scholars interested in the development of libraries throughout the world. For this reason, I have included much material and explanation that I felt would be necessary for any reader unfamiliar with the Ottoman Empire and its institutions. As the first comprehensive monograph on Ottoman libraries, this work will naturally have many defects and no doubt mistakes will have been made. I hope that in the future these deficiencies will be made good and mistakes corrected.

Some of the material in this book has been previously published in a number of articles in journals. I am grateful to these journals for allowing me to reproduce much of the material. Of course, with the passage of time, I have, in many places, reviewed my original findings and some passages have had to be rewritten to incorporate new research.

Introduction

Throughout the period with which this book deals (1299–1923) almost the entire network of religious and cultural institutions of the Muslim community in the Ottoman empire was established by means of charitable foundations. Mosques, schools, colleges, dervish convents, baths, clinics, hospitals and soup kitchens were invariably built as a result of a wealthy Muslim providing for the community by means of a foundation deed. To these charitable institutions we can also add markets, bridges, fountains, and caravanserais. Prominent among the objects of endowment we find collections of books and indeed, at a later date, complete libraries with buildings and large staff of librarians and other personnel.

The founder who wished to direct his charity towards the establishment of an institution did so by means of a foundation deed (*vakfiye*). This foundation deed documented the founder's wishes and described what was to be established. Usually, the founder would donate money to build the institution and at the same time provide sources of income to maintain not only the building, but also to pay for the personnel who would work in the building and other costs involved in running the institution. The foundation deed was an important document because it became the written constitution for the running of the institution and there was no mechanism for changing the terms of this type of document. Furthermore, the deed appointed an administrator (*mütevelli*) of the foundation, whose job it was to ensure that the trust was being properly run in accordance with the will of the founder as stated in the foundation deed. The administrators were responsible to the holders of particular posts in government such as the chief mufti (*şeyhülislam*) or the grand vizier, or a palace official such as the chief eunuch, as the ex officio superintendents of the foundations (*nâzır*). A foundation was in legal theory a donation to God and its provisions therefore immutable. The sole exception to this principle were imperial foundations where succeeding sultans could rearrange their organization and redraft the original deed.

The early Ottomans were a group of nomadic warriors expanding on the fringe of the Byzantine empire in Anatolia in the fourteenth century. As the Ottomans expanded their territory at the expense of the Byzantines, they came to be referred to as warriors of the faith (*gazi*). By the time of Orhan Gazi, the second Ottoman sultan, the Ottomans had captured ancient Byzantine cities which had no Muslim religious and educational institutions; these they had to establish by the means of religious foundations.

The Ottoman state was perilously situated between the Byzantine Empire and the stronger Turkish principalities (*beyliks*) to the south and east. It would certainly not have survived had they not expanded into Europe, where there were no Turkish principalities to rival their power. The Ottomans transferred their capital to Edirne after their conquest of the city and became an expanding European power with no Muslim rivals. Ottoman institutions, such as mosques, schools, colleges (*medrese*), and dervish convents (*tekke*), began to flourish in all the cities and towns where Muslims lived. These institutions were often small, but with the capture of Istanbul in 1453 by Mehmed II, the Conqueror, the Ottomans had acquired a throne city unrivalled in the world. A massive program of buildings was carried out so that the city should become the cultural as well as the physical center of the fast-expanding empire. Mehmed II's grandson, Selim I, expanded the empire over Syria, Egypt, Mesopotamia, and Arabia and ensured its dominant position in the Muslim world, which was to last into the nineteenth century. Selim I's son, Süleyman the Magnificent, expanded the empire in Europe, but more importantly consolidated his father's rapid gains. Süleyman's reign witnessed an immense building program, not least of all the creation of his mosque complex (*külliye*), which was called the Süleymaniye after the sultan himself. This complex of buildings contained the mosque in the center, with several colleges, schools, baths, soup kitchens, mausoleum built around it. It was not only a center of worship, but a center of learning.

During the next 250 years Ottoman cultural institutions continued to flourish throughout the empire. However, this expansion was not mirrored in the military domain. By the beginning of the eighteenth century, the Ottomans had ceased to have a technical advantage over their rivals and the borders of the empire began to contract. By the end of the century, Ottoman statesmen were aware that reform, if only technical and military reform, was a necessity if the survival of the empire was to be assured. However, the reform movement which gathered apace in the nineteenth century acquired a momentum of its own so that the very cultural and educational institutions that they were introduced to defend became increasingly irrelevant as the elite started to adopt Western cultural values. The mosques survived, but the classical educational structure withered and was finally abolished in the twentieth century.

Almost all libraries in the Ottoman empire were founded to service educational institutions. The Ottoman education system was based on the medieval Islamic curriculum. Primary school began with lessons in reading the Koran in the original Arabic and aimed to teach students to read and memorize the Koran and to read basic catechisms. On finishing primary school, students then went through two levels of college which were referred to as the lower and the higher colleges. In the lower colleges, the students started by studying Arabic grammar, rhetoric, logic, theology and jurisprudence. In the higher colleges, jurisprudence, the methodology of jurisprudence, and Koranic exegesis were studied. These subjects were taught at various levels. After Mehmed II (r. 1451–1481) founded his college called *Sahn-ı Seman* (the Eight Courtyards), it became the highest graded college in the empire. His great grandson, Süleyman the Magnificent, was to found a complex of colleges which taught specialized subjects at an even higher level. The curriculum, as defined in Süleyman's reign, continued with virtually no change until the end of the Ottoman empire in early twentieth century.[1]

The lower colleges could be found throughout the empire. The higher colleges, however, would only be established in the larger cities, such as Bursa and Edirne, while the very highest, as we have seen, were imperial foundations situated in Istanbul. The colleges were sometimes graded according to the salary of the teachers. While the salaries were paid monthly or quarterly, they were calculated on a daily basis. The lower colleges employed teachers who were paid perhaps twenty aspers (*akçe*) per day, and these came to be called "twenty-*akçe* colleges." The higher colleges would be referred to as "colleges of fifty" because the teacher would be paid fifty aspers per day. The higher the stipend of the teacher, the higher the status of the college.

---

1   See Halil Inalcık, *The Ottoman Empire: The Classical Age 1300–1600*, translated by Norman Itzkowitz and Colin Imber (London: Praeger Publishers, 1973), 168–169.

The textbooks in the curriculum were fixed and indeed it was the book that was being studied which defined the lesson. The textbooks were in Arabic, as were the plethora of commentaries and supercommentaries on the books. Rarely would a Turkish translation of the Arabic text be available. When libraries were established in a college, the founders would know exactly what books were needed. Books were often bought specifically for a particular college. However, some college collections reflect the taste of the founder who may have had a broader range of interest than was required by a given college.

We should keep in mind that in Ottoman the word for library (*kütübhane*) can mean library in our sense of the word, that is, a room or building dedicated to the storage or reading of books; but it can also have a broader meaning and cover any collection of books, be it a single bookcase or even a shelf of books. When a library was endowed to an institution, especially in the early Ottoman period, it may have been merely one or two shelves of essential books which were kept in a cabinet somewhere in a college or mosque. Access to the cabinet would have been restricted. As time passed, larger collections were endowed and may have required a special room for storage. The independent Ottoman library of the seventeenth century used the concept of a library in the present sense of the word: a reading room with storage facilities for the books and various members of staff to service it. As we would expect, the larger the collection the broader the number of subjects included, often beyond the immediate needs of the college curricula.

The collections in the libraries in the period under discussion were almost exclusively manuscripts. Books in Ottoman Turkish were printed only after the early eighteenth century and merely seventeen titles appeared in the first phase of the printing press between 1729 and 1742. These were not the type of books required by college students and teachers, so very few printed books entered the foundation libraries. The printing of books in Ottoman Turkish came to a halt for a brief period only to be revived at the end of the eighteenth century. Again, the printed works tended to be dictionaries, histories, and geographical works, as well as translations of Western scientific books, rather than college textbooks. These rarely made it onto the libraries' shelves. By the middle of the nineteenth century, book publishers began to print college textbooks, but the libraries had no funds set aside to implement an active acquisition policy, as they still depended on donations. Founders of libraries after the 1850s might have acquired and subsequently endowed printed books within their collections, but generally the printed book remained a rarity in foundation libraries.

As the textbooks of the Ottoman college libraries were exclusively in manuscript form, it was sometimes difficult for students to find a particular or rare text. They would not usually have the necessary funds to buy books, so they had to use one of many copies available in a library. They could either commit the text to memory or make a copy of it from an existent library copy. The very process of copying was an aid to the memorization of a text. These student copies were often of poor quality, written on inferior quality paper of varying sizes, usually not properly bound and often casually annotated. Only rarely would these student copies find their way into a library. Library books were usually copied by students or scholars intending to copy a book which would be used by others. The paper would be of high quality, properly sized, with uniform lines and wide margins and written in uniformly numbered fascicles. Professional copyists would sometimes be employed to copy a college text, when there was a special demand for it, or literary, historical, and philosophical works which were not used as textbooks in the colleges. Literary works which were mainly poetry required a copyist who could write in a special *talik* script in which poetry was frequently written.

Ottoman manuscript production can be viewed as a part of a longer Islamic manuscript tradition. By the fourteenth century, the practice of giving a book a title page with the title of the book and the author's name had ceased. There were often one or more blank fly leaves before the first folio. Folio 1ᵃ (1 recto) was usually blank with the text beginning on folio 1ᵇ (1 verso) which was frequently decorated. On this page, the title of the work and sometimes the author's name was recorded, either at the top of the page or in the text of the introduction to the work, which could extend for several folios. This was not invariably the case: in some works, there was neither mention of the title or the author. The owner of a book would sometimes identify the title and author of a work on the flyleaf. The accuracy of this identification could not always be relied upon. This casual practice of putting down the (occasionally incorrect) title of the works created problems for librarians.[2]

Another problem for librarians was that books were often referred to by several different names. The author would usually give his work a poetic and rhymed title which would allude to the content of the work. The famous bibliographical work by Katib Çelebi, for instance, is entitled *Keşfü'z-Zünûn an Esamii'l-Kütübi ve'l-Fünûn*, which means "The Removal of Doubts about the Names of the Books and Sciences." In practice, this title was shortened to simply *Keşfü'z-Zünûn* [The Removal of Doubts]. Even shortened titles such as the *Miftâhu'l-Ulûm* [The Key to the Sciences] was further shortened to *Miftâh* [The Key]. As there were several books beginning with the word *Miftâh*, confusion

---

2 For this problem see: İsmail E. Erünsal, "Yazma Eserlerin Kataloglanmasında Karşılaşılan Güçlükler 1: Eser ve Müellif Adının Tesbiti," in *Hakkı Dursun Yıldız Armağanı* (Ankara: Türk Tarih Kurumu Basımevi, 1995), 233–243

was bound to arise. Famous works often acquired other, commonly used titles. The great scholar Nasreddin Ebu Said Abdullah b. Ömer b. Mehmed el-Beyzavi was generally referred to as Beyzavi, and his commentary, the *Envârü't-Tenzîl ve Esrarü't-Te'vîl* [The Lights of Revelation and the Secrets of Interpretation] was simply referred to as *Tefsir-i Kadî* [The Judge's Commentary] because the author was famous as a judge. The names of the authors themselves were often found in different forms due to authors being known by several names, adjectives, and attributes.

All these problems meant that the librarian was required to have wide bibliographical knowledge, and even then, he was bound to come across books which were difficult to identify. The compilation of a classified catalogue could become a nightmare with the daunting task of identifying works compounded by having to decide in which category a work should best be placed.

Another difficulty for librarians in cataloguing and classifying books was the Ottoman practice of binding smaller treatises together into a *mecmua*, a collection of several works. These works were occasionally on the same subject, but often they were not. Given that the practice of cross-referencing did not exist, the librarian had to make an arbitrary decision as to the classification under which a single volume of disparate essays should be placed. He could place it, for example, under the classification of the first essay in the collection, or under that of the longest essay, and so on. As there was no uniform practice, each librarian adopted his own method, or sometimes none at all.

A further problem for the librarian was the fact that it was not the custom to identify the title of the work on the binding. In Islamic libraries, books were laid flat on shelves, and identified by writing the title of the work on the bottom or top edge. If the collection was large, the librarian often had difficulty finding a particular work. If the catalogue he was using did not have a shelf number, as was usually the case before the nineteenth century, he would have to check out a number of works before finding the volume that was required.

As cataloguing and locating Ottoman books demanded a high degree of knowledge, librarians were often college teachers, or at least very competent students, employed on a part-time basis. Even when independent libraries were established with full-time librarians, the posts were given to scholars. The danger of employing a scholar in a library is obvious. The inclination to treat the library as his own personal collection, spend his time reading, and reluctance to perform the more mundane duties of a librarian may have impeded the development of the profession.

Part 1

HISTORICAL DEVELOPMENT

Figure 1. "Turkish books," as depicted in Mouradgea D'ohsson, *Tableau général de l'Empire Othoman*, vol. 1 (Paris: Imprimerie de monsieur [Firmin Didot], 1787).

Chapter One

Early Ottoman Libraries
(1299–1453)

Before the conquest of Istanbul in 1453, the fledgling Ottoman state had already established itself in several towns and cities in Anatolia and the Balkans. As soon as they had consolidated their political control over a region, the Ottomans built mosques and colleges, some of which have survived to the present day. However, due to lack of any supporting evidence, historians could, in prior studies, only assume that some of these colleges and mosques had been endowed with libraries. In this chapter we will examine all the available evidence for the existence of these early Ottoman libraries.

The political events and chronology of the reign of Osman Gazi (d. 1324), the founder of the Ottoman dynasty, are far from clear, let alone the cultural history of the period. There is no evidence for, or indeed mention of, any cultural institution founded in his reign. As Paul Wittek (d. 1978) pointed out, the early Ottoman state was essentially a *beylik*, a small polity ruled by an insignificant potentate, established precariously on the Byzantine border, and principally engaged in a holy war against the Byzantine Empire.[1] It is probable that Osman Gazi's reign, which was entirely taken up by raids, battles, and the expansion of the fledgling state, witnessed no significant cultural development. In a small

---

1 P. Wittek, "Ankara Bozgunundan İstanbulun Zaptına" [translated by Halil İnalcık], *Belleten* 7, no. 27 (1943): 559.

principality, such as that ruled by Osman Gazi, the continual state of war produced conditions which were not naturally conducive to the establishment of institutions of education. Another factor which prevented cultural development was the lack of any common cultural or religious heritage in the territories they conquered from the Byzantines.[2]

The famous Ottoman biography of scholars and Sufi masters, the *Şakaik-i Nu'maniyye*, which is classified by the reigns of the sultans, lists only two scholars for the reign of Osman Gazi, which would suggest that a scholarly class had yet to be established. Without scholars and scholarly institutions, one would hardly expect to find libraries or even collections of books; indeed, we have evidence suggesting that Osman Gazi himself possessed no books.[3]

With the death of Osman Gazi, his son, Orhan (r. 1324–1360), was to consolidate his father's conquest and continue to expand the borders of his state successfully. This created an environment of confidence in the prospects of the Ottoman principality which attracted not only *gazis* who had already arrived during Osman Gazi's reign, but also scholars such as Mevlana Sinan and Kara Alaaddin. Some years later, with the conquest of İznik (Nicea), the first Ottoman college was established (1331), and Davud-ı Kayseri was invited to be its principal teacher.[4]

We may assume that in this college, books were available for use by teachers and students, but without specific information, we cannot talk of a library room, or even a book cabinet. It has not been possible to support with evidence this claim that Orhan Gazi founded libraries in various institutions in Bursa, İzmit, and İznik.[5] The extant foundation deeds and account books for these institutions make no reference to a library or a librarian, nor is there any mention of libraries or librarians in any of the extant records for the institutions in Bursa and İznik during the reign of Orhan.[6] Scholars have naturally assumed that these Ottoman institutions would have been endowed with books just as they were in many

---

2 It may be noted that Islamic cultural activities developed rapidly in the Ottoman state only after it had annexed other Islamic territories, principally the Germiyan *beylik*, which itself had already developed an Islamic cultural infrastructure.

3 The Ottoman historian, Neşrî, gives a list of his effects when he died. This list includes such humble items as a salt cellar, a cutlery box, a herd of sheep, etc., but no books. *Kitab-ı Cihannüma* I, ed. Faik Reşit Unat and Mehmed A. Köymen (Ankara: Türk Tarih Kurumu Basımevi, 1949), 147. The image of Osman Gazi offered by the list is that of a simple man leading a simple life.

4 Wittek, "Ankara Bozgunundan İstanbulun Zaptına": 166.

5 İsmet Parmaksızoğlu, "Türk Kütüphanelerinde Gelişmeler," *TKDB* 12, no. 2 (1974): 88.

6 E. H. Ayverdi reconstructed a floor for the college built by Süleyman Paşa, Orhan Gazi's son, in Yenişehir, on the plan of which he indicated a room set aside as a library; see *Osmanlı Mimarisinin İlk Devri* (İstanbul: İstanbul Fetih Cemiyeti, 1966), 207–208. However, as no

colleges and mosques in other Islamic lands. However, we ought to bear in mind that as the Ottomans were conquering areas which had never been under the rule of Muslims. They had to bring scholars in from other areas and book production would have only just begun. In view of this lack of educational infrastructure it is not surprising that we have no mention of libraries at this early stage.

The reign of Murad I (1360–1389) witnessed several significant developments. With the conquest of Edirne, the Ottomans had proven themselves established enough in European soil to encourage scholars to migrate into Ottoman territories. The growing Ottoman state attracted further waves of scholars together with their books. Ottoman scholars for their part travelled to the long-established Islamic cultural centers to increase their knowledge; for example, Mevlana Musa b. Mahmud travelled to Khorasan and Transoxiana, while Molla Fenarî went to Egypt.[7] As a result of these scholarly relations with established Islamic centers and the influx of scholars, it is likely that books began to come into the Ottoman dominions in significant quantities. The Şakaik-i Nu'maniyye notes that Molla Fenarî left behind ten thousand volumes on his death.[8] Although this figure should be treated with caution, it nevertheless suggests that books were becoming increasingly available.

The Ottoman scholars themselves began, in this period, to write books and commentaries on the established classics of Islamic scholarship. At the same time, their students began to copy the books which had been chosen as the class texts. Despite the increase in books there is still no evidence to suggest that libraries were established in the reign of Murad I. We must assume that books were made available to the students on an informal basis out of the private collections of the teachers. The Şakaik-i Nu'maniyye, recounts that students of this period, wanting to read Sa'deddîn Teftazanî's works, were unable to buy copies. Molla Fenarî therefore increased the college holidays from two to three days a week to allow students more free time in which to copy texts.[9]

During the reign of Bayezid I (1389–1402), the Ottomans not only established themselves firmly in the Balkans but also annexed most of the remaining small independent Turkish states in Anatolia. This gave Ottoman scholars and educational institutions access to the private collections and book markets which could be found in centers of Islamic culture, such as Kütahya, Manisa, and Kastamonu. At the same time, the older Ottoman cities of Bursa

---

reference to a library can be found either in the account books of this college (BOA, MAD, 626, 29–30) or in other sources, we must assume that the library belonged to a later period.

7   Şakaik, 14 and 23.
8   Ibid., 25.
9   Ibid., 27–28.

and Edirne began to acquire dominant positions as the new centers of Islamic scholarship in Anatolia and Europe, and consequently they attracted scholars who had previously taught in the older centers of Anatolia. During Bayezid I's reign, the Ottoman state also began to produce its own scholars in significant quantities. Of the nineteen scholars during the reign of Bayezid I, whose origins are given in the Şakaik-i Nu'maniyye, eleven were educated within the Ottoman territories and eight were immigrants.[10] To the five colleges which had been established in Bursa before the reign of Bayezid I, the following colleges were added in his reign: Ali Pasha, Ebu İshak, Gülçiçek Hatun, Eyne Bey, Eyne Bey Sübaşı, Ferhadiyye, Molla Fenarî, Vaiziyye, and Yıldırım.[11] In the college of Eyne Sübaşı, there was an upper room set aside for books.[12] Unfortunately, the deeds for this college have not survived and consequently we have no information on its organization or collection. It is very likely that other colleges also had libraries, but it is difficult to find any reference to them as their foundation deeds and all other relevant documents were probably destroyed during the period of the invasion and occupation (1402) led by Timur Leng.

Apart from Bursa, other cities were also endowed with colleges during Bayezid I's reign.[13] In one of these, Eyne Bey Sübaşı College in Balıkesir, a library was established and a librarian appointed.[14] Another college to be furnished with a collection was Bayezid I's own foundation in the city of Bolu. Although there is no mention of a librarian being on the staff,[15] there is conclusive evidence that Bayezid established a library in this college.[16]

With the defeat of Bayezid I by Timur Leng in 1402, the Ottoman presence in Anatolia was weakened considerably and a period of civil war, which lasted for eleven years, began. During this interregnum, the Ottomans spent most of their efforts on consolidating their political position, leaving little time for the expansion of their educational infrastructure. With the emergence of Mehmed I as the undisputed ruler of the Ottoman state, we see the establishment of some more colleges, but in only one of these do we have evidence of a library: in the college built by Sultan Mehmed at Merzifon, a bookbinder was appointed,[17] suggesting the existence of a library.

---

10 Ibid., 22–58.
11 Mustafa Bilge, İlk Osmanlı Medreseleri (İstanbul: Edebiyat Fakültesi Basımevi, 1984), 102–115.
12 Ayverdi, Osmanlı Mimarisinin İlk Devri, 444.
13 Bilge, İlk Osmanlı Medreseleri, 161–207.
14 BOA, Ruus 64, 295.
15 Ayverdi, Osmanlı Mimarisinin İlk Devri, 381.
16 Documents to this effect are in the private collection of Turgut Kut.
17 Belediye Library (now Atatürk Library), Mc. O. 70, 335.

On the death of Mehmed I, Murad II inherited a state which enjoyed political unity, and the Ottomans began to enjoy a period of cultural resurgence, especially after the relocation of the capital to Edirne in Europe.[18] Murad II was a patron of scholars and poets, and it is claimed by Latîfî, the famous biographer of poets, that he spent two days a week in their company.[19] As a result, many books were written in this period, most of which were dedicated to him.[20]

In 1430, Murad II built Darü'l-Hadis College in Edirne on the banks of the Tunca river.[21] In the deed for this college, drawn up on 24 March 1435, it is stated that the sultan endowed books for the benefit of the students and teachers of the college.[22] Although the deed makes no mention of a librarian, we observe from an account book for the years January 1489 to June 1491 that a certain Sinan was paid two aspers daily to act as a librarian, the money coming from the surplus funds for that period.[23] This would suggest that as no post of librarian was envisaged in the deed, the shortcoming was made up on an ad hoc basis by paying a person out of surplus revenues of the foundation. According to the deed, this library was open to students and teachers of the college.[24] As all of the seventy-one volumes were in Arabic, the language of scholarship, it is unlikely that there would have been much demand for access to the library by the lay community.

Murad II also founded the Saatli Medrese in Edirne, which was to become the most important Ottoman college of its day, and maintained its reputation as the leading institution of higher education up to the time of the foundation of the *Sahn-ı Seman* College in 1470 by Mehmed II in Istanbul.[25] Although the deeds are not extant, we can see from some later documents that a librarian had been appointed at a daily stipend of two aspers.[26] According to a record dated 1586, when the administration of the college was amalgamated with that of the Darü'l-Hadis College mentioned above, the posts of the librarians were reorganized so

---

18 Stanford J. Shaw, *History of the Ottoman Empire and Modern Turkey*, vol. 1 (Cambridge: Cambridge University Press, 1976), 142.

19 Latîfî, *Tezkiretü'ş-Şu'ara ve Tabsıratü'n-Nuzama*, ed. Rıdvan Canım (Ankara: Atatürk Kültür Merkezi Başkanlığı, 2000), 138.

20 Uzunçarşılı gives a list of these books in *Osmanlı Tarihi*, vol. 1 (Ankara: Türk Tarih Kurumu Basımevi, 1972), 539–542.

21 Mustafa Bilge, *İlk Osmanlı Medreseleri*, 140.

22 TSA, D. 7081.

23 Belediye Library (now Atatürk Library), Mc. O. 91, 263 and 270.

24 TSA, D. 7081.

25 Şahabettin Tekindağ, "Medrese Dönemi," *Cumhuriyetin 50. Yılında İstanbul Üniversitesi* (1979): 11–12.

26 Ömer L. Barkan, "Edirne ve Civarındaki Bazı İmaret Tesislerinin Yıllık Muhasebe Bilançoları," *Belgeler* 1, no. 2 (1965): 322.

that in the amalgamated structure of the colleges, one of the librarian's posts was made into that of assistant librarian.[27]

Two further libraries were established in Edirne during the reign of Murad II. The first, a mosque library, founded by Gazi Mihal Bey in 1422, is known to us through a reference to the appointment of a librarian to this mosque.[28] The second, also a mosque library, was founded by Fazlullah Pasha, who appointed a librarian to it with a stipend of three aspers daily.[29] Libraries were also established outside Edirne during the reign of Murad II. In Skopje, a library was founded in the college of İshak Bey, the first Ottoman library to be established in what is present day north Macedonia.[30] One of Murad II's viziers, Saruca Pasha, founded a college in Gelibolu (1443) and endowed it with eighteen books. The foundation deed of the college makes no provision for a librarian.[31]

The best documented library in this period is that founded by Umur Bey, son of Kara Timurtaş Pasha, who endowed some textbooks to his college in Bergama and several Turkish books to his mosque in Bursa. Deeds drawn up in different years by him for endowments in Bursa, Bergama, and Biga are available to us. According to the earliest deed prepared in April of 1440, Umur Bey donated some Arabic textbooks to the college, which he had founded in Bergama, for the use of students and teachers, and thirty-three volumes of Turkish books to the mosque he had built in Bursa, to be used by the congregation.[32] In his endowment deed, he divides the books into two categories: Arabic books which were destined for the college where they would be used as texts and Turkish books which were to be sent to the mosque where they were to be available for the commoners who had little or no knowledge of Arabic or Persian. In this deed, we find that the books are endowed on the condition that they may not be taken out of the college or mosque.[33] For the safekeeping of the Turkish books he provided a salary of one asper per day for the muezzin of the mosque, who was placed in charge of the collection.[34]

---

27 BOA, MAD, 5455, 18.

28 BOA, Ruus 64, 145.

29 BOA, Ruus 13.

30 Hasan Kaleşi, "Yugoslavyada İlk Türk Kütüphaneleri," *Türk Kültürü* 5, no. 38 (1965): 169; Hasan Kaleşi, *Najstariji vakufski dokumenti u Jugoslaviji na arapskom jeziku* (Priština: Zajednica naučnih ustanova Kosova, 1972), 89–109.

31 M. Tayyib Gökbilgin, *XV-XVI. Asırlarda Edirne ve Paşa Livası* (İstanbul: Üçler Basımevi, 1952), 248–252.

32 VGMA, no. 591, 181.

33 Ibid.

34 Bursa Eski Eserler Library, Ulu Cami Section, No. 436, f. 329a-b.

Umur Bey later changed his mind and allowed his books to be borrowed. In a deed record written in Arabic in 1449, he made the deposit of a pledge, a condition of borrowing, and emphasized that his books should remain within the city of Bursa.[35] A further document concerning his books can be found on the last folio of a commentary entitled *Enfesü'l-Cevahir,* one of the books he had endowed. In this document he lists the names of "sixty volumes of books" and places the following conditions on their keeping, borrowing, and control:

> It is furthermore a condition that these books should be placed in his ancestral foundation and whosoever be şeyh of the foundation should be the supervisor and keep the books. Students and reciters of the Koran and others should benefit from these books at ease, and the learned people who are not associated with this foundation should not benefit from the books unless they provide a reliable guarantor. If any such person uses the books without providing a guarantor, he should be cursed both in this world and the next, and his use of any book should be interdicted. And it is also a condition that as long as [Umur Bey] lives he should be able to use his books both while on campaign and while in residence. Whosoever be the şeyh of the foundation should check the books every six months.[36]

In this document, Umur Bey seems to have changed his original deposition, removed the books from his own mosque, placed them in his father's mosque and appointed the şeyh of the foundation as guardian of the collection.

In the last of the endowment deeds prepared by Umur Bey in 1454 all the endowments are codified in their final form.[37] Of the two copies of this endowment deed, one is inscribed in stone on both sides of the main doorway to his mosque.[38] The inscription placed in 1455 represents a Turkish translation of part of the deed, the original having been prepared in Arabic four months previously.

---

35 Bursa Eski Eserler Library, Ulu Cami Section, No. 435 f. 1a.
36 Ibid.
37 A recent article by Tim Stanley gives list of books in this foundation deed: "The Books of Umur Bey," *Muqarnas* 21 (2004): 323–331.
38 The transcription of the stone inscription can be found in several publications, the best version being in Ayverdi's book *Osmanlı Mimarisinde Çelebi Mehmed ve II. Sultan Murad Devri* (İstanbul: İstanbul Fetih Cemiyeti, 1972), 339–340.

In these two versions of Umur Bey's codification, we find his final instruction for the care of the books. In the complete Arabic version[39] Umur Bey states that the books, the titles of which are to be found on the obverse of the scroll, were for the benefit of all who could read and thereby profit from them. The administrator who was to be the guardian of the books was charged with distributing and collecting them.[40]

In the Arabic version, no provision is made for housing the collection which now numbered some three hundred volumes.[41] The Turkish inscription, however, adds the following condition which tells us where the books were to be kept: "I have detailed and endowed my books. They should not be taken from the mosque."[42]

From the examination of these four documents spanning two decades, we see Umur Bey changing the arrangements for the care of his books several times and we can note a significant increase in the size of the collection. In fact, the number of the books probably continued to increase after 1454, the date of the last document, for we have a book endowed by Umur Bey in 1456.[43]

The reason for the changes in the conditions placed on the lending, guardianship, and housing of the collection probably stems from the fact that at this period of Ottoman history there was little precedent for founding libraries on which Umur Bey could rely.

The libraries of this period were invariably endowed to colleges and mosques with the sole exception of the library at the tomb of Yazıcıoğlu Mehmed Efendi, the famous mystic poet buried in Gelibolu. We know little about this library, save that it was the first Ottoman library to be built at a shrine, and that it contained the works of Yazıcıoğlu Mehmed Efendi (including one autograph). Telhisîzade Mustafa Efendi, a judge, on his way to Manisa, visited the tomb in 1712 and noted the following in his diary:

> Sunday, beginning of the month of Ramazan 1124 [October 1712]. Anchored at Gelibolu. I left the ship and visited the tomb of Yazıcıoğlu Mehmed Efendi. I offered up a prayer at his tomb

---

39 The complete Arabic scroll, now in the Belediye Library (now Atatürk Library) in Istanbul (No. 38), measures 5.15 m in length by 27 cm. width. It bears the signature of the judge of Bursa, Molla Hüsrev.

40 Belediye Library, Mc. 38.

41 Ibid.

42 Ayverdi, Osmanlı Mimarisinde Çelebi Mehmed ve II. Sultan Murad Devri, 339.

43 Murat Yüksel, "Kara Timurtaşoğlu Umur Bey'in Bursa'da Vakfettiği Kitaplar ve Vakıf Kayıtları," Türk Dünyası Araştırmaları 31 (1984): 143.

and saw the autograph manuscript of his work which is very famous.[44]

A document from a later period indicates that the librarian at Yazıcıoğlu's tomb was unsalaried.[45]

Two further libraries established in this period are mentioned by Osman Nuri Peremeci, who, writing at the beginning of the twentieth century, claimed that Murad II and Şahabeddin Pasha founded libraries in Plovdiv.[46] However, there is no documentary evidence to support this assertion, which should therefore be treated with caution.

Thus, we see that the salient characteristics of the medieval Ottoman library was that it contained a small collection, and sometimes did not have a librarian appointed for its custody. When librarians were appointed, it was usually on a part-time basis and they were, therefore, poorly paid, the work often being carried out by the existing staff of the institution, usually a mosque or college, to which the library had been endowed.

In sum, the middle part of the fourteenth century witnessed a slow Ottoman expansion into Christian territories where there had been no tradition of Islamic book production. It is only towards the end of the century that we can confidently talk about an Ottoman library as such. The beginning of the fifteenth century saw little development due to the civil strife following the Ottoman defeat in 1402 by Timur's forces at the Battle of Ankara. During the second quarter of the fifteenth century the momentum behind the establishment of colleges, mosques, and libraries increased rapidly so that the Ottoman state was poised, on the eve of the conquest of Istanbul in 1453, for an explosion in the development of its cultural institutions.

With the conquest of Istanbul by Murad II's son, Mehmed II, the Ottoman state came of age and acquired a city fit for the endowment of numerous colleges and libraries. The conquest marked the end of the first stage in the history of Ottoman cultural institutions, a stage which witnessed its development from a fledgling Turkish principality in Anatolia to an empire straddling two continents with its capital in the ancient city of Constantinople.

---

44 BOA, Kepeci 7500, 32.

45 BOA, Cevdet-Maarif 5043.

46 Peremeci, *Tuna Boyu Tarihi* (İstanbul: Resimli Ay Matbaası, 1942), 191; Mihaila Stajnova, *Osmanskite biblioteki v bulgarskite zemi XV-XIX vek. Studii* (Sofia: NBKM, 1982), 154–156 and 178.

Chapter Two

From College and Mosque Libraries to the Independent Library (1453–1650s)

With the conquest of Istanbul in 1453, Mehmed II acquired a city which truly befitted a mighty empire. This spurred him on to establish institutions appropriate for the capital of a reinvigorated expanding Ottoman state.

The city which Mehmed II acquired was in a ruinous state.[1] He set about rebuilding the city by adopting various strategies. The first of these was the repopulation of the city with Muslim settlers.[2] The existing Greek and Armenian population were organized into distinct minorities with their own laws under the leadership of their respective patriarchs. As for the Muslim population, Mehmed II had to create a complete infrastructure of institutions where none had existed before. He did this by taking over existing churches and monasteries and turning them into mosques and colleges.[3] For example, the monastic cells in the Pantocrator Monastery became the Zeyrek College, with Molla Zeyrek as

---

1   Halil İnalcık, "The Policy of Mehmed II towards the Greek Population of Istanbul and Byzantine Buildings of the City," *Dumbarton Oaks Papers*, 23–24 (1968–1969): 231- 233.
2   This is explained in the foundation deed of Mehmed II: "No impediment was placed in the way of those subjects from Anatolia and Rumeli who wished to remain in the city, moreover a decree was sent out to the effect that artisans and craftsmen should be sent together with their families to the capital and in this way was the aforementioned city rebuilt. Couplet: Thus was accomplished the building of a city. Thus was gladdened the hearts of the subjects." *Mehmed II. Vakfiyeleri* (Ankara: Vakıflar Umum Müdürlüğü Neşriyatı, 1938), facsimile, 36.
3   Ş. Tekindağ, "İstanbul; Şehrin İmar ve İskanı," *İA* 5, no. 2 (1993): 1205.

its first professor with a salary of fifty aspers per day. Shortly afterward teaching began at Ayasofya (Hagia Sophia).[4] Naturally, books were donated to these institutions for the use of teachers and students.

There also began a vast program of mosque and college building throughout the city.[5] The most ambitious of these projects was the building of Mehmed II's own complex of a mosque and associated colleges and institutions. In the foundation deed of this complex, we see that while the capture of the city was termed the minor holy war (*cihad-ı asgar*), the rebuilding of the city was referred to as the major holy war (*cihad-ı ekber*).[6]

The historian, Kritovolous, tells us that it was not only Mehmed II who endowed religious institutions. He encouraged his statesmen to do likewise:

> Then he called together all the wealthy and most able persons into his presence, those who enjoyed great wealth and prosperity and ordered them to build grand houses in the city, wherever each chose to build. He also commanded them to build baths and caravanserais and marketplaces, and very many and very beautiful workshops, to erect places of worship, and to adorn and embellish the city with many other such buildings, sparing no expense as each man had the means and the ability.[7]

With the new sense of permanency that the conquest of Istanbul afforded the Ottoman state, it was natural that the palace, the administrative center of the empire, should be built in the center of the city in what is now called Beyazıt. It was very shortly afterwards relocated to the site of the present Topkapı Palace. The palace library was established there and books were brought from Edirne, the previous capital, to the new palace.[8] Apart from the Islamic books which formed the core of the palace library there were some non-Islamic books in a variety of languages including Greek, Latin, Armenian, Syriac, Italian, and Hebrew. In a list prepared in the sixteenth century, we have the titles of about

---

4 *Şaka'ik*, 74 and 71.
5 For Mehmed II's efforts to establish Istanbul as a center of learning and as a capital fit for a world power as reflected in Western sources see: Theoharis Stavrides, *The Sultan of Vezirs: The Life and Time of the Ottoman Grand Vezir Mahmud Paşa Angelović (1453–1474)* (Leiden: E. J. Brill, 2001), 20–28 and footnote 6.
6 *Mehmed II Vakfiyeleri* (Ankara: Vakıflar Umum Müdürlüğü Neşriyatı, 1938), facsimile, 37.
7 Kritovoulos, *History of Mehmed II*, translated from the Greek by Charles T. Riggs (Princeton: Princeton University Press, 1954), 140.
8 İsmail Baykal, "Fatih Sultan Mehmed'in Hususi Kütüphanesi ve Kitapları," *VD* 4 (1958): 77.

120 of these books.[9] The existence of Greek books in the palace library gave rise to legends of undiscovered ancient classics surviving from the earliest periods of the Byzantine empire.[10] The truth is far more mundane. Most of these books were of the religious nature and of little scholarly value. This did not deter Western ambassadors from attempting to obtain and purchase books from the library by bribing Ottoman officials.

To this library was appointed the leading scholar of the age, Molla Lütfi, who was charged with looking after the books. An interesting anecdote in Sehi's *Biography of the Poets* records an exchange between Molla Lütfi and Mehmed II which took place in the library:

> It is related that one day Sultan Mehmed came to the library for he wanted to read a book. To Molla Lütfi he said, 'bring down that book.' The book was in a high place beyond the reach of Molla Lütfi. But there happened to be a block of marble stone on the library floor upon which Molla Lütfi attempted to stand in order to reach the book. The late Sultan Mehmed prevented him from stepping on the stone, maintaining that this was the very block of stone upon which Jesus the Prophet had been born. Molla Lütfi kept his peace and somehow produced the book for the sultan. Later on, he found in a corner of the library a dust cloth, moth-eaten, threadbare and extremely dirty. This cloth he took with great care and respect and placed on the sultan's lap as he was reading. The sultan was annoyed and asked the reason for the Molla's behaviour to which the Molla replied: "why do you get angry, your Majesty, why, this is the very cloth in which Jesus the Prophet was swaddled after his birth."[11]

---

9   Speros Vryonis, "Byzantine Constantinople and Ottoman Istanbul," *The Ottoman City and Its Parts, Urban Structure and Social Order,* ed. Irene A. Bierman and Rifa'at A. Abou-El-Haj (New York: A. D. Caratzas, 1991), 37–40. Not all these 120 volumes were taken during the conquest of the city. Some were the result of a policy of purchasing books. We see in a document in the Dubrovnik Archives, Mehmed II thanking his grand vizier, Mahmud Pasha, for purchasing three titles from Italy and making a request for a further title. See: Ciro Truhelka, "Dubrovnik Arşivinde Türk-İslam Vesikaları," *İstanbul Enstitüsü Dergisi* 1 (1955): 51–52.
10 Emil Jacobs, *Untersuchungen zur Geschichte der Bibliothek im Serai zu Konstantinopel,* (Heidelberg: C. Winter, 1919).
11 The original Turkish version is in *Heşt Behişt,* ed. Günay Kut (Cambridge, MA: Harvard University Press, 1978), f. 40a–b.

It is accepted that the first Ottoman library to be established in Istanbul after its conquest was the palace library, but there are a number of differing opinions as to which was the first foundation library. The foundation libraries in Mahmud Pasha College (1474) and in the Eyüb Complex (1459) are both claimed to be the first foundation library in Istanbul by difference sources and historians.[12] However, a foundation deed indicates that a Sufi master by the name of Visali founded a dervish convent by the walls of the city at At İskelesi and donated to this institution a library of twenty books, mainly on mysticism, in 1454, but naturally it was not felt necessary to appoint a librarian for such a small collection.[13]

The library in the Eyüb Complex is, however, one of the earliest. In the foundation deed of this complex, there is provision for a librarian with a salary of one asper per day.[14] In an account book for the years 1489–1491, we find a scholar, by the name of Fakih, holding the post of librarian and receiving one asper per day.[15] Mehmed Pasha donated two books in February of 1480 and on the condition that they should be carefully checked on return to prevent fraud by substitution. He further stipulated that the books should not be transferred to another institution and that the books were not to be lent out for more than three months and never to the same person a second time.[16]

When Mehmed II completed his own complex in 1470 after eight years of intensive building, as might be expected he endowed his colleges with books.[17] Scholars have been misled by the scanty source material into believing that there were a number of libraries in the complex. Süheyl Ünver wrote that there were several libraries, the first in the mosque itself, the second in a separate building attached to the *Sahn-ı Seman* Colleges, while others were situated in the colleges

---

12 For differing opinions about this see *TKT*, 17.

13 VGMA, No. 625, 141. This document is published by the author: İsmail E. Erünsal, "Fetihten Sonra İstanbul'da Kurulan İlk Vakıf Kütüphanesi ve Vakfiyesi," *Prof. Dr. Mübahat S. Kütükoğlu'na Armağan*, ed. Zeynep Tarım Ertuğ (İstanbul: İstanbul Üniversitesi Edebiyat Fakültesi, 2006), 391–403.

14 Istanbul Court Registers Evkaf-ı Hümayun Müfettişliği, No. 46, 83–84.

15 Ömer Lütfi Barkan, "Ayasofya Camii ve Eyüp Türbesinin 1489–1491 Yıllarına ait Muhasebe Bilançoları" *İktisat Fakültesi Mecmuası* 23, no. 1–2 (1963): 375.

16 Süheyl Ünver, "Sadrazam Karamanlı Mehmed Paşa'nın Eyüp Sultan Medresesi Kütüphanesine Vakfettiği iki Kitaba dair," *Konya*, no. 74–77 (1945): 3–4.

17 Süheyl Ünver, *Fatih Külliyesi ve Zamanı İlim Hayatı* (İstanbul: [Kader Basımevi], 1946), 51; B. N. Şehsuvaroğlu, *İstanbul'da 500 Yıllık Sağlık Hayatımız* (İstanbul: İstanbul Fethi Derneği Neşriyatı, 1953), 29; Müjgan Cunbur, "Fatih Devri Kütüphaneleri ve Kütüphaneciliği," *TKDB* 4 (1957): 7–9; Halil İnalcık, *The Ottoman Empire: The Classical Age 1300–1600*, trans. Norman Itzkowitz and Colin Imber (London: Praeger Publishers, 1973), 167; Cahid Baltacı, *XV-XVI. Asırlarda Osmanlı Medreseleri* (İstanbul: İrfan Matbaası, 1976), 351.

themselves.[18] Müjgan Cunbur and other scholars have adopted Ünver's view with minor changes.[19] This misunderstanding arises from the fact that in various documents dating from different periods mention is made of a library which was situated in different places. Scholars have wrongly presumed that these are different libraries in the complex. However, more recent research would indicate that the documents refer to the same collection, which was housed in different locations in the early history of the complex.

Advocates of the thesis that there was more than one library have noted that in the earliest extant foundation deed, drawn in Arabic and dated 1470, four librarians with stipends of five aspers per day were appointed to the colleges.[20] The list of the books donated to these four colleges can be found appended to another copy of the same foundation deed now located in the Ottoman Archives.[21] According to this deed, Mehmed II founded four libraries in the four colleges of the *Sahn-ı Seman* at the outset. The next extant foundation deed used by Süheyl Ünver is from the period of Bayezid II, copied in 1496 and also in Arabic, in which there is no mention of the college libraries, but reference is made to books being located on the west side of the mosque and a six aspers per day librarian and a four aspers per day assistant librarian being appointed to look after them.[22] In a further foundation deed, which is a Turkish translation of the above-mentioned second Arabic deed, dating from the end of the sixteenth century, we also find the same information.[23]

However, another interpretation of these references to the library is possible. It seems probable that in 1470 the books belonging to the complex were located in the four colleges and required four librarians to look after them. By 1496, the books had been brought together into the mosque where they were cared for by a single librarian and an assistant librarian. There remains the problem of establishing when the change took place. We are lucky enough to have a third version of this second deed, which precedes the other two copies, having been written in 1482. This copy was recently donated to the Süleymaniye Library by Nuri Arlases and has up to now been unavailable to scholars. This

---

18 S. Ünver, *Fatih Külliyesi ve Zamanı İlim Hayatı* (İstanbul: [Kader Basımevi], 1946), 51–57. In some of S. Ünver's articles this figure raises to ten libraries. See: Süheyl Ünver, "Fatih'in Tuğrasıyla Bir Kitap Vakfı Hakkında," *TKDB* 9, nos. 1–2 (1960): 7.

19 See works cited in footnote 70.

20 Osman Ergin, *Fatih İmareti Vakfiyesi* (İstanbul: Belediye Matbaası, 1945), 13 and 63.

21 BOA, Ali Emiri, Fatih Devri, No. 70. A reproduction of this document can be found in S. Ünver's *Fatih Külliyesi ve Zamanı İlim Hayatı* (İstanbul: [Kader Basımevi], 1946), 23–27.

22 Tahsin Öz, *Zwei Stiftungsurkunden des Sultan Mehmed II. Fatih* (İstanbul: n.p., 1935), 14–15 and 119–120.

23 *Fatih Mehmed II Vakfiyeleri* (Ankara: Vakıflar Umum Müdürlüğü Neşriyatı, 1938).

deed was written in the second year of Bayezid II's reign and it was drawn up at his command when he was reorganizing his father's foundation.[24] There, it is mentioned that the books were to be found in one location, namely on the west side of the mosque, so it is clear that the college libraries had been merged by that time. If we are to speculate, we could suggest that the libraries were combined by Bayezid II on his accession for it was customary for the sultan to reorganize and recatalogue the existing imperial foundations on his accession. Yet this remains a hypothesis.

What is certain is that the collection referred to as being in the colleges in the first deed, and in the mosque in all three copies of the second deed, is one and the same collection. The evidence for this assertion lies in the list of books belonging to the library appended to the first deed and in a separate library catalogue prepared for the books lodged in the mosque. In these two catalogues, most of the titles belonging to the college libraries appear in the catalogue of the Mosque Library. This proves at least that the same titles were to be found in both libraries, though it does not prove that they are the same copies of the original titles. As many of the books were standard textbooks, it is not unlikely that they could have been different copies of the same title. Fortunately, it is the practice in the Ottoman cataloguing system to describe, often in some detail, the characteristics of the manuscripts in the library that a comparison is possible. Several couple of books are described in different catalogues with enough similar peculiarities to allow us to regard them as the same manuscript:

> List of the college libraries: "The *Kitabü'l-etraf*, five volumes, only three exist." Catalogue of the Mosque Library: "The *Kitabü'l-etraf*, but only volumes III, IV and V (f. 11a)."[25]
>
> List of the college libraries: "*Commentary on the Koran* by Zemahşeri, incomplete." Catalogue of the Mosque Library: "*Commentary on the Koran* by Zemahşeri, incomplete (f. 4a)."
>
> List of the college libraries: "*Camiü'l-usul*, but only first volume." Catalogue of the Mosque Library: "*Camiü'l-usul*, first volume (f. 9b)."

---

24 Süleymaniye Library, Nuri Arlases Section, No. 242.
25 This catalogue is to be found in the TSA, No. D. 9559. For a description of this catalogue see: chapter 9, "Catalogues and Cataloguing in the Ottoman Libraries."

The list of the college libraries has a very rare book entitled *The History of Genghis Khan* which can also be found on folio 39b of the Catalogue of the Mosque Library.

In the Catalogue of the Mosque Library, we also find a few books which have been transferred from Ayasofya and the Zeyrek college. This would indicate that the Mosque Library was a compilation of books from various sources.

Hoca Sa'deddin, the author of the famous history *Tacu't-Tevarih*, writing about a hundred years later noted that Mehmed II's Mosque Library had the peculiarity of containing many duplicate copies of the most popular textbooks. He came to the conclusion that Mehmed II had provided for duplicate copies, so as not to keep students waiting for books in demand.[26] We know, however, that the reason that there were many duplicates is that the library situated in the mosque was an amalgamation of books from the four colleges in the complex and books from Ayasofya and the Zeyrek College.

Finally, we have to accept the fact that in the many account books dealing with Mehmed II's complex there is no mention of librarians in the colleges among the list of personnel, which would suggest that in the following centuries there were no books in the colleges. For three hundred manuscripts, many of them valuable, to disappear without comment in these account books is hardly possible.[27] Having established his own palace library and having endowed a library in his complex, Mehmed naturally looked to establishing a larger library network for a city the size of Istanbul. This he did by encouraging the richest and most powerful of his entourage to endow and build mosques and colleges and even to complete complexes to which books would eventually be endowed. One of Mehmed II's grand viziers, Mahmud Pasha, founded a complex in Istanbul and endowed other cities in the empire with institutions and buildings.[28] Both in his complex in Istanbul and in his college in Hasköy there existed libraries. The résumé of the foundation deeds for each of these institutions, dated 1474, indicate that he endowed the complex in Istanbul with 195 books and the college in Hasköy with eighty-four books. Unfortunately, the titles of these books were not recorded; just headings of topics are given with the number of books in each category. A librarian was appointed to his Istanbul complex with a stipend of five aspers per day, but there is no mention of a librarian at the Hasköy College Library.[29]

---

26 *Tacü't-Tevarih*, vol. 1 (İstanbul: Matbaa-i Amire, 1279H), 580.
27 BOA, MAD, 5103, 108–109; No. 5305, 79, and 131; No. 5019, 49.
28 S. Ünver, "Mahmud Paşa Vakıfları ve Ekleri," *VD* 4 (1958): 65–76
29 İVTD, 42–45.

From a survey of foundations in Istanbul, we learn that Şeyh Vefa founded a library in his dervish convent in which there were a number of "bound and unbound books" and a librarian at a stipend of one asper per day.[30] This survey was carried out sixty-five years after the death of Mehmed II and leaves us in some doubt as to whether the library had been established in his reign. Fortunately, an earlier document recently came to light in which we discover that in 1485, only four years after Mehmed II's death, a certain Ala'addin was appointed to provide the endowment with a new foundation deed.[31] The inspector copied the information from existing records from the former foundation deed to the effect that a library existed and that the books had been endowed by Şeyh Vefa. In the list prepared by the inspector, the number of books in each category was given. It was further noted that there was a catalogue of the books bearing the seal of the military judge of Rumili, the second highest ranking religious functionary.

The report also gives interesting details about the conditions under which the books were to be lent. We have little idea as to what happened to the books in this library's collections save that it was noted by Evliya Çelebi, at the end of seventeenth century, that the library was operating.[32] However, in a report written in 1909, Mahmud Bey, an inspector of foundations, notes that this library was no longer open to readers. What happened to the books in the intervening two hundred years is still a mystery. Only two books exist which have been identified as belonging to the Şeyh Vefa Library collection; one is housed in the Köprülü Library,[33] while the other is now in the Şehid Ali Pasha collection.[34]

It was not only in Istanbul that libraries were built at this time, but also throughout the whole empire. Edirne, the former capital, was particularly fortunate in its endowments at this period. Çandarlızade İbrahim Pasha, a vizier of Mehmed II, endowed ninety-nine books to a complex he had built in this city,

---

30 İVTD, 15.

31 Istanbul Court Registers Evkaf-ı Hümayun Muhasibliği, No. 102, 150–151. This document has been published by the author: İsmail E. Erünsal, "Şeyh Vefa ve Vakıfları Hakkında Yeni Bir Belge," The Journal of Islamic Studies 1 (1997): 47–64.

32 He wrote: "El-Mevla Katibzade Zeynelabidin: because his father was secretary to Koca Mahmud Pasha they called him Katibzade [the secretary's son]. He was buried at the Şeyh Vefa Mosque to which he endowed all his valuable books and I was able to get from his endowment, book of the Mülteka and of Kohistanî from the librarian and was thus able to read them." Orhan Şaik Gökyay, Evliya Çelebi Seyahatnamesi, vol. 1 (İstanbul: Yapı Kredi Yayınları, 1996), 153.

33 Abdülkadir Erdoğan, Şeyh Vefa, Hayatı ve Eserleri (İstanbul: Ahmed İhsan Basımevi, 1941), 8–9.

34 Günay Kut, Nimet Bayraktar, Yazma Eserlerde Vakıf Mühürleri (Ankara: Başbakanlık Basımevi, 1984), 230.

consisting of texts on Koranic commentary, Prophetic tradition, jurisprudence, mysticism, a book on medicine and a book which could not be identified.[35] In a later survey from the period of Selim II (1566–1574), we see that a librarian continued to be employed to look after this collection.[36]

In 1480 Mesud Halife, a teacher and a Sufi master, established a library in his dervish convent in Edirne. Among the conditions, it was stated that the books were not to be restricted to the use of the members of the dervish order, but were to be made available also to outsiders.[37] In the same survey, carried out in the reign of Selim II, we see that only nineteen books had survived, three of which were about mysticism, the others about standard Islamic sciences.[38]

Another library in Edirne can be described as a local library. In 1470, Ali Fakih, the muezzin of the *Cami-i Cedid*, or the New Mosque, established a library in his own house for the benefit of "himself, his family, students and scholars." The library was to be in his care during his lifetime, and thereafter in the care of the *imam* of the New Mosque. In the same survey from the period of Selim II (1566–1574), we discover that most of the books had disappeared and only fifteen had survived.[39]

In Bursa, the first Ottoman capital, Molla Yegan, one of the most famous scholars of Mehmed II's reign (1451–81), founded a library which had an extraordinarily rich collection for that period. According to the foundation deed the library had 2,900 books the names of which were recorded in an appendix to a Koranic commentary, in the hand of Molla Yegan himself.[40] Unfortunately, this huge collection seems to have been broken up and most of the books have later found their way into other collections.

Other provincial towns also acquired libraries in this period. In Amasya, Hızır Pasha endowed a library in a building next to his college.[41] In Skopje, Isa Bey endowed three hundred books to a college he founded in 1469, and appointed a librarian with a stipend of two aspers per day.[42] Another grand vizier of Mehmed

---

35 M. Tayyib Gökbilgin, *XV-XVI. Asırlarda Edirne ve Paşa Livası* (İstanbul: Üçler Basımevi, 1952), 417–428.

36 BOA, Tapu-Tahrir Defteri, No. 1070, 434–435

37 BOA, Tapu-Tahrir Defteri, No. 1070, 19

38 BOA, Tapu-Tahrir Defteri, No. 1070, 19

39 BOA, Tapu-Tahrir Defteri, No. 1070, 220

40 Bursa Court Registers A. 156, No. 208, 24b.

41 Hüseyin Hüsameddin, *Amasya Tarihi*, vol. 1 (İstanbul: Hikmet Matbaası, 1327H), 261; BOA, Cevdet-Maarif No. 340.

42 The Foundation deed of Isa Bey's library is to be found in Glisa Elezovic's *Turski Spomenici*, book 1, vol. 2 (Beograd: Srpska kraljevska akademija, 1952), 13–29. Hasan Kaleşi has given subject-headings of this collection and the number of books under each subject-headings: "Yugoslavya'da İlk Türk Kütüphaneleri," *Türk Kültürü* 4, no. 38 (1965): 41–42

II, Gedik Ahmed Pasha, founded two complexes, one in Istanbul, no doubt at the behest of the sultan himself, and one in Afyon, his hometown. It was to the Afyon Complex that he endowed a library.[43]

With the expansion of the Ottoman state southwards into Anatolia, existing libraries in the principalities became part of the Ottoman library network. After the conquest of Konya, the former capital of the Karaman principality, the library of the dervish convent of the famous Sufi, Sadreddin Konevi,[44] the library of the Sübaşı Mosque in the district of Beyşehir and the library of the Hoca Ferruh Mosque became Ottoman libraries.[45]

After the period of expansion that the empire witnessed in the reign of Mehmed II, the reign of Bayezid II can be characterized as a period of consolidation, in which he avoided conflict with external forces and attempted to win over those members of society who had been alienated by the harsh measures of Mehmed II.[46] The period of peace allowed Bayezid II to promote his interests in patronizing scholarship and literature. Latîfî, the biographer of the poets, praised Bayezid II's patronage of the arts and noted that he would invite any scholar, even from as far as India and China, to come to Istanbul, using all necessary persuasion and inducements.[47]

The palace library, founded by Mehmed II, was expanded greatly by Bayezid II. In a record book from this period, we see many entries giving the name of persons who presented books to the sultan and received in return several gifts.[48] This indicates that Bayezid appreciated the books greatly. It is related that from time to time he would go through his collection and apply his seal to the front

---

43 İsmail Hakkı Uzunçarşılı, *Kitabeler* (İstanbul: Devlet Matbaası, 1929), 25; BOA, MAD, 626, 230 and MAD, 5455, 240; Afyon Court Registers 504, 130.

44 Belediye Library (now Atatürk Library), Mc. O. 116, No. 1, 6b–8b. See also Suraiya Faroqhi, "Vakıf Administration in Sixteenth Century Konya, The Zaviye of Sadreddin-i Konevî," *JESHO* 17, No. 2 (1974): 147; İrec Afşar, "Fihrist-i Kitabhane-i Sadrüddin-i Konevî," *Tahkikat-ı İslamî* 10, nos. 1–2 (Tehran, 1374, no. 1996): 477–502.

45 Feridun Nafiz Uzluk, *Fatih Devrinde Karaman Eyaleti Vakıfları Fihristi* (Ankara: Doğuş Matbaası, 1958), 20 and 38.

46 Sydney Nettleton Fisher, *The Foreign Relations of Turkey 1481–1512* (Urbana, IL: University of Illinois Press, 1948), 5; Halil İnalcık, *The Ottoman Empire: The Classical Age 1300–1600*, translated by Norman Itzkowitz and Colin Imber (London: Praeger Publishers, 1973), 30–33; Stanford J. Shaw, *History of Ottoman Empire and Modern Turkey*, vol. 1 (Cambridge: Cambridge University Press, 1976), 70.

47 Latifi, *Tezkiretü'ş-Şu'ara*, Rıdvan Canım (Ankara: Atatürk Kültür Merkezi Başkanlığı, 2000), 141–143.

48 For the content of this record book called İn'amat Defteri, see: İsmail E. Erünsal, "Türk Edebiyatı Tarihine Kaynak Olarak Arşivlerin Değeri," *TM* 19 (1980): 213–222; Erünsal, İsmail E., "Türk Edebiyatı Tarihinin Arşiv Kaynakları I: II. Bayezid Devrine Ait Bir İn'amat Defteri," *TAD* 10–11 (1981): 303–342.

and back flyleaves and would, in his own hand, inscribe his name as owner.[49] An account book from this period mentions that there was a librarian employed in this library and he was called *hafız-ı kütüb-i hassa* (keeper of the imperial books).[50] In the palace in Galata, there was a school in which the court staff were trained. Evidently, Bayezid II founded another library in this school.[51]

In 1488, when Bayezid II complex was founded, the foundation deed notes that the library was an integral part of it. Among the textbooks donated to this library there were medical books, probably for the use of the staff of the hospital which was a part of the complex.[52] Bayezid II's keen interest in preserving the collection was demonstrated in the following condition concerning borrowing placed in the foundation deed, where he tried to eradicate some of the sloppy practices which had endangered previous collections:

> Whenever a student in the college wishes a book he should present himself to the librarian, who should summon witnesses and in front of them count the fascicles and the pages and record them together with the size of the book and the quality of the binding, as well as recording the details of the borrower and the witnesses, all this so that fraud by substitution be avoided.[53]

Bayezid II also founded a complex in Amasya to which he donated a collection of books and appointed a librarian with a stipend of two aspers per day.[54]

His complex in Istanbul was built between 1500 and 1505.[55] However, it is not clear that he endowed it with a library. The historian Ata, claims in his history that Bayezid II founded a library in his mosque in Istanbul. Yet, the historian was writing in the seventeenth century and thus is not a reliable source.[56] However, in an account book for the foundation covering the period 1583–1595 we

49 Süheyl Ünver, "İkinci Selim'e Kadar Osmanlı Hükümdarlarının Hususi Kütüphaneleri Hakkında," *IV. Türk Tarih Kongresi* (Ankara, 1952), 309–311.

50 Ömer Lütfi Barkan, "H. 933–934 (M. 1527–1528) Mali Yılına Ait Bir Bütçe Örneği," *İktisat Fakültesi Mecmuası* 15 (1954): 308.

51 İsmail Baykal, "Topkapı Sarayı Müzesi Kitaplıkları," *Güzel Sanatlar* 6 (1949): 75.

52 M. Tayyib Gökbilgin, *XV-XVI. Asırlarda Edirne ve Paşa Livası* (İstanbul: Üçler Basımevi, 1952), facsimiles, 16.

53 Belediye Library (now Atatürk Library), No. Mc. O. 61, 44a.

54 Hüseyin Hüsameddin, *Amasya Tarihi*, vol. 1 (İstanbul: Hikmet Matbaası, 1327H), 261; BOA, MAD, 5455, 76 and 210.

55 R. Melül Meriç, "II. Sultan Bayezid Zamanı Binaları, Mimarları, Sanat Eserleri ve Sanatkarları," *Yıllık Araştırmalar Dergisi* 2 (1958): 8.

56 *Tarih-i Atâ*, vol. 1 (İstanbul: Yahya Efendi Matbaası, 1291H), 76.

observe that a librarian was working for a stipend of three aspers per day.[57] This modest salary would suggest that the collection was small and required only the attention of a single librarian. Three libraries founded by Bayezid II were furnished with small collections of books, a fact that is rather curious given that Bayezid II had a reputation as a lover of books. He had amassed a large collection of books in the palace library.

Many prominent people of this period emulated the sultan by founding their own libraries: Alaiyelü Muhyiddin donated seventy-one books to an unnamed institution and these were later transferred to the mosque of Mehmed II.[58] Atik Ali Pasha founded a college at Çemberlitaş in the center of Istanbul and donated 119 books and appointed a librarian at a stipend of three aspers per day.[59] Efdalzade Ahmed Çelebi founded a college near the mosque of Mehmed II to which he donated forty-two books and appointed a librarian with a stipend of one asper per day.[60] A scholar, Muslihiddin Çelebi Yegani, donated one hundred books with the provision that he should care for them in his own lifetime and thereafter his family should look after them. When this was no longer possible the books should be deposited in the Ulu Mosque in Bursa.[61] According to the famous biographical work, the Şakaik, Ahi Yusuf, a scholar of this period, donated many books to a mosque he had built close to his house.[62]

Koca Mustafa Pasha, a grand vizier of Bayezid II, founded a mosque in Istanbul. By 1606, there is mention of a library in some archival documents, but we cannot be sure that it was established during the lifetime of the Pasha.[63]

A library was founded by İshak Pasha, another grand vizier of Bayezid II in the complex he built in 1489 in İnegöl. To this complex a librarian was appointed with a stipend of one and a half aspers per day.[64] In 1492 in Edirne, Şeyh Mehmed b. Yusuf, donated 37 books, mainly on the subject of mysticism, to his dervish convent.[65] In 1485, another Sufi master, Abdurrahim Karahisarî,

57 BOA, MAD, 5103, 273 and 5761, 61 and 98.

58 İVTD, 338.

59 İVTD, 69.

60 İVTD, 199.

61 İVTD, 172.

62 Şaka'ik, 275.

63 Hüseyin Ayvansarayî, Hadikatü'l-Cevamî, vol. 1 (İstanbul: Matbaa-i Amire, 1281H), 162; Osmanzâde Tâ'ib, Hadikatü'l-Vüzera (İstanbul: n.p., 1271H), 21.

64 Vehbi Tamer, "Fatih Devri Ricalinden Ishak Paşa'nın Vakfiyeleri ve Vakıfları," VD 4 (1958): facsimile, 12.

65 BOA, Tapu-Tahrir Defteri, No. 1070, 270–272.

mentioned in the foundation deed for his complex at Afyon that he had donated 159 books.[66]

The most interesting library to be established in this period, in terms of the founder and the books making up the collection, is certainly the library that Kıssahan Muslihiddin founded in the village of Çavlı Hacı in the vicinity of İzmit.[67] Kıssahan Muslihiddin was storyteller to Bayezid II and when he retired after long years of service, covering the reigns of three sultans, he returned to his village and there founded two mosques and rooms for students. He donated 210 books to these mosques and set conditions for their use and protection. The collection includes the usual standard college textbooks in Arabic, but what is far more interesting, it includes books by Muhyiddin ibni Arabi, the famous mystic philosopher, Feridüddin-i Attar, the poet and author of many works on ethics, Mevlana Celaleddin-i Rumi, the mystical poet, and another well-known mystic Kuşeyri. There are also Turkish works and five books on mathematics and astronomy and nine books on medicine.[68] This library is not the library of a college teacher, but the collection of a widely read person who was obviously collecting books as an aid to his profession as storyteller to the sultan. It would seem that he retired with his books to the peace and quiet of his village, where he donated them to the mosque so that others could benefit from them.

One of Bayezid II's wives, Hüsnü Şah, built a mosque in Manisa in 1490, while her son, Şehinşah, was the governor of the city.[69] Şehinşah donated 140 books to the library which his mother had established in the mosque.[70]

Libraries were also established in the Balkans in this period. In 1506, Abdullah Yakup Pasha, one of Bayezid II's viziers, donated 135 books to an institution he built in Salonica.[71] However, no mention of a librarian is made in the foundation deed. In the same year, the judge of Salonica and Bitola, a certain İshak Çelebi, established a library in the college which he had previously founded.[72] This is

---

66 Edip Ali Baki, *Mısırlıoğlu Abdurrahim Karahisarî* (Afyon: Yeni Matbaa, 1953), 101–103; Afyon Court Registers 514, 94b–96a.

67 VGMA, No. 579, 218.

68 VGMA, No. 579, 224–227.

69 Çağatay Uluçay, *Padişahların Kadınları ve Kızları* (Ankara: Türk Tarih Kurumu Basımevi, 1980), 23; İsmet Parmaksızoğlu, "Manisa Kütüphaneleri," *TKDB* 8, no. 1 (1959): 18.

70 Manisa Court Registers 113, 237–238.

71 VGMA, No. 740, 305–312.

72 Hasan Kaleşi, "Ishak Çelebi von Bitola und seine Stiftungen" in *La Macedonia et les Macedoniens dans la Passe* (Skopje: n.p., 1970), 149–162; Dr. Hasan Kaleşi, *Najstariji vakufski dokumenti u Jugoslaviji na arapskom jeziku* (Priština: Zajednica naučnih ustanova Kosova, 1972), 172–185; Ekrem Hakkı Ayverdi, *Avrupa'da Osmanlı Mimari Eserleri, Yugoslavya* 3, no. 3 (1981): 100–101; Hasan Kaleşi, "Yugoslavya'da İlk Türk Kütüphaneleri," *Türk Kültürü* 4, no. 38 (1965): 170.

the earliest Ottoman library to be established in Bitola. Another library was established by Suzî Çelebi, a Turkish poet, in the mosque which he had built in Prizren.[73]

Apart from foundation libraries, which were in the public domain, there are also records of private collections. One of Mehmed II's viziers, Sinan Pasha, a famous author and an esteemed scholar, apparently owned a very rich collection of books which he willed to a foundation following his death. Another equally esteemed scholar, Molla Lütfi had the responsibility of ensuring that the books reached the foundation to which they had been endowed. Whether or not Molla Lütfi delayed the process so as to allow himself exclusive use of the collection is not certain, but he was accused of doing so by, Ahmed Pasha, in two letters addressed to the sultan. Ahmed Pasha even went as far as to accuse Molla Lütfi of selling some of the books.[74] Bayezid II's son, Prince Korkud, a renowned poet and scholar, also had a very rich collection which required a camel caravan to move it from one location to another.[75] This collection was housed in the citadel of Manisa when Korkud died[76] and his collection was confiscated. Some, if not all, of the books were placed in the palace library.[77] The Prince's şarabdar, that is, the chief taster of drinks, a certain Piyale Bey, had a private collection and left the books to an elementary school which he had founded in Manisa.[78] One of the books from this collection can now be found in the Atıf Efendi Library (no. 1835). It bears the seal of Piyale Bey which consists of the following Persian couplet: "Piyale, the slave of Prince Korkud / Had nothing in this world save his chosen friends."[79]

An extremely important private library was that belonging to a famous scholar, Müeyyedzade Abdurrahman Efendi, who if the author of the Şakaik is to be believed, had a library of over seven thousand books. The author of

73 BOA, Tapu-Tahrir Defteri, No. 495, 417; Hasan Kaleşi, "Oriental Culture in Yugoslav Countries from the Fifteenth Century until the End of the Seventeenth Century," in *Ottoman Rule in Middle Europe and Balkan in the sixteenth and seventeenth Centuries*, Edited by Jaroslav Cesar (Prague: Oriental Institute in Academia, 1978), 391; Agah Sırrı Levend, *Gazavatnameler* (Ankara: Türk Tarih Kurumu, 1956), 203–204; Olga Zirozeviç, "Prizren Şehri," *XI. Türk Tarih Kongresi, Kongreye Sunulan Bildiriler* 5 (1994): 2116.
74 İsmail E. Erünsal, "Fatih Devri Kütüphaneleri ve Molla Lütfi Hakkında Birkaç Not," *TD* 33 (1980–1981): 74–78
75 Feridun Bey, *Münşe'at-ı Selatîn*, vol. 1 (İstanbul: Darü't-Tıbaati'l-Amire, 1274H), 373; İsmail Hakkı Uzunçarşılı, *Osmanlı Tarihi*, vol. 2 (Ankara: Türk Tarih Kurumu Basımevi, 1972), 644
76 Feridun Bey, *Münşe'at-ı Selatîn*, vol. 1 (İstanbul: Darü't-Tıbaati'l-Amire, 1274H), 373.
77 İsmail Hakkı Uzunçarşılı, "Sultan Korkut," *T. T. K. Belleten* 30, no. 120 (1966): 601; Feridun Emecen, "Korkut, Şehzade," *DİA* 26 (2002): 207.
78 BOA, Tapu-Tahrir Defteri, No. 398, 27.
79 Atıf Efendi Library, No. 1835

the *Şakaik* goes on to note that not only had he not read many of these works, he had not even heard of their names.[80] The famous historian Hoca Sa'deddin wrote that this collection consisted of "precious and rare books, and apart from the duplicates it is well known that there are more than seven thousand works" in the collection.[81]

We do not know if this reputed seven thousand book collection Türk was an exaggeration or the truth. However, it seems that the collection was extraordinarily rich, even if it did not amount to seven thousand works. Müeyyedzade during his lifetime had apparently incurred enormous debts in building up this collection and upon his death in 1516 the books went to his family, who apparently sold some of them. Sultan Selim I decided to confiscate this library and he appointed one of his servants, a certain Aydın, to appropriate as many of the books as he could lay his hands on. Aydın duly did so and noted the names of the books which he could find; these amounted to 2112. The titles of these books are noted in an account book now housed in the Topkapı Palace Archive. The sultan took the rarest of the books into his own palace collection and had the remainder sold in order to clear Müeyyedzade's debts.[82]

We have from Bayezid II's reign two proper independent catalogues which have survived. Up to this period, there were inventories appended to the foundation deeds which functioned as catalogues. The first is not dated, but from external evidence we can say that it was prepared at the beginning of the sixteenth century.[83] It belongs to the library of the mosque of Mehmed II. This catalogue, which consists of fifty-six folios, has an introduction covering two folios the first of which has unfortunately been torn and the bottom half lost. In the remaining part of the folio, the cataloguer advises the reader that the catalogue has been drawn up on the order of the reigning sultan, whose specific orders were to inspect the library which the late Sultan Mehmed II had endowed. After this missing section, folio two begins with a discussion of how the books were to be shelved. We know that Mehmed II endowed books to four of the eight colleges that surrounded the mosque he built. His successor, Bayezid II, relocated the books to a single location in the mosque, probably for ease of administration and better protection. The compiler of the catalogue may

---

80 *Şaka'ik*, 294; İsmail Hakkı Uzunçarşılı, *Osmanlı Devletinin İlmiye Teşkilatı* (Ankara: Türk Tarih Kurumu Basımevi, 1965), 232.

81 *Tâcü't-Tevârih*, vol. 2 (İstanbul: Matbaa-i Amire, 1279H), 556.

82 TSA, No. D. 9291, No. 2, 10a.

83 BOA, HMH, SFTH, No. 21, 941, No. B.

have been involved in physically allocating space to the books, and that this preoccupation was foremost in his mind when he drew up the catalogue.[84]

The second catalogue, dated 1502, belongs to the palace library and consists of 340 folios.[85] The first two folios contain a list of contents, followed by five folios containing a Turkish introduction, which lays down the principles by which the catalogue was organized and the classification rules. This is followed by a single folio containing a preface in Arabic, which says that this catalogue was prepared on the orders of Sultan Bayezid II. The introduction talks about the problems confronting librarians of the time, for example, how to deal with several books bound together and how to classify a book in which two distinct categories overlap. Classification is the overriding priority in this catalogue; no importance is given to the physical description of the books. It would seem that the reason for classification being so important was that the palace library was built to house a collection which was intended for the court. If information was needed it was important that the required book could be located quickly. To ensure this, an efficient system of classification was needed.

Selim I's reign is extraordinary in that, despite lasting only eight years, 1513–1521, the Ottoman territories expanded into Syria, Egypt, and the holy cities of Mecca and Medina. This allowed Selim I to buy and confiscate books whenever the opportunity arose. By the end of his short reign the palace had become much richer, and these books were, in later reigns, to become the core of foundation libraries. Selim I's reign was too short to allow him to establish educational institutions bearing his name, but we do have evidence for his love of books and reading. Hoca Sa'deddin recounts in his history, that while on the Egyptian campaign (1516) he took many books with him. One night in the desert some camels carrying equipment were stolen by Bedouins. Among the baggage was a chest of books among which was Vassaf's *History*, which the sultan was reading at the time. When he arrived in Egypt he had one of the palace teachers, Mevlana Şemseddin, famous for the speed at which he could copy (he was reputed to be able to copy the whole Koran in ten days), write another copy of the *History of Vassaf* for him.[86] There are some documents which

---

84 For a description of this catalogue see author's articles: "Fatih Camii Kütüphanesine Ait En Eski Müstakil Katalog," *Erdem* 9, no. 26 (1996): 659–664 and "The Oldest Extant Ottoman Library Catalogue," *61st IFLA General Conferance*, booklet 7 (1995): 58–62.

85 Magyar Tudomanyos Akademia Künyvtara Keleti Gyüjtement (Konyvtara Library of the Hungarian Academy of Sciences), Török F. 59. I related the discovery of this catalogue in the following article: "The Catalogue of Bayezid II's Palace Library," *Kütüphanecilik Dergisi, Belge, Bilgi Kütüphane Araştırmaları*, no. 3 (1992): 55–66

86 *Tacu't-Tevarih*, 2:610.

show his keen interest in books. A document dated 1517 takes the form of a report on the books housed in the citadel of Aleppo, the first part of which is a list of books which the anonymous author believes should be sent to the palace library. The second part of the report deals with those books which although not very valuable may be acquired by the palace, while the third section gives the titles of books which are of no interest to the palace and should be disposed of on the open market. The report requests that the sultan should make his decision clear.[87]

Another document is a letter from the governor of Egypt, who had found some books which Selim I had lost while in Damascus. The governor mentions that he had sent one book already, and now he had found another four, but, as the letter was going by sea, he was not sending the books with it, lest they become damp, but would await the first opportunity to send them by land.[88]

Selim I's short reign witnessed the establishment of comparatively few foundation libraries. One of these was founded by Mevlana Bali in his mosque in Istanbul. Attached to the mosque were rooms designated for scholars and students, for the benefit of whom he endowed, in 1519, a library of 620 books to be kept by the imam of the mosque.[89] Ahmed Pasha donated some books to his college in Bursa and thus established a library.[90] In a survey of the foundations of Edirne, it has been noted that a certain Hasan Halife left nineteen books, his house, and some money with the provision that after his death his descendants should look after the books, and thereafter they should be entrusted to the judge of the city. On no account were the books to leave the house. Trustees were appointed to manage the foundation.

İsmet Parmaksızoğlu, in his article entitled "The Libraries of Manisa" reports that Süleyman the Magnificent's mother, Hafsa Sultan, built a mosque and dispensary in Manisa and founded a library in both institutions.[91] A library was also established in a mosque complex in Trabzon, built in the name of Sultan Süleyman's grandmother, Gülbahar Hatun.[92]

---

87 TSA, No. D. 9101
88 TSA, No. D. 5596
89 İVTD, 243
90 Bursa Court Registers A. 83, No. 97, 48a; Tahsin Özalp, *Sivrihisar Tarihi* (Eskişehir: Tam-İş Matbaası, 1960), 124.
91 "Manisa Kütüphaneleri," *TKDB* 8, no. 1 (1959): 19. In a survey carried out in Manisa in September 1567, it was noted that the collection consisted of 311 titles. See Manisa Court Registers 113, 237–238.
92 Heath W. Lowry, *Trabzon Şehrinin İslamlaşma ve Türkleşmesi*. Translated from his English thesis by Demet and Heath Lowry (İstanbul: Boğaziçi Üniversitesi Matbaası, 1998), 68.

In the first years of Süleyman I's reign, as in the whole reign of his father, Selim I, there was a recession in the development of libraries. This may perhaps be attributed to the enormous social and economic dislocation witnessed in the reign of Selim I.[93] Although we see several libraries established in Edirne during the early years of Süleyman I's reign, there is no evidence of such activities in the capital, Istanbul. Most of the libraries founded by statesmen and scholars of the period happened in the latter part of his reign, due mainly to political and economic stability, which in turn encouraged development in culture and scholarship.

In Edirne, the tradition of establishing small collections for the use of the local inhabitants, which began in the reign of Murad II, continued. This is demonstrated in the case of a collection of 114 books, mainly to do with religion, donated by Hacı Hasan b. Ali to the school he founded, by means of an endowment deed dated 1521. In the deed, Hacı Hasan b. Ali includes the condition that "the books should be lent freely to the teacher and to anyone who is able to read them, but they should not be given to anyone from outside the mentioned locality."[94]

Again in Edirne, a library was founded by Kasım b. Abdullah in January 1528, similar to that of Hacı Hasan b. Ali's library, but containing in the foundation deed the further stipulation that the teacher should not lend a book without first obtaining a pledge from the borrower.[95] In both foundation deeds, we can observe that, as in previous periods, the teacher is responsible for conserving and administering the collection, there being no specific post of librarian.

At the beginning of Süleyman I's reign a library was founded in Gebze, near Istanbul, by Çoban Mustafa Pasha, the governor of Egypt, in a complex which he completed in 1522.[96] The collection, consisting of 165 books mainly on religion, with some works on medicine,[97] was to be cared for by a librarian, who was to receive a daily stipend of three aspers.[98] In the complex founded by Çoban Mustafa Pasha, as in most complexes and colleges of this period, a library was considered a necessary constituent of the educational organization. For this reason, throughout Süleyman I's reign, we see a library established in

---

93 M.Tayyib Gökbilgin, "Süleyman I," İA 11 (1940–1986): 149.

94 BOA, Tapu-Tahrir Defteri, No. 1070, 239–241. Although the library was located in a house and could be considered a school library, when we look at the types of books in it and the stipulation in the foundation deed, it is best to view this library as a local public library.

95 BOA, Tapu-Tahrir Defteri, No. 1070, 211.

96 Muallim Cevdet, Zeyl ala fasli'l-ahiyyeti'-fityani't-Türkiyye fi rıhleti İbni Batuta (İstanbul: Kurtuluş, 1932), 211.

97 Süheyl Ünver, Tıp Tarihimiz Yıllığı (İstanbul: İstanbul Üniversitesi Tıp Fakültesi, 1966), 18.

98 BOA, MAD, 22, 151; MAD, 5455, 29; MAD, 5070, 4, 24, 114, 126.

each of the following colleges: Hayreddin Pasha's college in Istanbul (1534),[99] Abdülvasi b. Hızır's college in Edirne (before 1538),[100] Hadım Süleyman Pasha's college in Cairo (950, no. 1543),[101] Kasım Pasha's colleges in Istanbul and in Bursa,[102] Rüstem Pasha's colleges in Istanbul (1547) and in Tekirdağ (1553),[103] Sofu Mehmed Pasha's college in Sofia (1547),[104] Sultan Süleyman I's college in Rhodes,[105] İbrahim Pasha's college in Istanbul (1549),[106] Sekban Kara Ali's college in Istanbul,[107] Hüseyin Ağa's college in Amasya,[108] Şehzade Mehmed's college in Istanbul,[109] and Semiz Ali Pasha's college in Istanbul (1556).[110]

Records indicate that books were not only donated to the colleges, but also to mosques. Thus we see Makbul İbrahim Pasha, one of Sultan Süleyman I's grand viziers, donating some books and appointing a librarian to his mosque in Hezargrad,[111] as did Hüsrev Pasha in Diyarbakır,[112] Kiremitçizade Sinan

---

99 VGMA, No. 571, 185.
100 Şaka'ik, 393. The books in this icular college were endowed by Abdulvasi Çelebi. He was expecting to be appointed to the post of the chief mufti and when he found that the position was given to rival candidate, he endowed his books to his college and thereupon emigrated to Mecca. See: Enîsü'l-Müsamirîn, ed. Ratip Kazancıgil (Edirne: Türk Kütüphaneciler Derneği Edirne Şubesi, 1996), 150.
101 Ahmed M. El-Masry, Die Bauten von Hâdim Sulaimân Pascha (1468–1548) (Berlin: Klaus Schwarz, 1991), 111.
102 İVTD, 431–432; BOA, Ruus No. 1, 145; Ruus No. 80, 446; MAD, 626, 174; Bursa Court Registers A. 82, No. 96, 43b.
103 BOA, Ruus No. 66, 5; Ruus No. 80, 546; Ruus No. 82, 230; İ. Aydın Yüksel, "Sadrazam Rüstem Paşa'nın Vakıfları," in Ekrem Hakkı Ayverdi Hatıra Kitabı (İstanbul: İstanbul Fetih Cemiyeti, 1995), 219–281. Rüstem Pasha donated a mere 120 books to his college in Istanbul. His own private collection was legendary in his day. The historian Peçevi claims that his collection exceeded five thousand books (Tarih-i Peçevî, vol. 1 [İstanbul: Matbaa-i Amire, 1283H], 23), while the historian Ali notes that besides these five thousand books, there were further copies of the Koran of which 131 were richly decorated. See: Heinrich Friedrich von Diez, Denkwürdigkeiten von Asien in Künsten und Wissenschaften, Sitten, Gebräuchen und Alterthümen, Religion und Regierungverfassung aus Handschriften und eigenen Erfahrungen (Berlin: n.p., 1811), 95–96.
104 VGMA, No. 988, 51–64. For his complex see: Abdülkadir Özcan, "Kanuni Devri Vezirlerinden Sofu Mehmed Paşa'ya ve Sofya'daki Külliyesine Dair," Balkanlar'da İslam Medeniyeti Milletlerarası Sempozyumu Tebliğleri, Sofya 21–23 Nisan 2000 (2002): 267–276.
105 BOA, MAD, 626, 189.
106 BOA, Ruus No. 78, 10; BOA, Cevdet-Maarif No. 580; In a Mühimme record dated November 1584, it is mentioned that İbrahim Pasha had endowed some books to the Cami-i Ezher in Egypt (BOA, Mühimme Defteri, No. 55, 48).
107 BOA, Cevdet-Maarif No. 5465.
108 BOA, MAD, 22, 125; BOA, İbnülemin-Evkaf, No. 718.
109 TSA, No. EH. 3003, 100b-106a.
110 VGMA, No. 585, 16–20.
111 BOA, Cevdet-Maarif No. 100; BOA, Ruus No. 84, 201.
112 BOA, Ruus No. 84, 110; Ruus No. 85, 95; İbnülemin, Tevcihat, No. 1010.

Bey in Bursa,[113] and Tercüman Yunus,[114] Ferruh Kethüda,[115] and Cihan Bey[116] in Istanbul. According to a foundation record, Çadırcı Hayreddin established a position of librarian with a daily stipend of one asper at the Bezzaz-ı Cedid Mosque at Mercan district in Istanbul.[117]

Besides local and college libraries, there are particular libraries which are worthy of note: the library in the mausoleum complex of Caliph Ali and Musa Kazım in Baghdad,[118] the library of Yorganî Dede in his dervish convent (1564) near the Gül Mosque in Istanbul[119] and Feridun Bey's library located in the primary school bearing his name, also in Istanbul.[120]

The libraries we have come across so far all fit within the established classification of libraries: libraries found in colleges, mosques, schools, dervish convents and mausoleums.[121] However, there is a further type of library, examples of which can only be seen in the fifteenth and sixteenth centuries, one instance in Mehmed II's reign, and one in Selim's, and several in Sultan Süleyman I's reign. These are the libraries founded by members of the learned class of *ulema* in their own houses or in small buildings, the deeds of which stipulate that the founder will have priority in the use of the books, thereafter his family, scholars of the locality, righteous persons and, finally, anyone able to profit from the books.

One example of such libraries is the one donated by Mevlana Emir Hüseyin b. Mehmed, a teacher at the Darü'l-Hadis College in Edirne, who, by means of an endowment deed, dated February 1535, specified that his seventy-seven books should be available not only to himself, but to scholars, students and any person able to profit from them. Although the deed does not state clearly where the books are to be housed, when the extant copy of the deed was made it was noted that the books were currently in the hands of Muslihiddin Dede in the district of Sevündük Fakih. A clause in the deed shows that the founder expressly wished the books to be used as widely as possible:

---

113 Bursa Court Registers A. 83, No. 97, 82a.
114 BOA, Kepeci-Ruus No. 217, 161.
115 VGMA, No. 570, 60; BOA, Ruus No. 9, Ruus No. 32, 308; BOA, Cevdet-evkaf, No. 711; BOA, İbnülemin-Evkaf, No. 5990.
116 Istanbul Court Registers Evkaf-ı Hümayun Muhasibliği, No. 7, 23b; BOA, Cevdet-Evkaf, No. 24 290; BOA, Ruus No. 33, 11, Ruus No. 91, 168.
117 BOA, İbnülemin-Evkaf, No. 97; Istanbul Court Registers Evkaf-ı Hümayun Muhasibliği, No. 7, 28a, No. 9, 39b.
118 BOA, Bağdad Tapu Defteri, No. 386, 117–118, 124–127, and 161.
119 Istanbul Court Registers Rumeli Sadareti, No. 8, 55a–b.
120 VGMA, No. 570, 198.
121 Özer Soysal, "Cumhuriyet Öncesi Dönemi Türk Kütüphaneciliği" (Habilitation Thesis, Ankara University, 1973), 17–21.

> The books are not to be lent without a deposit or pledge and it is
> a condition that they must not remain in the hands of a person
> for an extended period. Indeed, when a person is finished with a
> book, the librarian should take it from him and give it to another
> person so that the books do not go out of use and do not become
> lost.[122]

Similarly, Mevlana Alaaddin b. Hacı Sinan donated twenty-five books in 1545 and placed similar conditions in his deed, but also added that upon his death the imam of the Haseki district mosque in Istanbul was to look after the books and that the congregation of the mosque was to act as supervisor.[123]

Another example appears in the foundation deed, dated November 1562, in which Kadı Alaaddin b. Abdurrahman donated his house in the district of Balat in Istanbul, together with his books and a sum of money. Here, the condition was that the local imam or someone appointed by him would live in the house, read every day one *cüz* (a thirtieth part) of the Koran for the soul of the founder and maintain the books.[124]

In a document dated 1536, we see a certain Sinan Bey and Mehmed b. Sinan, co-owners of a collection of books, donating their books in a similar way: that the books be for the use of their sons and the scholars of the district and those who may profit from them. However, what is different in this document is that the price of every book is entered after each title. This is explained thus:

> As for the one who has need of a book, it shall not be given to
> him without taking the full value of the book or a pledge which
> should not be worth less than the value of the book. Books
> should thus be lent and should a book be lost then it should be
> replaced with the money or pledge taken.[125]

When Şeyh İshak b. Abdürrezzak endowed forty-one of his books, mainly on mathematics, medicine, and astronomy, for the use of himself, his sons, and his friends who could benefit from them, he made it a condition that the books not leave the confines of Istanbul.[126]

---

122 BOA, MAD, 557, 11–12.
123 İVTD, 341.
124 Istanbul Court Registers Balat Mahkemesi, No. 2, 5a.
125 VGMA, No. 578, 318.
126 İVTD, 439–440.

Despite the fact that many a locality could boast a library, no matter how small, and that the libraries were established in the complexes Sultan Süleyman I built for his son Şehzade Mehmed and his daughter Mihrimah Sultan, it is ironic that no collection was endowed when his own vast complex was built at the Süleymaniye. However, according to the Süleymaniye foundation deed, probably drawn up in 1557, it was planned that a library should exist at some future date:

> Thus, it is stipulated that when the books are provided for the above-mentioned colleges, a librarian and assistant librarian are to be appointed by the grand vizier and their duties to be determined by him.[127]

We do not know when the library was founded in the Süleymaniye Complex nor when the staff were first appointed. Müjgan Cunbur has claimed that a library was operating soon after the completion of the complex, relying on a list of books appended to the foundation deed, but it is apparent that this list was drawn at a later date.[128] It is not therefore possible, on the basis of this document, to claim categorically that the library was functioning shortly after the deeds were drawn up. However, in a document found in the Topkapı Palace Archive, dated 1561, it is recorded that some books were sent from the palace to the college of the sultan, that is, to the Süleymaniye.[129] In another document in the same archive, dated 1565, there is a list of the titles of fifty-five books under the heading: "The list of books given to the teachers, which were needed by the colleges of the Süleymaniye, by order of the sultan."[130] With these documents we can presume that within a few years of the completion of the Süleymaniye Complex, books began to come to the library from the palace.

The oldest reference so far noted for the appointment of a librarian and assistant librarian to this library is dated 1583. In an account book of the Süleymaniye foundation, there are records of a staff member by the name of Şeyh Şemseddin Mahmud, with a daily stipend of six aspers and an assistant librarian at four aspers. In the same account book, a record, dated 1589, shows that the above-mentioned Şemseddin had resigned and on the petition of the

---

127 Kemal Edib Kürkçüoğlu, *Süleymaniye Vakfiyesi* (Ankara: Vakıflar Umum Müdürlüğü, 1962), facsimile, 151–152.

128 Müjgan Cunbur, "Kanuni Devrinde Kitap Sanatı, Kütüphaneleri ve Süleymaniye Kütüphanesi," *TKDB* 17, no. 3 (1968): 139.

129 TSA, No. E. 861, No. 1.

130 TSA, No. E. 2803, No. 1.

Judge of Istanbul a certain Osman b. Hüdaverdi was appointed.[131] From the account books of later years it is seen that these salaries remained steady[132] until 1649, when the librarian started to receive ten aspers and the assistant librarian seven.[133] In addition to their daily stipend, the staff of the Süleymaniye library were entitled to receive one meal a day from the kitchen of the complex.[134]

Similarly, when Gazi Hüsrev, whose mother was Selçuk Sultan and grandfather Sultan Bayezid II, founded a complex in Sarajevo he stipulated in an endowment dated 1537 that a library was to be established at a future date with the funds remaining after the building was completed.[135] We are informed that another library was established in 1550 in the town of Foča on the river Drina.[136]

A library built in 1559 in Kayseri by a scholar, Bedreddin Mahmud b. Mevlana Süleyman b. Alaaddin Ali, has attracted the attention of researchers because of its peculiar location. It has been claimed that this was the prototype of a new category of library, namely the *"bedesten"* or *"bazaar library."*[137] However, we should examine the establishment of this library more closely before accepting this new category of "bazaar library." In the foundation deed, dated 1559, Bedreddin Mahmud specified that the books were to remain in his possession until his death and, thereafter, in the possession of his children and brother's children, to be used both for their benefit and that of students, and thus they were to remain in the hands of his descendants until they died out, whereupon the books were to be located in a place in a bazaar called the *bezzazistan*, or cloth bazaar. Furthermore, it is clearly stipulated that this collection, which comprised four hundred volumes, mainly in Arabic and dealing with religious sciences or the Arabic language, was to be used by "seekers of knowledge," in other words, students.[138] It is therefore a collection appropriate to a college library, although it is located in the bazaar.

---

131 BOA, MAD, 5103, 4.

132 BOA, MAD, 2056, 6, MAD, 5761, 26, MAD, 1018, 9–10.

133 BOA, MAD, 994, 10, MAD, 5019, 88.

134 BOA, MAD, 19 342, 1.

135 Kasim Dobrača, *Katalog arapskih, turskih i perzijskih rukopisa* (Sarajevo: Starješinstvo islamske vjerske zajednice za SR Bosnu i Hercegovinu, 1963), xxi–xxiv; M. Tayyib Okiç, "Saraybosna Gazi Hüsrev Beğ Kütüphanesi Yazma Eserler Kataloğu," *İlahiyat Fakültesi Dergisi* (1964), 144; İlhan Polat, "Saray-Bosna'da Gazi Hüsrev Bey Kütüphanesi," *TKDB* 18, no. 4 (1969): 244–248; Lamija Hadziosmanovic, *Biblioteke u Bosni i Hercegovini za vrijeme austrougarske vladavine* (Sarajevo: Veselin Masleša, 1980), 64–69.

136 Dobruca, *Katalog Arapskıh, Turkish ı Perzıjskıh Rukopisa*, xxi.

137 Özer Soysal, "Cumhuriyet Öncesi Dönemi Türk Kütüphaneciliği," 110; M. Cunbur, "Tarihimizde Anadolu'da Kütüphane Kurma Çabaları," *TKDB* 15, no. 3 (1966): 130; M. Cunbur, "Kayseri'de Raşit Efendi Kütüphanesi ve Vakfiyesi," *VD* 8 (1969): 185.

138 VGMA, No. 581, No. 1, 31–33.

Other collections were endowed during the period of Sultan Süleyman I's reign. According to the famous biographer of Ottoman scholars, Ataî, a certain Şah Ali (d. 1553) was reputed to have performed his morning prayers for forty years in the front row in the Ayasofya Mosque. He is said to have left his books for the benefit of students. Where he donated them is not mentioned and therefore we do not know if he donated them to the Ayasofya Mosque or to some other institution.[139] A court record indicates that a teacher called Kasım b. Habil donated sixty-five books to the library of Mehmed II and stated in his foundation deed that his books might be lent out provided that the person borrowing them took a pledge to return them.[140]

The period from the death of Süleyman I until the end of sixteenth century saw the spread of libraries throughout the empire, as the reigning sultans and their statesmen endowed libraries to institutions they had founded in large cities, or in places to which they had been appointed, or to their place of birth. Except for the Selimiye Mosque Library, the libraries were comparatively small and had just a single librarian, but these were to become the core collection of libraries, which were to expand in the following century as the numbers of students increased, creating a need for more books.

İsmihan Sultan, the daughter of Selim II and wife of the Grand Vizier Sokollu Mehmed Pasha, founded a college at Eyüp in Istanbul to which she donated some books with the provision that they be kept in a cabinet in her mausoleum.[141] As in the case of Bedreddin Mahmud's library in Kayseri, the books were placed in the mausoleum purely out of convenience. Some scholars have, in an attempt to classify libraries according to the location of the books, coined the phrase "mausoleum library," analogous to mosque library or dervish convent library. It must be emphasized that in the absence of a purpose-built library, books were placed in a convenient and secure location. The mausoleum was as secure as any building in a complex. The catalogue of this library is a particularly good example from this period, giving a detailed physical description of each book in the collection.

The Grand Vizier Sokollu Mehmed Pasha established three libraries, one in his college in Istanbul, another in a dervish convent he had established, also in Istanbul, and a third in his college in Bergos.[142] As in the case of his wife's endowment, the catalogue of these libraries is very detailed in the physical

---

139 *Hadaikü'l-Haka'ik*, vol. 1 (İstanbul: n.p., 1268H), 72.
140 Istanbul Court Registers Balat Mahkemesi No. 2, 81b–82a.
141 VGMA, No. 572, 141.
142 VGMA, No. 572, 27–63 and Kasa No. 103.

description of the books. He makes a further provision for necessary precautions to be taken to prevent theft by substitution and provides money in order to replace any book which becomes worn out due to overuse. [143]

Selim II established a library in the college which he built in İzmir, a few years after ascending the throne.[144] When he completed his complex in Edirne in 1575, he endowed it with a library. The foundation deed (1579) demonstrates that the catalogue and the richness of the collection are of great interest, but so are the provisions for staffing the library.[145] He provides for three librarians, two of whom were to be trained calligraphers and ornamentors, and whenever necessary they were to repair the books and replace missing text and ornamentation.[146] We learn from the introduction to the catalogue, which is appended to the foundation deed, that unlike Süleymaniye, where the books were donated to the complex some years after its completion, the volumes were collected beforehand and were ready to be used as soon as the Selimiye complex opened.[147]

Nurbanu Sultan, the senior wife of Selim II and mother of Murad III, built a complex in Üsküdar. From an account book we see that a library was located there in the mosque with a librarian at a stipend of two aspers per day.[148]

Koca Sinan Pasha, the grand vizier who led the conquest of Yemen, used much of his wealth in building numerous religious foundations,[149] four of which were endowed with libraries. An endowment deed dated 1586 tells us that he endowed books to four separate institutions, a college in the İshak Pasha district in Istanbul, a college in Aydın and a college in Malkara where he had been exiled on several occasions, and a dervish convent in Kulaksız in Istanbul. The college in Istanbul provided for a head reciter of the Koran to be given the responsibility to look after the books with an extra salary of one asper per day, while the others had no particular provisions in terms of a librarian.[150]

---

143 VGMA, Kasa No. 103, 1–80.
144 VGMA, No. 741, 84; Münir Aktepe, "İzmir Şehri Osmanlı Devri Medreseleri Hakkında Ön Bilgi," *TD* 26 (1972): 26, 114, and 117.
145 VGMA, No. 1395, 87–114.
146 VGMA, Kasa No. 169, 76–77; M. Cunbur, "Osmanlı Çağı Türk Vakıf Kütüphanelerinde Personel Düzenini Geliştirme Çabaları," in *VII. Türk Tarih Kongresi*, 7 (1973), 679.
147 VGMA, No. 1395, 91; BOA, Maliye-Ahkam Def. KK. 67, 776.
148 BOA, MAD, 5455, 91, MAD, 6483, 5; Nina Cichocki, "The Life Story of the Çemberlitaş Hamam: From Bath to Tourist Attraction" (PhD diss., University of Minnesota, 2005), 364, 371, 383.
149 Şerafettin Turan, "Sinan Paşa," *İA* 10 (1940–1986): 674.
150 BOA, Haremeyn Dosyası No. 1 (Süleymaniye); M. Cevdet, 188.

As for Sinan Pasha's personal library: it was housed after his death in his mausoleum in Divan Yolu in Istanbul. An account book notes that a librarian there received a salary of eight aspers per day, which suggests that the collection may have been quite sizable.[151] As his mausoleum is located in the vicinity of several colleges, we may also presume that the library was for the use of students studying in the surrounding colleges.

Towards the end of the century, three prominent men, Chief Mufti Zekeriyya Efendi,[152] Chief Eunuch Gazanfer Ağa,[153] and Hadım Hafız Ahmed Pasha[154] founded colleges each endowed with a library. Zekeriyya Efendi's library was located in his mausoleum and his son the Chief Mufti Yahya Efendi augmented the librarian's salary by three aspers per day in 1638.[155]

Besides college libraries, there were a number of mosque libraries founded for the benefit of teachers and students and the congregation. In 1568, Ali b. Receb founded a library in his mosque in Yiannitsá, in the deed of which he placed a strict stipulation for lending: the librarian should obtain from the reader a deposit twice the value of the book and refuse to lend to inhabitants of other cities or the surrounding villages.[156] Hemşinzade donated some books to Ulu Cami in Bursa in 1585 and provided that books might be lent on deposit of a pledge and with a known person standing as guarantor.[157] Pertev Pasha drew up an endowment deed providing money for a mosque to be built in the town of İzmit wherever it was felt necessary and endowed twenty-one books for the use of the congregation. The mosque was completed in 1579 and a librarian with a stipend of one asper per day appointed.[158] In 1584, Mehmed Efendi b. Abdullah Molla Çelebi endowed a library to the mosque in Fındıklı in Istanbul. The purpose was to serve the needs of the students of a college which he intended to build nearby.[159] Another library was endowed in 1591 by Mehmed Ağa for his mosque in Çarşanba in Istanbul. The books were exclusively for the use of

---

151 BOA, Ruus No. 25, 161.
152 VGMA, No. 571, 165; Bursa Court Registers B. 63, No. 259, 95a-97a.
153 Istanbul Court Registers Davud Paşa Mahkemesi, No. 129, 33–34; VGMA, No. 571, 11–22; BOA, Ruus No. 92, 353.
154 Hüseyin Ayvansarayî, *Hadikatü'l-Cevami'*, vol. 1 (İstanbul: Matbaa-i Amire, 1281H): 87–88; Mübahat Kütükoğlu, "1869'da Faal İstanbul Medreseleri," *Tarih Enstitüsü Dergisi*, no. 7–8 (1977): 53.
155 İstanbul Üniversitesi Kütüphanesi, İbnülemin Section, No. 3151, 10b.
156 Istanbul Court Registers Rumeli Sadareti, No. 3, 38.
157 Bursa Court Registers A. 143, No. 170, 240.
158 Beyazıt Umumi Kütüphanesi, No. 5157, 62a–b; BOA, MAD, 626, 351; Abdülkadir Erdoğan, "Kanuni Süleyman Devri Vezirlerinden Pertev Paşa ve Eserleri," *VD* 2 (1942): 235–236.
159 VGMA, No. 624, 5; Cengiz Orhunlu, "Fındıklı Semtinin Tarihi Hakkında Bir Araştırma," *TD* 7, no. 10 (1954): 66–68; M. Baha Tanman, "İstanbul'un Ortadan Kalkan Tarihî

college teachers, a condition clearly stated not only in the endowment deed, but also on the seal attached to each book.[160]

One of the most interesting mosque libraries was endowed in 1593 by a certain Mahmud Bey whose thirty-nine-book library was given to the Cihangir Mosque in Istanbul. With a few exceptions all the books are in Turkish and mostly of a nonreligious nature, consisting of anthologies of folk tales and famous love epics. The books were to be lent, but the loan was restricted to a period of a month. Although housed in a mosque, this is a public library intended for the use of the local people.[161]

Cerrah Mehmed Pasha founded a library in his mosque in Istanbul in 1594. Based on the contents of the books, the library was probably intended for the two colleges, Gevher Sultan and Haseki, situated nearby.[162]

Although there are no archival records, recent research indicates that the following mosques and colleges had libraries endowed towards the end of the sixteenth century. These endowments were made by the following benefactors: Zal Mahmud Pasha in Eyüp (1570), Karagöz Bey in Mostar (1570),[163] Abdurrahman Pasha in Tosya (1584),[164] Mesih Pasha in Istanbul in the Eski Ali Pasha Mosque (1586),[165] Murad III in the Muradiye Mosque in Manisa (1586),[166] Lala Mustafa Pasha in Ilgın (1591),[167] and Dervish Pasha in Mostar (1593).[168]

Two specialist collections are noted in this period. The first is the collection of the chief physician to the palace. In a document of 1576, we have a list of the books given to the Chief Physician Molla Kasım. In 1580, we see the same

---

Eserlerinden Fındıklı'da Hatuniye Külliyesi," in *Prof. Dr. Yılmaz Önge Armağanı* (Konya: Selçuk Üniversitesi, 1993), 139–161.

160 TSA, No. xxx, EH, 3028; Süleymaniye Kütüphanesi, Mehmed Ağa Camii, No. 134.

161 Istanbul Court Registers Galata Mahkemesi, No. 17, 187–188.

162 Ayvansarayî, *Hadikatü'l-Cevamî*, 1:71; Belediye Kütüphanesi (now Atatürk Library), No. Mc. O. 70, 446.

163 Hafzija Hasandedic, "Muslimanske Biblioteke u Mostaru," *Annali Gazi Husrev-begove Biblioteke1* (1972): 107–108; Hadziosmanovic, *Biblioteke u Bosnı ı Hercegovina Za Vrijeme Austrougarske Vladavıne*, 73–75.

164 A. Gökoğlu, *Paphlagonia-Pagflagonya* (Kastamonu: Doğrusöz Matbaası, 1952), 228–229.

165 VGMA, 746, 83; Halit Dener, *Süleymaniye Umumi Kütüphanesi* (İstanbul: İstanbul Maarif Basımevi, 1957), 43; Süleymaniye Kütüphanesi, Mesih Paşa, No. 37.

166 İsmet Parmaksızoğlu, "Manisa Kütüphaneleri," *TKDB* 8, no. 1 (1959): 19. From a record in Manisa Court Registers No. 11, 237–238), it is learnt that an inspection of books was carried out in September 1657. The author would like to thank Prof. Feridun Emecen for providing this information.

167 Ilgın Court Registers No. 261, 186; M. Cunbur, "Yusuf Ağa Kütüphanesi ve Kütüphane Vakfiyesi," *TAD* 1, no. 1 (1963): 206.

168 Hasandedic, "Muslimanske Biblioteke u Mostaru": 108.

books passed onto Molla Kasım's successor on his retirement.[169] While not a library in the strict sense of the word, it is a collection for the use of the chief physician. A second specialist collection was attached to the observatory built by Takiyüddin (d. 1585) in Istanbul while he was the sultan's chief astronomer.[170] We see that the sultan took special interest in the collection and occasionally expanded it. A certain Lutfullah left some books on astronomy to be cared for by the muezzin and imam of the mosque in the Mimar Sinan district in Istanbul. Sultan Murad III ordered that these books be placed in the observatory for the benefit of the chief astronomer.[171] Another decree commanded that the books of the astronomer, Kurd, should be sent with all due haste by the Governor of Saruhan and Judge of Manisa to Istanbul, presumably again to be added to the collection at the observatory.[172]

From the beginning of the seventeenth century all the major cities of the empire were well-endowed with mosques, colleges and institutions associated with religious and cultural institutions, among which we include libraries. It was now the turn of the smaller cities and towns to develop libraries. At a first glance, this expansion of libraries throughout the Balkans and Anatolia may suggest an increase in literacy, but the contents of these libraries are mainly college texts, Arabic books and commentaries and translations into Turkish which would suggest that the expansion of the library system merely reflects the expansion of the college system. The libraries were established to meet the needs of the students. Some of these small town libraries were established by the following benefactors: Mustafa Dede in his dervish convent on the island of Lesbos (1602),[173] Müeyyedzade Pîrî Çelebi in Amasya in the vicinity of the Hatuniye Mosque (1609),[174] Kaçanikli Mehmed Pasha in his mausoleum in Skopje (1608),[175] Ali Ağa b. Yahya in his college in Mostar,[176] Tavlasunlu Halil Pasha in the village of Tavlasun in Kayseri (1617),[177] Şeyh Hüsameddin in his

---

169 TSA, No. D. 8228.
170 Aydın Sayılı, "Alauddin Mansur'un İstanbul Rasathanesi Hakkındaki Şiirleri," *Belleten* 20, no. 79 (1956): 411- 428; Süheyl Ünver, *İstanbul Rasathanesi* (Ankara: Türk Tarih Kurumu Basımevi, 1965), 47–48.
171 Ahmet Refik, *Onaltıncı Asırda İstanbul Hayatı: 1553–1591* (İstanbul: İstanbul Devlet Basımevi, 1935), 36.
172 BOA, Mühimme Defteri, No. 49, 44.
173 Istanbul Court Registers Evkaf-ı Hümayun Müfettişliği, No. 8, 105.
174 Hüseyin Hüsameddin, *Amasya Tarihi*, vol. 1 (İstanbul: Hikmet Matbaası, 1327H), 262.
175 BOA, Ruus No. 78, 152; Hasan Kaleşi-Mehmed Mehmedovski, *Tri vakufnami na kačanikli Mehmed-Paša* (Skopje: Nova Makedonija, 1958), 20–21; Ekrem Hakkı Ayverdi, *Avrupa'da Osmanlı Mimari Eserleri: Yugoslavya*, vol. 3.3 (İstanbul: İstanbul Fetih Cemiyeti, 1981), 259.
176 Istanbul Court Registers Evkaf-ı Hümayun Müfettişliği, No. 50, 149.
177 Kazım Özdoğan, *Kayseri Tarihi* (Kayseri: Kayseri Erciyes Matbaası, 1948), 107–108.

dervish convent in Bursa (1612),[178] the Chief Eunuch Bosnalı Ahmed Ağa in his college in Mostar (1653),[179] Köprülü Mehmed Pasha in his mosque in Bozcaada (1660),[180] Merzifonlu Kara Mustafa Pasha in his mosques in Merzifon (1668),[181] and İncesu (1670),[182] Mehmed IV in his mosque in Crete,[183] the Grand Vizier Mehmed Pasha in his complex in Erkilet in Kayseri (1671),[184] and Hüseyin Ağa in Eyne Bey Sübaşı college in Bursa (1674).[185]

In the seventeenth century, established institutions also began to receive collections through gifts and endowments, which were usually documented in an endowment deed.[186] When a small endowment of, for example, a single book or two or three books, was made, it was more usual to record the endowment on the flyleaf of the book.

Until the establishment of independent libraries beginning with the Köprülü Library in 1678, all major colleges in Istanbul had their own libraries. Indeed, the founders of new colleges did not, as in previous times, found a college in the hope that a library would be donated at a later date, or that the students

---

178 Kamil Kepeci, *Bursa Şer'iyye Sicilleri Kütüphaneler Defteri*. According to a record made in 1622, these books were moved to the Temenye Mosque (Bursa Court Registers B. 41, No. 235, 160a). For the list of books in this collection see: Hasan Basri Öcalan, *Bursa'da Tasavvuf Kültürü* (Bursa: Gaye Kitabevi, 2000), 252–253.

179 Hafzija Hasandedic, "Muslimanske Biblioteke u Mostaru," *Anali Gazi Hüsrev-begove biblioteke* 1 (1972): 108.

180 Köprülü Library, Vakfiye, No. 1, 15b.

181 Istanbul Court Registers Evkaf-ı Hümayun Müfettişliği No. 63, 28. For an appointment of a librarian to this mosque see: BOA, Ruus No. 16, 351.

182 BOA, Cevdet-Maarif No. 404; BOA, Ruus No. 84, 471; Abdullah Kuran, "Orta Anadolu'da Klasik Osmanlı Mimarisi Çağının Sonlarında Yapılan İki Külliye," *VD* 9, no. 5 (1971): 239–243.

183 BOA, Süleymaniye, No. 2918, 1b-2a.

184 Özdoğan, *Kayseri Tarihi*, 108.

185 In some of the books donated to Eyne Bey Subaşı College in Bursa, the donor's seal reads "The endowment of Hüseyin Ağa, son of Mustafa, known as the son of the late Grand Vizier Fazıl Ahmed's uncle. 1085" [1674]. Which means that Mustafa has to be Fazıl Ahmed Pasha's uncle. This, the most famous of families to supply a line of grand viziers is well documented. Nowhere, save in this seal, is there mention of Fazıl Ahmed Pasha's having an uncle by the name of Mustafa. This puzzling reference still remains a complete mystery to me. This has caused some scholars to ascribe the endowment of books to this library to Grand Vizier Amcazade Hüseyin Pasha (see Kazım Baykal, *Bursa Anıtları* [Bursa: Aysan Matbaası 1950], 97; Mefail Hızlı, *Osmanlı Klasik Döneminde Bursa Medreseleri* [İstanbul: İz Yayıncılık, 1998], 44; Ömer S. Kurmuş, "Bursa'da Yazma ve Eski Basma Eserler Kütüphaneleri," *Evliyaları ve Abideleriyle Şehirler Sultanı Bursa* [Bursa: Uludağ Yayınları, 2003], 212–213). The reason for this is that they have confused him with Hüseyin Ağa who is referred to in a court record dated 1093 [1682] as "late Hüseyin Ağa," (Bursa Court Registers B. 107, 138a–b). As Amcazade Hüseyin Pasha did not die until 1114, No. 1702, the two Hüseyins must be different persons.

186 For examples of this see *TKT*, 56.

of the college would benefit from the collections of other institutions nearby, but ensured that the college was provided with its own library from the outset. Thus we see new colleges being founded with a library: Kuyucu Murad Pasha (1610),[187] Sultan Ahmed I (1617),[188] Kazasker Hasan Efendi (1630),[189] The Chief Mufti Abdurrahim Efendi (1650),[190] Yeni Cami (1663, 1666),[191] Mimarbaşı Kasım Ağa,[192] Abbas Ağa b. Abdüsselam (1670),[193] Mustafa Efendi b. Abdüsselam (1677),[194] and Bayram Pasha (1636).[195]

In the middle of the seventeenth century, two libraries were established in existing mosques where these collections were not created by means of an endowment deed, but were gifted in the will of the deceased donor. The conditions attached to the administration of these collections are extremely unusual and worth mentioning. The first of these was a donation of seventy-one books made to the Üsküplü Mosque in Cibali in Istanbul by Mehmed Pasha on behalf of a certain Mustafa Efendi. The will, dated 1667, stipulates that the books should only be lent out to poor scholars and that the supervision of the endowment should be in the hands of the whole congregation of the mosque acting as a committee.[196] Another library was established in the İplikçi Mosque in Konya by a teacher Ali Efendi, acting as the executor of Mahmud Efendi's will. The will, dated 1672, provided for seventy-eight books to be donated on the condition that they be lent out to poor students and scholars of the İplikçi College for a period not exceeding six months on the deposit of a pledge, and should the book be lost the pledge was to be sold and a "reliable version" of the book should be bought. Again, the supervision of the collection was in the hands of the congregation, who were not to receive payment for their efforts.[197]

---

187 Şemim Emsem, "Osmanlı İmparatorluğu Devrinde Türkiye Kütüphanelerinin Tarihçesi," *TKDB* 9, nos. 1–2 (1960): 32.
188 Istanbul Court Registers Evkaf-ı Hümayun Müfettişliği, No. 57, 49–50; BOA, MAD, 6888, 6 and 66–67; VGMA, No. 71, 3.
189 BOA, Süleymaniye, No. 2864, 14b; BOA, Ruus No. 55, 5.
190 BOA, Ruus No. 80, 220 and Ruus No. 82, 84.
191 VGMA, No. 744, 23–24 and 112–135.
192 BOA, Ruus No. 89, 184.
193 Istanbul Court Registers Evkaf-ı Hümayun Müfettişliği, No. 63, 16–22.
194 Istanbul Court Registers Bab Mahkemesi No. 26, 103b–105b and Bab Mahkemesi, No. 29, 129b–131a.
195 M. Kütükoğlu, "1869'da Faal İstanbul Medreseleri," 32; Zeynep Nayır, "İstanbul Haseki'de Bayram Paşa Külliyesi," in *Ord. Prof. İsmail Hakkı Uzunçarşılı'ya Armağan* (Ankara: Türk Tarih Kurumu, 1976), 397–410.
196 Istanbul Court Registers Ahi Çelebi Mahkemesi, No. 19, 36b–37a.
197 Istanbul Court Registers Ahi Çelebi Mahkemesi, No. 29, 23a–b.

The attitude of the religious authorities to the donation of books is well exemplified in the following, rather unusual, case. A certain Abdulkadir Efendi died without leaving a will regarding his private collection of books. Two persons appeared in front of the judge in Istanbul responsible for dealing with the estates of deceased persons and claimed that Abdülkadir Efendi had orally pledged his collection, in front of witnesses, to the dervish convent which he had founded in Karagümrük in Istanbul. This oral testament had apparently been made in a remote town while he had been travelling to Istanbul. The judge ruled in favor of the dervish lodge rather than the other beneficiaries of his estate, and the books were sent to his dervish convent.[198]

From its humble beginnings, the Ottoman library system had, by the end of the seventeenth century, developed into a large, sophisticated entity which provided for libraries not only in the major cities of the empire, but also in many small towns. With the establishment of the independent libraries the Ottoman library system was to take a new direction.

---

198 Istanbul Court Registers Kısmet-i Askeriyye, No. 8, 62a–b.

Chapter Three

Independent and Large College Libraries (1650s–1730)

The second half of the seventeenth century witnessed a new development: the establishment of independent libraries which were not attached to specific institutions and intended for the public at large. In other words, libraries were established as libraries rather than as an ancillary adjunct to an educational or religious institution.[1] Not only did these libraries have their own buildings, but more importantly they had staff whose sole responsibility was dealing with books and readers. Whereas previously the librarian in a mosque or college would work in the library on a part-time basis and would most likely have held a position as an imam or teacher, depending on what type of institution the library was attached to, in the independent library the staff would primarily function as professional librarians. This change is reflected in the salaries of the librarians. In the colleges and mosques, the librarians were given a small stipend to reward them for the extra hours they devoted to library work, but in the independent library the librarians received a full salary.

There are examples of independent library buildings before the mid-seventeenth century, but they were part of a larger institution or complex. It is the status of the staff which defines the status of the independent library.

---

1   Müjgan Cunbur has discussed institutional and independent libraries in "Vakfiyelerine Göre Eski Türk Kütüphanelerinin Yönetimi," *TKDB* 11, nos. 1–2 (1962): 3–4.

Many mosques and colleges were built within a complex of buildings. Some of these complexes had devoted a particular building to the storage of books, and in the strictest sense, these buildings can be considered libraries. However, the personnel who serviced the library were members of the staff of the larger institution and worked in the library on a part-time basis. The foundation deed setting up the complex often intended that a particular building be used as a library, but the endower saw the library as a part of a larger whole, not as an independent institution. Examples of such libraries can be found in the complex of Eyne Bey Sübaşı, established in the fifteenth century in Bursa and Çoban Mustafa Pasha in Gebze in the sixteenth century.

FIGURE 2. Köprülü Library, Istanbul, est. 1678.

Ottoman historians generally accept that the first independent Ottoman library was the Köprülü Library established in the second half of the seventeenth century.[2] It is one of the many ironies of history that its establishment as an independent institution was purely accidental. Grand Vizier Köprülü Mehmed

2 Müjgan Cunbur, "Türk Kütüphaneciliğinin Tarihî Kökenleri," *TKDB* 12, nos. 3–4 (1963): 115; Cevdet Türkay, "İstanbul Kütüphaneleri," *Belgelerle Türk Tarihi Dergisi* 13, nos. 74–76 (1974): 69.

Pasha was intending to establish a complex of buildings in which there would be a mosque, a college, public baths, and a library building surrounding his own mausoleum. He built the public baths, the college and mausoleum before his death in 1661. His son Fazıl Ahmed Pasha attempted to complete the complex on the terms of his father's will.[3] He not only built the library building, but added his own large book collection to that of his father's.[4] The library would have been incorporated into the larger complex had not Fazıl Ahmed Pasha died at a relatively young age in 1676. Fazıl Ahmed Pasha's brother, Fazıl Mustafa Pasha, was left with the responsibility of completing the task originated by his father, namely, to prepare endowment deeds for the library and open it to the public.[5] However, the college, public baths, and mausoleum were already functioning, and more importantly already had foundation deeds. As he could not amend the original deed for the other institutions, the practical step was to establish a specific foundation deed for the library, allowing it to have its own staff who would be, in effect, totally independent of the other institutions. Thus, the first independent Ottoman library was born. It was originally envisaged by the founder as a library for the college, and indeed the sort of books endowed were college textbooks, which were mainly Arabic. A general library, intended for the public, would have had a different type of collection.

The foundation deed prepared by Fazıl Mustafa Pasha provided for three librarians, a bookbinder, and a doorman, each paid on a full-time basis and, for the period, very adequately.[6] The deed also stated the conditions on which books were to be lent, that is, on a limited basis with safeguards to ensure the return of books. This particular clause attracted the attention of previous historians and led them to tentatively regard the Köprülü Library as the first to institute a lending policy, thus making it, in effect, the first Ottoman lending library.[7] However, by looking at a wider selection of foundation deeds for libraries, we discover that the lending of books was already widespread and the norm in Ottoman libraries at the time of the Köprülü Library's founding. Far from being the first library to lend books, it was instead one of the first to restrict lending. In fact, the Köprülü

---

3 M. Tayyib Gökbilgin, "Köprülüler," İA 6 (1940–1986): 902.
4 Defterdar Sarı Mehmed Paşa, Zübde-i Vekayi'at, ed. Abdülkadir Özcan (Ankara: Türk Tarih Kurumu Basımevi, 1995), 76–77.
5 Köprülü Kütüphanesi, Vakfiye, no. 2 (1678).
6 Muzaffer Gökman, Kütüphanelerimizden Notlar (İstanbul: Kardeşler Basımevi, 1952), 33.
7 Ibid., 35; M. Cunbur, ""Vakfiyelerine Göre Eski Türk Kütüphanelerinin Yönetimi," TKDB 11, nos. 1–2 (1962): 17; Necati Gültepe, "Vakıf Kütüphaneciliğinin Müesseseleşmesi," Türk Yurdu 8, no. 6 (1987): 25.

Library was a watershed in the practice of lending books, for whereas before its foundation it was the norm to lend books, after Köprülü Library restrictions on lending become increasingly stricter, until by the mid-eighteenth century the practice had almost disappeared.

The question of lending books had been a thorny problem for generations of founders of libraries. Instinctively, they wished to prohibit lending books outside library premises. But they were unable to restrict the reading of the books to within the library, mainly because of the Islamic tradition that no impediment should be placed on a scholar's access to knowledge. While successive foundation deeds put increasingly tighter controls on the way books were to be lent, the principle that they should be lent remained sacrosanct. The Köprülü Library started off with the principle that books should not leave the building and then placed exceptions for certain persons and students in certain circumstances. Whereas in effect the practice of lending books may not have been very different to that of previously established libraries, the principle governing lending was radically altered.[8]

As we have noted, the Köprülü Library became independent through an accident of fate, because of the untimely death of the founder's son. As an exceptional instance, it played little part in the development of the independent library at large. In the period in which the Köprülü Library was founded, most libraries which were endowed were generally established within a large college and continued to be so for another half century. We must wait more than a half century before we see the emergence and development of the institution of the independent Ottoman library.

Large college libraries continued to be the favored endowment of rich benefactors. When Köprülü's son-in-law, Grand Vizier Merzifonlu Kara Mustafa Pasha, began a complex of buildings in Çarşıkapı in Istanbul before the second siege of Vienna in 1683, he intended it to function as a college; the books that he wished to endow would form the basis of the college library. However, when he died the building he had designated for the college was not yet complete and the foundation deed specified that until it was completed the books were to be kept in a storehouse, and a librarian was to open the storeroom once a week for the benefit of readers.[9] The college buildings were completed in 1690[10] by his

---

8 For the lending of books in Ottoman libraries see chapter 9, "Services Offered."
9 VGMA, 641, 95.
10 Mübahat S. Kütükoğlu, "1869'da Faal İstanbul Medreseleri," *Tarih Enstitüsü Dergisi* 7–8 (1977): 83.

son Ali Bey, who made provision for teaching staff and two librarians to take care of the books.[11]

A different member of the Köprülü family, Amcazade Hüseyin Pasha, founded a college in Saraçhane, in Istanbul, to which he endowed a collection of five hundred books in 1700 and provided not only for two librarians to look after the books, but also, and somewhat exceptionally for a college library of this period, a bookbinder.[12] The famous scholar, the chief mufti Feyzullah Efendi, built a college in 1699 in the Fatih district of Istanbul, to which he endowed a library worthy of a scholar of his status. The collection consisted of almost two thousand books, making it the richest college library, on a par with the Köprülü Library.[13] Three librarians were provided for, all at the same salary,[14] whereas the normal practice would have been to have a senior librarian with two assistants and an appropriate differential in salary. It is reported elsewhere that not all his books went to his college, but that a large number of books were also endowed to a college in Medina.[15]

Although the large college library was the main development in the Ottoman library system in late seventeenth-century Istanbul, in Anatolia small collections of about one hundred to three hundred books would be endowed as the basis of a mosque or college library. Scholars wishing to endow similar small collections in Istanbul would tend to gift them to an already existing institution. The reason would seem to be that in Anatolia there was a need for colleges with their own libraries. Istanbul, on the other hand, was well provided with mosques and colleges with or without libraries. Small collections tended to be endowed to an already existing mosque or college as a basis for its library, or to an existing library to enrich its collection.[16]

11 BOA, Ruus No. 42, 303; Ruus No. 43, 58; Ruus No. 78, 359, 498; Ruus No. 85, 76; Cevdet-Maarif 8213; İbnülemin-Tevcihat, 2531.

12 VGMA, 502, 1–12; S. Nail Bayraktar, "Amcazade Hüseyin Paşa Kütüphanesi," İstanbul Ansiklopedisi 2: 799.

13 Millet Kütüphanesi, Feyzullah Efendi, 2196, 121a. Orhan Köprülü gives the number of books in this collection as 2, 193 (İA 4, 599) and Sabra F. Meservey as 2,279 (Feyzullah Efendi: An Ottoman Şeyhülislam [PhD thesis, Princeton University, 1966], 158). These figures do not indicate the number of books endowed by Feyzullah Efendi but gives the number of books existing in the library at a later date, which may include later endowments. See also: Mehmed Serhan Tayşi, "Şeyhülislam Seyyid Feyzullah Efendi ve Feyziye Medresesi," Türk Dünyası Araştırmaları, no. 23 (1983): 9–100.

14 VGMA, 571, 119.

15 Mehmed Süreyya, Sicill-i Osmanî, vol. 4 (İstanbul: Matbaa-i Amire, 1308–1315H), 34. According to the Hicaz Salnamesi (p. 307) the number of books in this library in 1309H (1891) was 1,247.

16 Examples of small endowments can be found TKT, 66–68.

The period of Sultan Ahmed III's reign (1703–1730) is called the "Tulip Period" in Turkish history, and saw many cultural developments, including the introduction of printing and translations of books into Ottoman Turkish, and a general flourishing of arts.[17] Libraries did not benefit from this sudden burst of creativity, which affected the intellectual life of Istanbul in this period. While they continued to evolve slowly, they did witness developments,[18] not least of which is the foundation of the truly independent library.

FIGURE 3. Şehid Ali Pasha Library, Istanbul, est. 1716.

The first of these is the Şehid Ali Pasha Library, which has attracted the attention of several scholars because of the peculiar circumstances in which it was founded. Ali Pasha was grand vizier and son-in-law of Sultan Ahmed III. He was also a great bibliophile who, while in office, forbade the export of

17 See for the cultural activities of this period: Wilhelm Heinz, "Die Kultur der Tulpenzeit des Osmanischen Reiches," *WZKM* 61 (1967): 62–116.
18 For a general survey of the libraries established in this period, see Müjgan Cunbur, "Lale Devrinde İstanbul Kütüphaneleri," *Türk Kültürü* 9 (1971): 363–368 and *TKT*, 68–83.

books from Istanbul.[19] He was himself credited with a very large collection of books on all subjects, including philosophy, history, literature, and astronomy. He prepared a foundation deed before his death for a library, which he conceived of as an independent institution in which his books would be housed.[20] We now know that in 1715[21] Ali Pasha had established a building in Şehzadebaşı for a library in which he had placed about two thousand books. However, he had in his house in Sultanahmet and in his waterside residence in Kuzguncuk/Beylerbeyi two separate collections of books. The library at Şehzadebaşı had an endowment deed and the two collections in Kuzguncuk and Sultanahmet had another endowment deed.[22] These endowment deeds are simple documents couched in the vaguest of terms; one would have expected a man with such a large private collection to be very specific about how his library was to be run. These deeds can be understood to represent a temporary arrangement for endowing the books until such a time that he could bring his three collections together and give the necessary time and attention to the future running of his endowment. However, his wishes were not to be realized, as he was killed at the battle of Peterwardein in 1716 before he could bring his collections together.

Unfortunately, the books in Sultanahmet and Kuzguncuk never reached their intended destination, as following his death all his property was confiscated by order of the sultan.[23] But a problem quickly arose with the acquisition of the books. The sultan was unable to confiscate his son-in-law's collection directly because they had already been endowed. According to Islamic principles the sultan had to acquire a *fetva*, a legal opinion which would determine that the endowment of certain books was not allowed and consequently the endowment was invalid. A *fetva* is always couched in abstract terms in the form of a question to which the answer is invariably "permitted" or "not permitted" and the protagonist in the *fetva* is invariably named "Zeyd," In this case, the *fetva* reads:

> If Zeyd [and we understand this refers to Ali Pasha] says that
> his books are to be entrusted to knowledge and if he surrenders

---

19 *Râşid Tarihi*, vol. 4 (İstanbul: Matbaa-i Amire, 1282H), 238.
20 Two copies of his first endowment deed exist: VGMA, 628, 639–646 and Istanbul Court Registers, Rumeli Sadareti,188, 128–132. Of his second foundation deed only one copy is extant: Rumeli Sadareti,189, 47a-50b.
21 See for the chronograms for completion of the library building: Ayşen Aldoğan, "Şehit Ali Paşa Kütüphanesi," *Türkiyemiz*, no. 35 (1982): 2 and Ahmet Küçükkalfa, "Şehid Ali Paşa Kütüphanesi," *TKDB* 33 (1984): 140.
22 See abovementioned foundation deeds.
23 *Râşid Tarihi*, vol. 4 (İstanbul: Matbaa-i Amire, 1282H), 284.

them to a trustee and registers the deed trust and dies, is it permitted for Zayd's books on Philosophy, History, Literature, and Astronomy, which are full of lies, to be included in the endowment. Is it proper that such books be included in an endowment of books and on this subject an opinion is requested?

To which the answer was "it is not permitted," with an explanation that "it is not the established practice to endow such books."[24]

Adnan Adıvar, an eminent scholar, in his *Osmanlı Türklerinde İlim* [The Ottoman Turks and the Sciences], accepted the *fetva* at its face value and commented on it thus:

This demonstrates a mentality which prevailed as late as the beginning of the eighteenth century, that far from regarding Philosophy, History, Literature, and Astronomy books as useful or even acceptable, banned them from public libraries.[25]

So powerful is an idea as simple as this that we find it repeated until it has become part of the corpus of received ideas about the Ottoman attitude to knowledge.[26] Adnan Adıvar of course approached his material looking for an answer as to why the Ottomans should remain behind Europe in terms of technological development. A simple solution lies in a single *fetva*: religious reaction to new ideas banned science books and even books on history from public libraries and thus the Ottomans remained in the scientific Middle Ages.

Having had the advantage of viewing the lists of books in mosque and college libraries of the centuries preceding this *fetva*, I have noticed that there did not

---

24 Ahmet Refik, *Alimler ve Sanatkarlar* (İstanbul: Kütübhane-i Hilmi, 1924), 332.
25 Adnan Adıvar, *Osmanlı Türklerinde İlim* (İstanbul: Maarif matbaası, 1943), 139.
26 Adnan Adıvar was working in a period where it was not fashionable to say anything positive about Ottoman attitudes and this should be taken into consideration. But to find the incident accepted at face value in more recent works is puzzling; Bernard Lewis, *The Muslim Discovery of Europe* (New York: W. W. Norton, 1982), 240; Halil İnalcık, *The Ottoman Empire: The Classical Age 1300–1600*, trans. Norman Itzkowitz and Colin Imber (London: Praeger Publishers, 1973), 180; Fatma Müge Göçek, *East Encounters West, France and the Ottoman Empire in the Eighteenth Century* (Oxford: Oxford University Press, 1987), 109. Fatma Müge Göçek refers to the religious authorities' concern that these books on history, literature, astronomy, philosophy, etc. should not be available to the public: "The moment these private libraries were endowed for public use, however, the religous authorities closely scrutinized the contents of the books. Only religous books were permitted to be endowed for public use. The nonreligous books were sold out [sic] by Ottoman collectors" (109). Such a view flies in face of all our observations on the contents of Ottoman libraries.

appear to be any such prejudice.[27] Indeed, the reign of Ahmed III was marked for its openness to Western ideas. I found the contents of the *fetva* extremely curious, especially in view of the Islamic scruples about impeding the scholar's access to knowledge. It was these very scruples that created the Ottoman lending library against the better judgment and instinct of the founders. I felt that this *fetva* could not be taken at face value, that there had to be some explanation other than a completely uncharacteristic and atypical action on the part of a single chief mufti.

I therefore set out to find out everything I could about Ali Pasha's books and discovered that the collection of his books was divided into three, each of which had a catalogue. In his lifetime he had drawn up and registered trust deeds for all three libraries, one of which had an independent building.[28] When he died the sultan ordered that all his goods be divided into two lists; those effects which were endowed and those that were not. The sultan issued a firman ordering that "the books which Ali Pasha was about to endow should be examined and those suitable for the palace should be sent there and those that were valuable should be kept and a list of their names sent to the palace, and the remainder should be sold."[29] However, the sultan, to his great disappointment, discovered that the books were all endowed and therefore, by Islamic law, were protected from confiscation.[30] The only solution was to have the chief mufti declare by *fetva* that the endowment of such books was not permitted by Islamic law, consequently making the foundation deed invalid. The *fetva* quoted above was the instrument whereby the sultan was able to confiscate his son-in-law's magnificent collection. Notably, the sultan was unable to confiscate the books in the library in Şehzadebaşı which was already functioning as, presumably, it was well known among the population of the city that these books had been endowed. The books in the collection that escaped confiscation also included many books on philosophy, history, literature, and astronomy. The two libraries that were confiscated were still in Ali Pasha's private residences in the Sultanahmet and Kuzguncuk areas of the city, and presumably it was not generally known that they had been endowed.

It is hard to view this *fetva* as anything other than extremely exceptional. For years, books on science, astronomy, history, and literature had been endowed without

---

27 There are numerous examples of these types of books being endowed. Even mosques were endowed with fictional works, dream interpretations, and even romances. An example of this is the Cihangir Mosque to which books of romances, folktales, and dream interpretation were endowed. See Istanbul Court Registers, Galata Mahkemesi 17, 187–188.

28 See footnote no. 271.

29 For this decree see: A. Refik, *Alimler ve Sanatkarlar* (İstanbul: Kütübhane-i Hilmi, 1924), 334.

30 Muhammed Abdullah el-Kebisî, *Ahkâmu'l-Vakf fi'ş-Şeriati'l-İslamiyye* (Baghdad: Matbaatü'l-İrşad, 1977), 377.

objection. The cataloguers in the Ottoman libraries for many centuries made no attempt to hide these books and created classification headings such as astronomy, poetry, history, and philosophy (*ilm-i kelam*).[31] After this incident the practice continued, and such books were endowed with no religious hesitation whatsoever. Indeed, the very books that were confiscated were endowed only a few years later by Ahmed III! We cannot even entertain the idea that this was a single act of bigotry on the part of a chief mufti. The fact remains that in Islamic law any item which is not fit for endowment is not fit to be sold, and in the imperial decree it is clearly stated that some of the books were to be sold. The *fetva* was, then, merely an instrument whereby the sultan could confiscate his son-in-law's library and has very little to do with either Islamic law or the Ottoman attitude to scientific knowledge. This incident, far from showing any hostility towards or fear of public access to books of this type, shows that they were in fact highly prized and coveted, even if it required a bogus religious sanction for the sultan to get his hands on them.

In 1718, the Ottoman Empire concluded the war with Austria, and with the treaty of Passarowitz a period of peace began. Grand Vizier İbrahim Pasha, son-in-law of the reigning Sultan Ahmed III (1703–1730), set out to tackle the problems of the empire and encourage cultural activities. Among these activities were the formation of committees of scholars tasked to choose and translate some classical works into Turkish and the establishment of a printing press.

As part of this cultural revival there was, as we would expect, the expansion and reorganization of the sultan's own Palace Library. The Palace Library had, up to Ahmed III's reign, no fixed site and the books were housed in various locations.[32] Furthermore, the collection would be periodically depleted whenever a sultan was founding a library, with books going from the palace collection to become the basis of a new library in a new foundation. Ahmed III gathered the major collections of books in the palace and constructed a library building to house them. Furthermore, he endowed them so that they could not be transferred elsewhere. In the introduction to the foundation deed of this library Ahmed III explains the reason for establishing this library:

> From the first days of the sublime Ottoman State books of boundless beauty and value, which were acquired by purchase or were presented to the imperial treasury in the new Imperial Palace, became priceless jewels of great worth but were rendered unavailable and unusable by men of knowledge and these books were closeted

31 See, for instance, catalogue of Fatih Library, TSA, 9559.
32 İ. Baykal, "Topkapı Sarayı Müzesi Kitaplıkları," *Güzel Sanatlar* 6 (1949): 76.

and forgotten in the dusty corners of cabinets and men who were desirous of knowledge were left bereft of any hope of using them.[33]

FIGURE 4. Sultan Ahmed III Library at Topkapı Palace, est. 1719.

---

33 VGMA, Defter 90, 3. In fact, it was not merely benign neglect that was endangering the books, but the far more serious harm caused by pilfering and theft, not least of all at the behest of foreign embassies and visitors. Pietro della Valle noted in 1615 that the Palace Library had an intact work of Titus Livy and in a letter to his friend Mario Schipano revealed that the doge of Venice was determined to acquire it, and had offered five thousand piastres for it. Della Valle claims that the offer of such a sum would alert the Turks to the fact that the book might be even more valuable, and they would not sell it. The Venetian ambassador had therefore offered the custodian of library ten thousand Scudi to steal the book and hand it over. However, the book was never delivered because the custodian could not find it. Apparently, according to Della Valle, the only way to acquire books from the Palace was bribing a palace official. Della Valle seems to imply that the ambassador had already acquired a number of Greek and Hebrew books in this manner. Della Valle Pietro, *Viaggi* (Venice: Baglioni, 1667), 179. We learn from a letter of Greaves written in 1638 that this plundering continued for sometime: "I have procured, among other works, Ptolemy's *Almagest*, the fairest book that I have seen; stolen by a spahy, as I am informed, out of the king's library in the seraglio." Quoted in Robert Walpole, *Memoirs Relating to European and Asiatic Turkey*, Edited from Manuscript Journals by Robert Walpole (London: Longman & Co., 1817), xvii.

Before the library building commenced, preparations were made by various palace officials for the books to be readied. They were taken from the treasury and handed over to the palace librarian.[34] We get a rare insight into how these preparations were carried out from a document dealing with the binding of the books. It is from a palace official to the sultan himself:

> My Majestic, Esteemed, Magnificent and Puissant Benefactor Sultan!
>
> This binder is not like other idlers and takes his work seriously. If now, in accordance with Your Imperial Decree, ten books were to be given to him he would complete and return them upon which a further ten books could be given to him. When your Blessed Imperial Decree came, the binder was in the presence of the treasurer and I said to him thus, "You are charging too much, you shall do each book of my Majestic Esteemed Sultan for 20 *para* a piece" and I insisted on this. He replied thus, "Everyone knows I did Ali Pasha's books for 40 *para* a piece; but as you insist, I shall do the books of Our Sultan for 20 *para* a piece. Should a position become vacant, you will give me a stipend of some aspers per day." If therefore ten books were to be sent to me, I will give them to him immediately.

The decision of the sultan is inscribed on the top of this document in Ahmed III's own hand:

> Let us give to this man a position of repairer in the library at ten aspers per day. Mehmed of Bursa wants this post, but he is not sufficiently diligent. Let ten books be sent now.[35]

Records exist describing various ceremonies and expenses involved in the building of the library.[36] When the foundation stone was laid a certain teacher in the palace said a prayer and was rewarded with 190 pieces of gold.[37] The total cost of the library as recorded in a document dated 1719, came to 19,750 piastres.[38] The historian Raşid Efendi notes that when the library, which was to

---

34 TSA, D. 2362, 132, 3a–b.
35 BOA, İbnülemin, Hatt-ı Hümayun, 388.
36 TSA, D. 2362, 9; D. 2002, 2b; D. 2362, 2; D. 2363, 8–12; D. 2184, 14a.
37 TSA, D. 2362, 10.
38 TSA, D. 2363, 10, 2b.

be used as a classroom as well, was opened, Selim Efendi, a palace teacher, gave an inaugural lecture, and the Sufi masters of the period said prayers. The sultan completed the celebrations by distributing money to all who had taken part in the building of the library and to the Sufi masters.[39] This library differs from other foundations in two aspects. Its use is restricted to members of the palace and its administration was to be in the hands of existing palace officials.

Ahmed III also donated some books to the Yeni Cami Mosque at the mouth of the Golden Horn. He first housed the books in the relative security of the mausoleum of Turhan Valide Sultan but, as recorded by the historian Küçükçelebizade, he realized that access to the books was restricted and he therefore built a library building next to the same mosque to house them (1725).[40] According to the endowment deed the library was staffed by four librarians[41] and a catalogue was prepared at the sultan's command (dated March 1725).[42] In a document it is stated that Ahmed III also sent to his college in Anapoli, in Morea, sixty-two books.[43]

Sultan Ahmed III's grand vizier, İbrahim Pasha, shared his love of books and we have records of his many book purchases, in which it is noted that he hired copyists to copy history books.[44] As we would expect he also founded libraries; the first was situated in Istanbul in the college which he founded at Şehzadebaşı.[45] The foundation deed provides for a staff of four librarians, one assistant librarian, and a further librarian responsible only for the books donated by Kazasker Sünbül Ali Efendi. There was also a binder, a cleaner, and a doorman.[46]

Following an old Ottoman tradition, İbrahim Pasha also built a complex in his birthplace, Nevşehir (1728).[47] The chronogram celebrating the completion

---

39 Raşid Tarihi, 176–177; TSA, D. 2184 and 2363, 12.
40 Tarih-i İsmail Asım Efendi (İstanbul: Matbaa-i Amire, 1283H), 250–251.
41 Süleymaniye Library, Yeni Cami Section 1200, 122a; BOA, Ruus 1, 57.
42 Süleymaniye Library, Yazma Bağışlar Section 2742.
43 Istanbul Court Registers, Evkaf-ı Hümayun Müfettişliği, 110, 78.
44 BOA, Cevdet-Dahiliye 8797. So great was his love of books that when he was killed in the Patrona Halil uprising of 1730 it was found that he had amassed a collection of more than nine hundred books. See Lale Uluç, "Ottoman Book Collectors and Illustrated Sixteenth Century Shiraz Manuscripts," Revue des Mondes Musulmans et de la Méditerranée, no. 87–88 (1999): 89.
45 Raşid Tarihi, vol. 5, 207–209.
46 VGMA, Defter 39, 90; VGMA, Defter-i Hazine-i Nevşehirli, 2–3; V. Minorsky, A Catalogue of the Turkish Manuscripts and Miniatures (Dublin: Hodges Figgis, 1958), 74–77; Şinasi Tekin, "1729 Yılında Vakfedilmiş Bir İstanbul Medresesinin Öğretim ve İdare Kadrosu Hakkında," Türk Kültürü 6, no. 71 (1968): 836–839.
47 Abdullah Kuran, "Orta Anadolu'da Klasik Osmanlı Mimarisi Çağının Sonunda Yapılan İki Külliye," VD 9 (1971): 243–247; M. Münir Aktepe, "Nevşehirli Damad Ibrahim Paşa'ya Aid İki Vakfiye," TD 11 (1960): 149–160.

of the library was written by Nedim, one of the most celebrated poets of his time.[48] We have no idea of the size of the collection, but as only one librarian was appointed we may presume that it was fairly modest. [49]

The period between the treaty of Passorowitz (1718) and the end of Ahmed III's reign was a period marked by a flowering of all cultural activities and conspicuous consumption, in which the palace took the lead. However, while library foundation continued in the capital,[50] fewer libraries seem to have been founded in the provinces.[51]

The second half of the seventeenth and first quarter of eighteenth centuries act as a transitional period in the history of Ottoman libraries. It is a time in which we see the continuation of the foundation of small mosque and college libraries side by side with the foundation of independent libraries. The following period, the reign of Mahmud I (1730–1754), represents the golden age of Ottoman libraries where we see a definite trend towards the foundation of large libraries dominating over the huge network of smaller libraries which by now dotted every district of Istanbul.

---

48 Ahmed Refik, "Damad Ibrahim Paşa Zamanında Ürgüp ve Nevşehir," *TTEM*, no. 80 (1340H): 175; Ahmet Sevgi, "Nedim'in Nevşehir İle İlgili Tarihleri Üzerine," *Yedi İklim* 4, no. 36 (1993): 29.

49 VGMA, 64, 37.

50 VGMA, 623, 76; Istanbul Court Registers, Evkaf-ı Hümayun Müfettişliği, 107, 99–102. VGMA, 734, 43; VGMA, 571, 92; Istanbul Court Registers, Bab Mahkemesi, 82, 50b-53a; VGMA, Kasa 188, 388–389; Süleymaniye Kütüphanesi, Gülnuş Valide Sultan 27, 29, 30, 31; Tahsin Özalp, *Sivrihisar Tarihi* (Eskişehir, 1960), 76–77.

51 For some of the small mosque and college libraries founded in this period see: BOA, Cevdet-Maarif, 6581, Ruus 63, 205; Ruus 29, 430; Lamija Hadžiosmanović, *Biblioteke u Bosni i Hercegovini za vrijeme austrougarske vladavine* (Sarajevo: Veselin Masleša, 1980), 75–76; VGMA, 744, 393; VGMA, 730, 86; Kasim Dobrača, *Katalog arapskih, turskih i perzijskih rukopisa* (Sarajevo: Starješinstvo islamske vjerske zajednice za SR Bosnu i Hercegovinu, 1963), xxi; Tahsin Özalp, *Sivrihisar Tarihi* (Eskişehir: Tam-İş Matbaası, 1960), 76–77.

Chapter Four

The Expansion and Reorganization of the Ottoman Library System (1730–1839)

Mahmud I's reign began ominously. His father had been deposed and his father's grand vizier Damad İbrahim Pasha had been killed in a brutal riot in the Ottoman capital. Furthermore, his reign saw defeats on the Austrian, Russian, and Iranian fronts. But despite all the turmoil, there is one area in which cultural activities reached their apogee during this time: the development of the library system. Of all the sultans, Mahmud I truly deserves the epithet of bibliophile. We can observe his keen interest in books in a decree concerning the organization of libraries of Kastamonu, the capital city of one of the central Anatolian provinces, which he sent to its judge:

> Whereas the order and basis of the World and Religion is given currency by the means of knowledge and science and associated with the acquisition of skill and virtue, and all depends on the collecting of books and making them available for the students … and for this reason … libraries were established.[1]

---

1   BOA, Mühimme, No. 152, 136.

Thus did Mahmud I express his view that the basis of Ottoman civilization, no less, was the library. In the following pages, we will see how he set out to make his philosophy a reality.

Mahmud I first opened a paper factory at Yalova, conveniently situated on the opposite shore of the Marmara sea from Istanbul, ensuring a steady supply of paper for the printing press in Istanbul, which he had reopened.[2] In the capital, he founded large libraries, including the Fatih, Galata Palace, and Ayasofya Libraries, setting an example for his statesmen to follow.

FIGURE 5. Ayasofya Library inside the Hagia Sophia, built by Sultan Mahmud I, Istanbul, est. 1740.

---

2   It is recorded in the diary of the sultan (*ruzname*) that he discussed the quality of the paper being produced at Yalova with the pioneer of the Ottoman printing press, Ibrahim Müteferrika. The sultan was particularly interested in the technological innovations behind the production of this paper, was pleased with the "new paper," and demonstrated his pleasure with a gift of a purse of gold. It is recorded that Ibrahim Muteferrika was pleased with the gift but more in the fact that he had found favor with the sultan. Özcan Özcan, "Kadı Ömer Efendi, Mahmud I Hakkında 1157, No. 1744–1160, No. 1747 Arası Ruzname" (BA Thesis, Istanbul University, 1965), 41–42.

Of all the libraries founded by Mahmud I, Ayasofya is the most interesting in terms of its furnishings,[3] staffing,[4] and the collection itself.[5] This is quite appropriate when we consider the special position that the Ayasofya Mosque and College had acquired in Ottoman religious and cultural life. The name Ayasofya is the Turkish version of the Greek Hagia Sophia, the (Church of the) Holy Wisdom. As the largest building in Istanbul when it was taken, Mehmed II turned it into a mosque-college. In successive reigns, it was extensively repaired, as well as endowed with four minarets and a host of buildings including a college in the surrounding area. The Ayasofya Mosque acquired a particular status, so that while there is no concept of a "cathedral mosque" in Islam, the Ayasofya Mosque came close to fulfilling that role, and was not only the largest mosque, but remained the "senior" and most respected of all the mosques in the Ottoman world. Its position as the mosque closest to the imperial palace also reinforced its close connection with the ruling dynasty. The college at Ayasofya also played a significant role in the educational system. The teachers at this college had a particularly high status, on a level with the teachers at the Mehmed II's College and the Süleymaniye College. It is no surprise then that it is to this mosque that Sultan Mahmud I devoted much of his energy.

In January 1740, a foundation deed was drawn up and many of books were endowed in that year.[6] Two months later, the library was officially opened in a ceremony attended by the sultan himself and all the high officials of the state. The ceremony opened with a silent reading of Buharî's collection of the Prophet Muhammed's sayings.[7] This was achieved by allocating a section of the work to each of the many attendant scholars. Each read their section silently and upon finishing recited a prayer. Each of the teachers appointed to the library – for this was to be a teaching library (see below)—gave an inaugural lesson, and the preacher of the mosque gave a sermon and concluded the ceremony with a prayer. After the lessons, the sultan distributed largess, in the form of gold coins, to the staff of the library. Many of the state officials attending the ceremony presented the sultan with books, which he in turn presented to the library.[8] The opening of the library has found a reflection in folklore. In a particular genre of

---

3   Azade Akar, "Ayasofya'da Bulunan Türk Eserleri ve Süslemelerine Dair Bir Araştırma," *VD* 8 (1969): 284–286.
4   VGMA, Defter No. 87, 1–2 and 28; TSA, E. 1767.
5   According to the historian Subhi, there were four thousand works housed in the library and the several catalogues prepared in this period verify this figure.
6   VGMA, Kasa No. 47; TSA, D. 1067.
7   Subhi, *Tarih* (İstanbul: Raşid Mehmed Efendi Matbaası, 1198H), 174b–175a.
8   The names of these donors can be found in the list prepared by Süheyl Ünver. See Süheyl Ünver Archive in the Süleymaniye library, Ayasofya File.

versification, which is particularly recited in coffeehouses and in streets during Ramadan, reference is made to the decoration of the library:

> The glory of the Ottoman line
> All other states to it supine
>
> From every corner comes great praise
> For the library's design
>
> Its decor famed in every clime
> Praiseworthy be it through all time
>
> In the Mosque of Ayasofya
> The sultan's made something sublime
>
> Its success ensured by the Almighty
> Let it be worthy of the Almighty
>
> And all who viewed this library
> Uttered praise to the Almighty [9]

FIGURE 6. The interior of Ayasofya Library, Istanbul, est. 1740.

---

9 Muhtar Yahya Dağlı, *İstanbul Mahalle Bekçilerinin Destan ve Mani Katarları* (İstanbul: Türk Neşriyat Yurdu, 1948), 59–60.

On several occasions, the sultan visited the library and distributed bounties, again in the form of gold coins, to the staff.[10]

At the beginning, the staff of the library consisted of four librarians, one assistant librarian, several teachers, two doormen, three cleaning staff, one binder, and two repairmen for the upkeep of the library building.[11] Within a year of its opening, it was realized that even this large staff would not suffice and we see that the number of librarians was increased from four to six and that their stipend was also raised.[12] In a clause appended to the foundation deed, dated August 1741, provision is made for the post of *buhurî*, that is, a thurifer, who would take burning incense around the library so that it would smell pleasant. An allowance of five aspers per day was made for the purchase of incense.[13]

In the foundation deed dated January 1740, provision was made for classes to be taught in the library, but in a better organized and on a more regular basis than was carried out in other libraries. The foundation deed specifies which books would be taught at what time, on what days, and allowances were to be given to all students who attended the classes.[14]

After inaugurating Ayasofya Library, Mahmud I's energy was focused on the establishment of a new library adjacent to Mehmed II's mosque. He first ordered a building to be constructed at the southeastern end of the mosque, a decision explained in one of the original catalogues to the library: "the noble mosque of Mehmed Han being the gathering place of the most eminent of scholars and a source of the religious sciences."[15] The opening ceremony was held in May 1742: *muezzins* recited prayers and professors held inaugural classes. İzzî, the imperial chronicler, was at the scene and recorded that the scholars in attendance were each given a robe of honor and money was distributed to the poor. He adds that the opening of the library was a cause of rejoicing and inspiration to the students of the district.[16]

When this library was first opened, its collection was not large, some two thousand books in all.[17] But throughout his reign, Mahmud I regularly endowed books to the library in order to build up its collection.[18] Furthermore, he ordered that all the books in the mosque should be transferred to the new

---

10 TSA, D. 1067, 8a, 16a, and 19a.
11 VGMA, Kasa No. 47.
12 VGMA, No. 639, 62.
13 VGMA, No. 638, 7.
14 VGMA, Defter 87, 2–3; VGMA, No. 638, 7.
15 Süleymaniye Library, Yazma Bağışlar, No. 242, 1b.
16 İzzi, *Tarih* (İstanbul: Mehmed Raşid ve Ahmed Vasıf [Matbaası], 1199 H), 219b–220a.
17 Süleymaniye Library, Yazma Bağışlar, No. 243, 63b.
18 Süleymaniye Library, Yazma Bağışlar, No. 242.

library building and he also had the books from the nearby Şehzade Mosque join the new collection.[19] It is not known how many books were in the library by the time Mahmud I died (1754), but some eighty years later a survey of this library recorded that there were more than 5,500 works in the collection.[20]

The staffing of Fatih Library was markedly different from that of Ayasofya. Fatih already had a large staff of teachers in its well-established college, so there was little need to appoint teaching staff. The staff of Fatih Library consisted of six librarians, one assistant librarian, one cleaner, and one doorman.[21]

Having made provision for the Ayasofya and Fatih Libraries, Mahmud I then focused his attention on Süleymaniye Library together with Grand Vizier Köse Mustafa Bahir Pasha.[22] There are very few records of what Mahmud I did in terms of organizing Süleymaniye Library. It appears that he moved all the books from various cabinets in which they were stored and created a central storage space, created by putting large iron gratings between the pillars at the southeast corner of the mosque. All the books were brought here.[23] From a later record, we see that the library had fixed opening times from sunrise to the afternoon prayer, five days a week. Five librarians had also been appointed. Books were not to be lent out, but presumably read in the mosque itself.[24] With the organization of the Süleymaniye, Istanbul was now endowed with three large well-staffed and well-organized libraries, one of which (Ayasofya) was at the southeast point of the city next to the palace, and the other (Fatih) geographically at the center of the city. Given that much of the city was uninhabited between the land walls and the Fatih Mosque, it was in fact located at the opposite end of the populated area from Ayasofya. The third mosque, the Süleymaniye, lies in the middle forming a

---

19 Süleymaniye Library, Yazma Bağışlar, No. 242, 75b and 135a.
20 Süleymaniye Library, Yazma Bağışlar, No. 252; TSA, D. 3310.
21 TSA, E. 1767; VGMA, Defter 87, 5–6. An American lady who visited this library at the end of nineteenth century describes its inner decoration thus: "The library that seemed to me the most beautiful of all belonged to the mosque of the Conqueror. There was a wonderful carpet on the floor, in pale blue and old rose, that had been sent as a gift to Sultan Mahmud II from the Shah of Persia. A very curious and interesting brass ornament hung from the dome. There was an illuminated scroll suspended on the wall, beginning, 'O Ye Eternal Being,' the golden letters of which shone in the dim light. The books were old manuscripts of great value, some of them containing rare specimens of Arabic and Persian illumination" (Mary Mills Patrick, *Under Five Sultans* [London: Williams and Norgate, 1930]), 96.
22 Hüseyin Ayvansarayi, *Hadikatü'l-Cevami'*, vol. 1 (İstanbul: Matbaa-i Amire, 1281H), 18; Halit Dener, *Süleymaniye Umumi Kütüphanesi* (İstanbul: İstanbul Maarif Basımevi, 1957), 35.
23 N. Bayraktar, "İstanbul'daki Vakıf Kütüphaneler ve Süleymaniye Kütüphanesi," *TKDB.* 15, no. 3 (1966): 134–135; Müjgan Cunbur, "Kanuni Devrinde Kitap Sanatı, Kütüphaneleri ve Süleymaniye Kütüphanesi," *TKDB* 17, no. 3 (1968): 139.
24 BOA, Müteferrik Section No. 89, 114a–115b.

triangle of three centers of learning, and acting as a core for all the other smaller institutions of higher education in Istanbul.[25]

These three libraries housed collections that specialized in the college curricula, and can essentially be viewed as the library system for Ottoman higher education in Istanbul. For the training of palace officials and future generations of statesmen, a different type of collection was necessary, as the college libraries did not generally house the types of books necessary for government training. Galata palace had been, for over two centuries prior to Mahmud I's rule, the school for palace personnel, traditionally including the people who would become provincial governors, army officers and viziers. We must presume that, from an early stage, books were available for students to read; the historian Ata notes that many books had been donated to the palace by successive sultans.[26] Apart from this brief note, we have no information about the early stages of this collection.

It was Mahmud I who organized the books into a proper library. He also endowed more books, established a staff, and made provision for its functioning in an endowment deed. He first built a separate library building to which he appointed three librarians and three teachers, who were to give lessons in the library.[27] A catalogue drawn up in 1753 describes a rather rich collection of about two thousand works; but it is the subject matter of these works which is most remarkable. Although the collection contains some works one would expect to find on the college syllabus, the main emphasis is on grammar, literature, and history.[28] This school was not there for the study of religious subjects, but to educate students in Ottoman culture, as they would be the next generation of Ottoman officers and statesmen.

Apart from these four libraries in Istanbul, Mahmud I also set up libraries in Cairo,[29] Belgrade,[30] and Vidin,[31] where he not only sent books, but also provided

---

25 In an interesting book on the topography of Ottoman Buildings, Maurice Cerasi demonstrates that many of the colleges, mosques and libraries tended to cluster in a ridge in the center of Istanbul, stretching from the palace walls to the walls of the city. Ayasofya is at one end of this cluster, the Fatih Library in the middle and the Süleymaniye set slightly aside from the main cluster: *The Istanbul Divanyolu* (Würzburg: Ergon-Verlag in Kommission, 2004), 80–82.

26 Fethi İsfendiyaroğlu, *Galatasaray Tarihi* (İstanbul: n.p., 1952), 60–61, 114, 267.

27 VGMA, Defter No. 87, 9–10.

28 Süleymaniye Library, Ayasofya Section, Fihrist, No. 5.

29 According to the Cairo foundation deed, which is dated 1754 (VGMA, 639, 29), provision was made for the building of a college, school, public fountain, and a library, which was to be housed in this college, for which a librarian and a binder were to be appointed. I am grateful to Mathilde Pinon for providing me with the reference to this foundation deed.

30 VGMA, No. 638, 190; Mihaila Stajnova, "Ottoman Libraries in Vidin," *Etudes Balkaniques*, no. 2 (1979): 57.

31 BOA, Cevdet-Maarif 7730; İsmail Hakkı Uzunçarşılı, *Osmanlı Tarihi* 4a (Ankara: Türk Tarih Kurumu Basımevi, 1978): 328.

for librarians to look after them. He also provided books for establishments built by others. When the ruler of Crimea, Selamet Giray Han, built a mosque near to his palace it was Mahmud I who provided books for the library,[32] and when the mother of Ahmed III built a mosque on the island of Chios the books for the library were again provided by the sultan.[33] In 1746, he sent a decree to the judge of Kastamonu ordering him to make a survey of the city's libraries and to catalogue the collections and to send these catalogues to the palace. This was all with a view to uniting all libraries in this city into a single collection which could be better maintained.[34]

Throughout his reign Mahmud I actively acquired books at every opportunity. This was done in three ways: he received many books as gifts,[35] he enlarged the palace library by confiscating the book collections of officials who died or fell out of favor and thirdly, and, perhaps most conventionally, he purchased books on the open market from booksellers through palace officials.[36]

For Mahmud I's officials, collecting books and subsequently founding libraries became an important charitable act during this period. Thus we see Hekimoğlu Ali Pasha, the grand vizier, founding a library in 1738 next to his mosque, which he had built in 1734 in the Davud Pasha district of Istanbul.[37] Although we have no information as to how many books the library contained, it had a relatively large staff of three librarians and other personnel, and he provided for teachers to give lessons in the library.[38] In 1740, Şeyh Mehmed Rıza Efendi donated his large collection of books to this library, and provided for extra staff to look after the expanded collection.[39]

---

32 Zafer Karatay, "Bahçesaray," DİA 4 (1991): 482.

33 VGMA, 639, 57.

34 BOA, Mühimme, No. 152, 136.

35 Examples of these gifts are: a former vizier, Abdullah Pasha presented, in 1750, 186 books, the governor of Sayda, Mehmed Pasha, eleven books. Another official, Hüseyin Bey presented thirty-eight books. The governor of Tripoli, İsmail Pasha, presented 312 books in 1753 and Hacı Ahmed Pasha fifty-eight books. A presentation of 3,252 books was made sometime in Mahmud I's reign. (Günay Kut, "Sultan I. Mahmud Kütüphanesi (Ayasofya Kütüphanesi)," in Osmanlı Devleti'nde Bilim Kültür ve Kütüphaneler, ed. Özlem Bayram (Ankara: Türk Kütüphaneciler Derneği, 1999), 99–12. This enormous collection was presented by the chief eunuch, but which one is not indicated. There were two famous collectors of books who rose to this position, and both were called Beşir Ağa. This collection certainly belonged to one of them.

36 For several examples, see TKT, 99.

37 Hüseyin Ayvansarayi, Hadikatü'l-Cevami', vol. 1 (İstanbul: n.p., 1281H), 81–82.

38 VGMA, No. 736, 67–70. Millet Library, Feyzullah Efendi Section No. 2197.

39 VGMA, No. 629, 37–41.

FIGURE 7. Hekimoğlu Ali Pasha Library, Istanbul, est. 1738. SALT, Ali Saim Ülgen Archive.

Of all of Mahmud I's officials, the most active in the field of creating charitable foundations seems to have been the chief eunuch of the palace, Hacı Beşir Ağa. As a recipient of a relatively large income, Beşir Ağa seems to have spent most of it on building mosques, fountains, colleges, and not least of all libraries. Like his patron, he was also a bibliophile and built up large collections of books, which he then endowed to his libraries. In the Eyüp district of Istanbul, he founded a college, to which he donated a collection of books and provided that the library should be staffed by three librarians and an assistant librarian. According to the foundation deed, the senior librarian should be from outside the college, but the other librarians and assistant librarian should be chosen from the best of the students. His library was to be a teaching library and he provided for one teacher and also for a specialist to teach prophetic tradition (*hadis*). Students who attended the lectures were also to receive five aspers scholarship per day. It was determined that the library should be open every day, the librarians taking turns to be on duty.[40] The library was further enlarged by a donation of books made by a certain woman named Rabia Hatun. This

---

40 VGMA, No. 736, 4.

collection had originally been donated to Ayasofya, but when it was realized that the books would be more useful at Eyüp they were transferred there in 1743.[41]

Very close to Ayasofya and the Topkapı Palace, in the district of Cağaloğlu, Hacı Beşir Ağa founded a complex consisting of a mosque, a college, a dervish convent, a primary school, and a library. The library consisted of a room adjoining the mosque. The foundation deed, dated 1745, provided for four librarians, of which the third librarian also had the duty of doorman. The deed forbade lending books.[42] However, it seems that despite the prohibition, later librarians acceded to the plea of scholars to be allowed to take the books out of library for a limited period of five days. An inspection of the collection revealed that, likely due to the librarians' lenience, thirty-eight of the 714 books had gone missing. It was therefore decided to close the library and prepare a new catalogue. When the library reopened in 1784, instructions once more prohibited the practice of lending in the strongest terms possible.[43]

In Medina, Beşir Ağa built a college with a library attached to it.[44] We do not know how many books he donated to the library, but he evidently expanded the collection throughout his life. An example of this process is recorded in a document which notes that he dispatched seventy-two books to the library in September of 1739.[45] A hundred years later, the judge of Medina, Işkî Mustafa Efendi wrote a history of this city, in which he noted that bookbinders were sent by the sultan to repair the books in all the libraries of Medina. In Beşir Ağa's library, the binder repaired 961 books.[46] This gives us some indication of the extent of the collection. When the orientalist Richard Burton wrote his account of his travels to the city in the mid-1800s, he noted that Beşir Ağa Library was known for its large collection.[47]

In the Balkan town of Sistova (Svishtov), Beşir Ağa built a college and library in response to a request for books on the religious sciences to be available for

41 VGMA, No. 638, 187–188.
42 Süleymaniye Library, Hacı Beşir Ağa Section No. 682, 105b–118a.
43 VGMA, No. 639, 128–150.
44 VGMA, No. 638, 141–142.
45 Istanbul Court Registers, Evkaf-ı Hümayun Müfettişliği, No. 130, 267.
46 Işkî Mustafa b. Ömer Kilisî, Ta'tirü Ercai'd-Devleti'l-mecdiyye, Istanbul University Manuscript Library, T. Y. 1490, 176b.
47 Richard F. Burton, Personal Narrative of a Pilgrimage to el-Medinah and Meccah, vol. 2 (London: Longman, Brown, Green, Longmans, and Roberts, 1855), 289.

both students and the people at large. As Sistova was a relatively small town, the collection consisted of a mere ninety-eight books.[48]

Beşir Ağa collected and donated books throughout his life. Already existing libraries received quantities of books from time to time. It is recorded, for example in a document dated 1734, that Beşir Ağa donated a quantity of books to a library attached to the mausoleum of the Imam A'zam Abu Hanifa, the founder of the Hanefi school of law, in Baghdad.[49] He also allocated to the librarian in al-Azhar College, in Cairo, an amount of money in one of his foundation deeds.[50] The sultan also received books as a gift from Beşir Ağa. We may presume that these were particularly fine copies or rare books.[51] However, some of the finest and rarest he kept for himself. On his death (1746) in one of his several residences 150 valuable and rare books were found including the autograph copy of the *Cihannüma*, a renowned Ottoman geographical work.[52]

Another of Sultan Mahmud I's statesmen, Atıf Mustafa Efendi, who was *defterdar*, a post corresponding to minister of finance, also emulated his sovereign by founding a library in the Vefa district of Istanbul. This library is a good example of an independent library not attached to a mosque or college. It seems that Ayasofya served as a model for the organization and activities of Atıf Mustafa's library. As it was established with several foundation deeds, we have a rare insight into how a library was established in this period. The first three of these deeds provide for the future income of the library.[53] Another deed from May 1741 makes provision for the books to be donated,[54] a further deed from September 1741 provides for the building,[55] and the last deed, later that same month, provides for the organization of

48 VGMA, No. 638, 141–142.
49 VGMA, No. 735, 169.
50 Hamza Abd al-Aziz Badr-Daniel Crecelius, "The Awqaf of al-Hajj Bashir Agha in Cairo," *Annales Islamologiques* 27 (1993): 294. When Volney visited el-Ezher College, he noted that there were many old volumes of which a considerable number were still being issued to the students. However, as a Christian, he himself was forbidden to handle the books. *Travels through Syria and Egypt, in the Years 1783, 1784 and 1785*, vol. 2 (London: G.G.J. and J. Robinson, 1788), 449.
51 Zeren Tanındı, "Bibliophile Aghas (Eunuchs) at Topkapı Sarayı," *Muqarnas* 21 (2004): 339.
52 TSA, D. 23, 36a–b, 37a. The *Cihannüma* had a number of maps and was so highly esteemed that it was one of the first books to be set in print.
53 Atıf Efendi Library, No. 2858, 1b–26b.
54 Fuad Sezgin, "Atıf Efendi Vakfiyesi," *İ. Ü. Edebiyat Fakültesi, Türk Dili ve Edebiyatı Dergisi* 6 (1955): 136.
55 Atıf Efendi Library, No. 2858, 27b–02b, 103a–104b. For the architectural characteristics of the library building see: Özden Çetinalp, "Atıf Efendi Library in Vefa," *Rölöve* 1 (1968): 31.

the library.[56] As the collection consisted of more than two thousand books, many of which were rare and valuable, such as autographs or books copied by famous scholars and calligraphers, Atıf Efendi was keen to see that they were properly cared for. To this end he made provision for three librarians, the senior to receive eighty aspers per day, the others seventy aspers each. The stipends were generous enough to allow him to make it conditional that they should not take up other employment and that they should reside in the accommodation provided for them next to the library. When Toderini visited the library some forty years later, he noted that the library had three resident librarians.[57]

FIGURE 8. Atıf Efendi Library, Istanbul, est. 1741.

As in Ayasofya, Atıf Efendi envisaged that teaching would be carried out in the library and provided for a teacher with a daily stipend of fifteen aspers to give lessons. As the library was independent, it was not attached to a mosque, so that prayers would have to be performed in the library itself. He therefore provided that the head librarian would lead prayers in the reading room and that the second librarian would act as *muezzin*. During his lifetime and after his

56 Atıf Efendi Library, No. 2858, 104b–109a.
57 G. Toderini, *De la litterature des Turcs, traduit de l'Italien en Français par l'Abbe de Cournand*, vol. 2 (Paris: Chez Poinçot, 1789), 86.

death, Atıf Efendi's family made additional bequests to the library and provided additional income.[58]

Another of Mahmud I's statesmen, Mustafa Efendi, the director of the Imperial Chancery, founded an independent library in Istanbul. He had originally demanded that his books should be divided between a college he had built in Kastamonu and a mosque he had built in Belgrade.[59] However, he later made another will (dated 1747) in which he donated all his books to a library to be founded in Istanbul and provided for two librarians and three teachers to work in the Valide and Mahmud Pasha Mosques until the library building was completed,[60] but he died before the building could be started. His son Aşir Efendi realized the construction of the building (1800) which consisted of a reading room and a classroom. We can see from the disposition of the staff that the teaching function was given more importance in this library. Beside reading and teaching, certain religious activities, such as reciting the *Mevlid*, a Turkish poem about the birth and life of the Prophet, and reading passages of the Koran for the soul of the founder were to be carried out there.[61]

Quite apart from the larger independent libraries in Istanbul and the larger towns, colleges and mosques continued to receive books by way of bequests. Almost every college could boast a library no matter how humble. Many mosques too had libraries, so that it could be said that the Ottoman library system had spread throughout the empire to all the cities and indeed to many small towns.[62]

However well the Ottoman library system may have been developed by the latter half of the eighteenth century, it is clear that some Ottomans were far from complacent. In 1769, a bureaucrat by the name of Penah Efendi was highly critical of donors who either founded libraries in Istanbul or bequeathed their books to existing institutions therein. According to him, the capital already had enough books and if bequests were to be directed to provincial libraries, science and knowledge would be more evenly spread throughout all the provinces. Furthermore, he argued, concentrating all the colleges and libraries in Istanbul would create a tendency for students to study in these colleges, rather than at

58 Atıf Efendi Library, No. 2858, 109b–134b.
59 VGMA, No. 736, 205–206.
60 VGMA, No. 738, 142.
61 Süleymaniye Library, Aşir Efendi Section No. 473, 7a–b; Süleymaniye Library, Yazma Bağışlar, No. 2783; VGMA, No. 738, 142; Virginia Aksan, *An Ottoman Statesman in War and Peace: Ahmed Resmi Efendi 1700–1783* (Leiden: E. J. Brill, 1995), 25–27.
62 For a list of bequests made to libraries in this period, see *TKT*, 96–98.

their local college and this would be one of the causes of overpopulation in the city.[63]

The reign of Mahmud I (1730–1754) established the independent library as the norm. The reigns of his five successors, Osman III (1754–1757), Mustafa III (1757–1774), Abdülhamid I (1774–1789), Selim III (1789–1807), and Mahmud II 1808–1839) were to see the spread of independent libraries not only in Istanbul, but also in the provinces as well. Apart from the libraries he established, Mahmud I had also begun to build his mosque complex in the well-established tradition of imperial endowments. He chose a site to the south of the Covered Bazaar (Kapalıçarşı) which was close to many of the existing colleges. The mosque is quite unusual for its rococo style and shows definite European influences. But it is most notable for the prominence of the library building, which, though part of the complex, was in effect designed to act as an independent library. Many books from the palace and other sources were designated for this library, and the imperial seal and endowment record of Mahmud I was applied to the flyleaf, indicating that the books had been endowed to the library. Unfortunately, Mahmud I did not live to see the completion of his complex or to give his name to the library which was to surpass all other libraries he had established. When he died in 1754, his brother, Osman III, completed the complex and gave his own name to it. Both the mosque and the library are known as the Nuruosmaniye, "the light of Osman."[64] Osman III sent the books which his late brother had chosen together with other books he himself selected to the library. Mahmud I's seal and endowment record were pasted over with paper and Osman III's own seal was placed on the books.[65] Osman III did not seem to have shared his brother's passion for library administration. In the endowment deed, in the section where we would normally expect to find the regulation for running the library, we find a short statement to the effect that the regulations applicable were to be the same as those which his brother had stipulated for the Ayasofya and Fatih Libraries.[66]

Nuruosmaniye Library was opened in December of 1755 with the usual ceremonies attended by the sultan, scholars, and high state officials.[67] At this point, the library had a collection of 5,031 books, making it the largest collection

63 Aziz Berker, "Mora İhtilali Tarihçesi veya Penah Efendi Mecmuası," *Tarih Vesikaları* 2, no. 12 (1943): 479.

64 *Şemdanîzade Fındıklılı Süleyman Efendi Tarihi, Mür'i't-Tevarih*, vol. 2, no. A, ed. M. Münir Aktepe (İstanbul: Edebiyat Fakültesi Matbaası, 1978), 4–6.

65 For some examples see: Nuruosmaniye Library, nos. 622, 1134, 2697, 3873.

66 VGMA, Dolap 49, 22.

67 *Mür'i't-Tevarih*, vol. 2, no. A, 5–6.

in Istanbul, the library of Ahmed III being a close runner-up with a collection approaching five thousand books.[68] The library was to have one general supervisor, six librarians, three doormen, one cleaning person, and one binder. Curiously, a further six member of staff whose actual duties were not defined[69] were also appointed. Their title *mustahfız* suggests that they were guardians and probably acted as security staff.

State officials also accumulated rich collections and established various libraries in this period. The grand vizier to Osman III and Mustafa III, Ragıb Pasha, was an ardent collector of books in addition to being a poet and writer. Having built up a large private collection, he made provision for an independent library to be built in the center of Istanbul. Before he endowed his collection, Ragıb Pasha employed a librarian to look after his books. However, this member of his household staff was not called *hafiz-ı kütüb*, which means "keeper of books," but was referred to as a *kitabçı*, a "book specialist."[70] This nuance reflects a different role. The primary role of a keeper of books was precisely to preserve the collection with the secondary duty of facilitating public access to it. The book specialist was a private servant whose duties covered everything to do with books, including not only classification, cataloguing, and general maintenance, but also buying them, and so forth. Ragıb Pasha completed his library in 1763.[71] The historian Vasıf Efendi noted:

> Ragıb Pasha, having for many years, collected, selected, searched, and had copies made of many books, and to preserve them from harm and loss and to make them available for the use of the people, furthermore, endowed a library in which he placed these books.[72]

Although these books were inalienably endowed to the library, Ragıb Pasha had reserved to himself the right to borrow books for his own personal use. On his death, twenty-eight of these books were found in his house and were dispatched to the library to rejoin the collection.[73] There were apparently more books

---

68 It should be noted that Toderini, usually a reliable informant on the subject of Istanbul libraries, has mistakenly given the number of books in this library as 1,693. G. Toderini, *De la litterature des Turcs, traduit de l'Italien en Français par l'Abbe de Cournand*, vol. 2 (Paris: Chez Poinçot, 1789), 97.
69 VGMA, No. 98, 10–12; TSA, D. 3311, 5b.
70 TSA, D. 6090.
71 *Mür'i't-Tevarih*, vol. 2, no. A, 54.
72 *Vasıf Tarihi*, vol. 1, 129.
73 TSA, D. 6090.

belonging to Ragıb Pasha, which were in the house belonging to his senior wife. In the Topkapı Palace Archives, there is a letter from Sultan Mustafa III to his grand vizier in which the sultan gives orders for a certain book to be found and dispatched to him. The style is informal:

> My Vizier,
> Summon Hatib-zade [presumably one of Ragıb Pasha's retainers] and his bookman Zihni Efendi and find out why the books on astrology have failed to appear among his books. There are apparently some books in the house of his senior wife. I have no interest in the household furnishings or the other books in the house, but there is a book on astrology from Persia which the late Ragıb Pasha had praised and promised to me. Ask that all the books in the house be taken away and we will search for the book on astrology and return the remainder of the books."[74]

As we would expect of a bibliophile statesman, Ragıb Pasha had definite ideas as to how a library was to be run. His first requirement was that the librarians should be full-time workers, and he allowed them an adequate stipend to ensure this. He also created a post of *"hafız-ı kütüb yamağı,"* an aide to the librarian, whose duties appear to have been retrieving books from and replacing them on the shelves. He required that the librarians should live in residences near the library, which had been built for this purpose, and even provided for the librarians to take turns staying overnight in the library. While other libraries were open five days a week at the most, Ragıb Pasha set down that his library should be open six days a week.[75]

Osman III's reign (1754–1757) was too short to allow him to do more than complete and open his brother's library. Mustafa III, on the other hand, reigned from 1757 to 1774, and this allowed him to see the completion of two important libraries. The first of these was the library that he endowed to the college situated in the complex of the Laleli Mosque.[76] Mustafa III also built a library in a section of Topkapı Palace, which is referred to as Bostancılar Ocağı

---

74 İsmail Hakkı Uzunçarşılı, "Osmanlı Tarihinde Gizli Kalmış veya Şüphe ile Örtülü Bazı Olaylar ve Bu Hususa Dair Vesikalar," *Belleten* 41, no. 163 (1977): 531.

75 Istanbul Court Registers, Evkaf-ı Hümayun Müfettişliği, No. 171, 1b–6b; Ahmed İhsan Türek, "Ragıp Paşa Kütüphanesi Vakfiyesi," *Edebiyat Fakültesi Araştırma Dergisi* 1, no. 1 (1970): 65–78.

76 VGMA, No. 642, 145.

Library.[77] This library was established for the benefit of the palace staff. It was not permitted to take books out of the library, so it essentially served as a reference library in which classes were given in certain subjects. Three part-time librarians were appointed to the library, and their comparatively low salaries reflects the part-time nature of their employment.[78]

We have additional information about this library from a rather unexpected source. In the retinue of the British ambassador, there arrived a certain Professor Carlyle in Istanbul in 1800. He had come in search of Byzantine manuscripts. Believing that palace library may have held some of these, Carlyle bribed a palace official to show him around the palace library. He described the library as cruciform in shape and stated that the building had been erected in 1767, but the library was no longer operating and was closed by 1800. He was, however, able to see the books on the shelves, but found no Byzantine manuscripts.[79]

He describes the library in a letter to the Bishop of Lincoln:

> After waiting some time for intelligence respecting the Bostangee Bashi, his deputy arrived, read the letters we had brought, and his principal was engaged in the Seraglio, took upon himself to send for the keeper of the library, and direct him to conduct us thither; we accordingly accompanied him and three other Moulahs to a mosque at a little distance, through which the entrance to the library lies. ... We passed through the mosque as we were directed, without speaking, and upon tiptoe; and at a length on the other side of it, arrived at the outward door of the library, which was locked, and a seal fixed upon the lock; above it is a short Arabic inscription, containing the name and titles of Sultan Mustapha, the present Emperor's father, who founded both the mosque and the library in the year 1767. The library is built in the form of a Greek cross, as in the margin; one of the arms of the cross serves as an anti-room, and the three remaining arms, together with the center, constitute the library itself. You proceed through anti-room by a door, over which is written in large Arabic characters, "enter in peace." The library is much

---

77 P. Ğ. İnciciyan, *XVIII. Asırda İstanbul*, trans. Hrand D. Andreasyan (Istanbul: İstanbul Fethi Derneği, 1956), 23.

78 VGMA, Kasa 187, 350–358; TSA, D. 330

79 Robert Walpole, *Memoirs relating to European and Asiatic Turkey*, Edited from Manuscript Journals by Robert Walpole (London: Longman & Co., 1817), 172.

smaller than Your Lordship could have any conception of; for from the extremity of one of the arms to the extremity of the opposite one it does not measure twelve yards. Its appearance, however, is elegant and cheerful. The central part of the cross is covered with a dome, which is supported by four handsome marble pillars. ... The bookcases, four of which stand in each of the three recesses are plain but neat. They are furnished with folding wire-work doors, secured with a padlock and the seal of the librarian. The books are laid upon their sides one above another, with their ends outwards, and having their letters written upon the edges of the leaves. Your Lordship may imagine I lost no time in examining the treasures enclosed in this celebrated repository, and the disposition of the books greatly facilitated my inquiries. I am very certain that there was not one volume which I did not separately examine; but I was prevented by the jealousy of the Moulahs who accompanied me from making out a detailed catalogue of the whole. I continued, however, to take an account of all writers on history and general literature, and I hope by means of a present to procure an accurate list of the remainder. The whole number of MSS, in the library amounts to 1294, much the greatest part of which are Arabic, these are, however, most of the best Persian and Turkish writers, but alas, not one volume in Greek, Hebrew, or Latin.[80]

Unfortunately, what Carlyle is describing as the palace library is in fact Bostancılar Ocağı Library. The palace library had been built earlier that century and was a rectangular building, which was not closed at that period. Carlyle had

---

80 Ibid., 171–172. Carlyle is merely one of the numerous foreign visitors determined to have access to ancient works inherited from the Byzantine period. In fact, the "Sultan's Library" acquired mythic proportions in the West. It harbored as yet unknown works of the ancients, and the Ottoman attitude of secrecy and suspicion towards foreigners only gave more credence to the myth. See, for instance, Michel Baudier, *Histoire Generalle du Serrail et de la Cour du Grand Seigneur Empereur des Turcs* (Paris: Chez Claude Caramoisy, 1626), 25; P. Ğ. İnciciyan, *XVIII. Asırda İstanbul Tarihi*, trans. Hrand D. Andreasyan (İstanbul: İstanbul Fethi Derneği, 1956), 23. There is much evidence that Mehmed II's library contained a substantial number of non-Islamic books, the majority of which were in Greek. However, these books were never catalogued together with the Islamic works. Succeeding Sultans seem to have taken little interest in these books and most gradually disappeared from the palace. (Speros Vryonis, "Byzantine Constantinople and Ottoman Istanbul," in *The Ottoman City and its Parts: Urban Structure and Social Order*, ed. Irene A. Bierman and Rifa'at A. Abou-el-Haj (New York: A.D. Caratzas, 1991), 37–39.

been duped into thinking that this now redundant staff library was the library of the sultan. But we are fortunate to get this information. In 1831, Mahmud II ordered that the books in this library be moved to Laleli Library.[81] The palace staff clearly had no great need of a special library for themselves, seeing that they had access to the main palace library. The library was closed after some thirty years of operation and after another thirty years the books were transferred elsewhere.

Another important library was built by Veliyüddin Efendi, twice chief mufti in Mustafa III's reign. He had originally endowed 150 books to Atıf Efendi Library in 1761, and at the same time raised the salaries of the librarians to compensate them for the extra work involved in looking after an enlarged collection.[82] However, this relatively small endowment did not satisfy him and he embarked upon a far more ambitious project; he built a library next to the Beyazıt Mosque and endowed it with 1,690 books, to which were added the 150 books of his original endowment to Atıf Efendi Library.[83] Although not very large when compared to the Fatih and Nuruosmaniye Libraries, the collection drew many scholars. Vasıf Efendi, the historian, noted that there were many rare books in the collection so that this library was busier than others in Istanbul. He also noted that Veliyüddin Efendi's son continued to search for rare books to add to his father's collection.[84] The conditions governing the running of the library were very much the same as those in the Atıf Efendi and Ragıb Pasha Libraries.[85]

Quite apart from the abovementioned large endowments, the foundation of smaller college libraries and the endowment of small collections to existing libraries continued during this period.[86] Libraries were either being founded anew, or existing collections were being enlarged throughout the empire.

The periods of Abdülhamid I (1774–1789) and Selim III (1789–1807) were marked by the growing realization that the Ottoman Empire was on the verge of collapse, after the disastrous treaty of Küçük Kaynarca with the Russians in 1774, and that sweeping and radical reforms were necessary to avert the unthinkable. New Western-style institutions were introduced in this period, mainly for the purpose of military training. To establish a new Western-style army and pay for the new expertise, the state became involved

---

81 VGMA, No. 642, 103–145.
82 Istanbul Court Registers, Evkaf-ı Hümayun Müfettişliği, No. 164, 381b–384b.
83 VGMA, No. 745, 79.
84 *Vasıf Tarihi*, vol. 1, 206–207.
85 VGMA, No. 745, 80.
86 For a detailed list of these libraries see: *TKT*, 106–107.

in an increasing amount of expenditure. This period is marked by a decrease in imperial endowments, partially compensated by an increase in endowments from prominent statesmen.

The decrease in imperial largess can be seen in the library built by Abdülhamid I in a small complex he built at Bahçekapı in Istanbul.[87] The library only housed 1,552 books and the staff consisted of only four librarians, one binder, one sweeper, and one doorman.[88] The collection was enlarged by an endowment of 750 books from Lala İsmail Efendi.[89] As for Selim III's endowments, they too are comparatively meager: he endowed thirty books to a library in Medina,[90] reorganized Laleli Library, erected a new building there,[91] and repaired Selimiye Library in Edirne and endowed it with some books.[92]

However, statesmen of this period continued the tradition of either building complete libraries or at least endowing books to existing institutions. While Istanbul benefited from much of the expansion of libraries, there seems to be a growing feeling that the city offered ample access to books with the existing collections, and thus we see a trend towards establishing or enlarging provincial libraries. The statesmen usually chose a provincial town or city that they had some connection with, either their birthplace or somewhere they had been appointed to in the course of their careers. For example Silahdar Seyyit Mehmed Pasha established a library in his birthplace, the village of Arabsun near Nevşehir.[93] Halil Hamid Pasha, grand vizier, established two libraries, one in Isparta,[94] one in Burdur.[95] Ahmed Ağa founded a library in Rhodes, his birthplace, in 1793, and specified that classes were to be given in it five days a week.[96] Mehmed Raşid Efendi, the director of the Imperial Chancery, founded a library with a collection of almost one thousand books in Kayseri in 1797, where he had been posted earlier in his career. This library is particularly interesting in

87 *Tarih-i Cevdet*, vol. 2 (İstanbul: Matbaa-i Osmaniye, 1309H), 46 and 81; Hüseyin Ayvansarayî, *Hadikatü'l-Cevami'*, vol. 2 (İstanbul: Matbaa-i Amire, 1281H), 179. See also Müjgan Cunbur, "I. Abdülhamid'in Vakfiyesi ve Hamidiye Kütüphanesi," *Dil ve Tarih-Coğrafya Fakültesi Dergisi* 22 (1964): 17–69. See also: Fikret Sarıcaoğlu, *Kendi Kaleminden Bir Padişahın Portresi: Sultan I. Abdülhamid (1774–1789)* (İstanbul: Tatav, Tarih ve Tabiat Vakfı, 2001), 27–29.

88 VGMA, No. 86, 1. Abdülhamid'in Hazine Defteri, 31.

89 VGMA, No. 746, 343–345.

90 TSA, No. E. 2885, No. 19.

91 VGMA, No. 93, 125–127.

92 BOA, Hatt-ı Hümayun, No. 16, 161.

93 VGMA, No. 742, 66.

94 VGMA, No. 628, 547, and 554.

95 M. Zeki Oral, "Mevcut Vesikalara Göre Burdur Kütüphaneleri ve Kitap Vakfiyeleri," *Belleten* 24, no. 94 (1960): 235–236.

96 VGMA, No. 743, 93–94, and 156.

that we see a development in the thinking about the operation through a series of added regulations each presumably there to correct some existing deficiency or abuse.[97] Other libraries were founded in this manner in Antalya by Hacı Mehmed Ağa (1797),[98] in Keban by Yusuf Ziya Pasha (1798),[99] in Akhisar by Zeynelzade Hacı Ali Efendi (1804),[100] in Manisa by Karaosmanoğlu Hacı Hüseyin Ağa (1806),[101] in Prizren by Mehmed Pasha (1805),[102] in Vidin by Pazvantoğlu Osman Pasha,[103] and in İzmir by Hatice Hanım (1806).[104]

Yusuf Ağa, the controller of the mint and holder of several other important positions, founded a library in Konya (1794), neither his birthplace nor a place to which he had been appointed at some time in his career. It seems that he wanted to establish a library in a city that needed one. The library he built was large by provincial standards: it had over one thousand books. The regulations for operating the library were the same as those in the Atıf Efendi, Ragıb Pasha and Hamidiye Libraries, save that the salaries were, for reasons unknown, to be paid six-monthly, and that it was stipulated that the librarian was to be from the city of Konya.[105] This stipulation would seem to be addressing a problem that was bothering the founders of libraries. An issue encountered by Raşid Efendi, among others, was that the librarians left to visit their families in other towns at intervals during the year. Locally based librarians would not require this type of leave. The sultan was so gratified by Yusuf Ağa's endowment that he allocated sources of state revenue to pay for the running of the library.[106]

Istanbul also benefited from the expansion of the network of libraries. In 1775, Mehmed Murad Efendi built an independent library in Çarşamba, which was to house his collection of books. They had previously been housed in a Nakşibendi dervish convent in the same district.[107] Unfortunately, we do not

97   VGMA, No. 579, 68.
98   S. Fikri Erten, *Tekelioğulları* (İstanbul: Hüsnütabiat Basımevi, 1955), 17–26.
99   VGMA, No. 579, 50.
100 Mehmed Emin Müderrisoğlu, *Akhisarlı Türk Büyükleri ve Eserleri* (İzmir: Piyasa Matbaası, 1956), 85–86.
101 Sadık Karaöz, *Manisa İli Kütüphaneleri* (Ankara: Ayyıldız Matbaası, 1974), 24; İbrahim Gökçen, *Manisa Tarihinde Hayırlar ve Vakıflar* (İstanbul: Marif Basımevi, 1950), 82; İnci Kuyulu, *Kara Osmanoğlu Ailesine Ait Mimari Eserler* (Ankara: Kültür Bakanlığı, 1992), 100–110.
102 İlhan Polat, "Osmanlı İmparatorluğu Devrinde Yugoslavya'da Kurulan Türk Kütüphaneleri" (Graduation thesis, University of Ankara, 1969), 40–42.
103 Mihaila Stajnova, "Ottoman Libraries in Vidin," *Etudes Balkaniques*, no. 2 (1979): 67.
104 İzmir Vakıflar Müdürlüğü, archive 2. Vakfiye Defteri, 40–45.
105 Istanbul Court Registers, Evkaf-ı Hümayun Müfettişliği, No. 261, 53–54.
106 Istanbul Court Registers, Evkaf-ı Hümayun Müfettişliği, No. 261, 57–58.
107 Muzaffer Gökman, *Murat Molla. Hayatı, Kütüphanesi ve Eserleri* (İstanbul: Cumhuriyet Matbaası, 1943), 12.

have the endowment deed and therefore we do not know the number of books in the collection when the library was opened. However, a later document shows that it was staffed with five librarians, a number which would suggest a sizable collection.[108]

Another library was founded by Selim Ağa, the controller of the imperial arsenals. He envisaged his independent library as primarily a teaching library and made it a requisite that two of the three librarians should be scholars capable of performing the duties of a teacher. The chief mufti was to choose them and ensure that they were well qualified for the task. We can see the influence of the Ragıb Pasha and Atıf Efendi libraries on the administration of this library. The librarians were expected to teach, to lead prayers and to reside in houses built for them close to the library.[109]

A third library was built by Said Efendi in Istanbul in the district of Saraçhane, in the precincts of the Dülgeroğlu Mosque. The collection consisted of 697 books, and it had a staff of four librarians for whom rooms were provided so that they could reside closeby. Unfortunately, the library building no longer exists and we have no record of what happened to the books.[110]

Another sizable library was founded in Istanbul in 1801 by İbrahim Efendi, who endowed 753 books to the Kılıç Ali Pasha College in Tophane. The collection is interesting in that most of the books were on Koranic exegesis, reflecting İbrahim Efendi's profession of teacher and scholar. The foundation deed is unusual in that he appoints four librarians from his family and mentions them by name. He stipulates that on their death other members of his family were to be the librarians and failing this the librarians would be appointed from people residing in the district of Tophane.[111] As a scholar he had insufficient capital to endow a building, so to ensure that his books would be available as a distinct collection he housed them in an existing college, and employed his family to act as librarians to ensure that the collection was properly looked after. He also seems to have wanted the librarians to reside close to the library. The first librarian was to be paid 40 aspers, the second and third 20 aspers and the fourth 16 aspers per day. This contrasts with large libraries of the period where the salaries were between 80 and 120 aspers.

One small collection is worthy of note, one endowed by Abdülkadir Bey to a court of law in Istanbul, in 1808. The books were mainly on jurisprudence

---

108 VGMA, dolap 1628.
109 VGMA, No. 579, 122.
110 TSA, No. D. 10, 294; VGMA, No. 743, 501.
111 Süleymaniye Library, Kılıç Ali Paşa Section No. 1049 and 1050; Istanbul Court Registers, İstanbul Kadılığı, No. 79, 6b–8b, 85a, 16b–18b.

and were most useful to the officers of the court. The collection was to be administered by the staff working there.[112]

Of course, we should not forget that throughout this period the existing library collections were growing larger through endowment made by relatives and descendants of the original founders. The salaries of the librarians were also increasing and sometimes the library staff was enlarged to meet the demands of growing collections. We also have examples of sons building libraries to fulfil the wishes of a deceased parent. As we have already noted, Mustafa Efendi, the director of the Imperial Chancery, in the reign of Mahmud I, had intended to found a library in the Bahçekapı district of Istanbul.[113] Unfortunately, he died before his wishes could be realized, and so when his son, Aşir Efendi, becoming the chief mufti in 1799, built the library in Bahçekapı and endowed to it his father's collection together with his own. In the foundation deed, dated 1800, he kept all the conditions stipulated by his father, but increased the salaries by providing new incomes.[114] The increase in salaries mirrored the changing economic conditions. Aşir Efendi's son, Hafid Efendi, in his turn, added both to the collection and activities of the library. When he became the military judge of Rumelia, he endowed 466 books which were not to be kept as a distinct collection, but were to be dispersed in the main collection, according to their subject classification. He also invested 1,500 kuruş so as to provide an income which was to pay for the recitation of the *Mevlid* poem on special occasions. Sweets and desserts were to be distributed to the congregation on these occasions.[115]

Again in 1805, we find Mehmed Asım Bey, a member of the Köprülü family and also the administrator of Köprülü Library, making provision for the expansion of the collection. He noted in an endowment deed that local college students were requesting certain popular textbooks which were unavailable in the library. To rectify the situation, he bought 350 of the books most in demand and provided money for the future purchase of necessary books.[116] The son of Selim Ağa also increased his father's initial collection.[117]

It is in this period we see libraries subjected to inspections and occasionally their activities being suspended for a period of time. The libraries would be closed by the inspector of foundations when he discovered irregularities in their

---

112 Istanbul Court Registers, Galata Mahkemesi, No. 584, 63b.
113 VGMA, No. 736, 205–206.
114 Süleymaniye Library, Aşir Efendi Section No. 473, 7a–b.
115 Süleymaniye Library, Hafid Efendi Section No. 486, 7a–9b.
116 VGMA, No. 580, 13–14.
117 Istanbul Court Registers, Üsküdar Mahkemesi, No. 564, 80.

operations. We have, for example, noted elsewhere that Hacı Beşir Ağa Library was closed when inspectors discovered that books were going missing as a result of practices contrary to the terms of the foundation deed.[118]

In 1776, when the first librarian of Nuruosmaniye Library died it was discovered that several books in his house belonged to the library. Immediately, the library's operations were suspended, and an inventory was made. In the words of the inspector:

> I, being the inspector of the Nuruosmaniye Library, hereby affirm that Yusuf Efendi, having been head librarian since the foundation of the library, and having died on the 2 Şevval in the year 1190 [14 November 1776], some [library] books were discovered among his belongings and it was further ascertained that he had lent out books, in violation of the conditions of the library and so the books which he had taken home were returned and the books which had been lent were retrieved as much as was possible and the books were checked against the list and a new inventory was prepared.[119]

In the list of missing books, it is noted that Yusuf Ziya Pasha, a former grand vizier, had borrowed and lost a book and that his receipt for borrowing the book was to be found in a certain box. The inventory was to show that nineteen books had gone missing, but none of these were of great value. However, fifteen valuable books bearing the sultan's seal were found to have been uncatalogued and there were also fourteen valuable pieces of calligraphy unrecorded.[120]

In the Mahmud Pasha College, the librarians seemed to have ceased fulfilling their duties and over a period of fifty years had allowed the 342 books belonging to the college to remain in the cabinets unattended and subject to dust and insects. The students at the college complained to the inspector of trusts and he sent some of his staff to investigate. He finally ordered the books to be cleaned, repaired, and catalogued and the librarian was instructed to fulfil his duty by allowing the students access to the books.[121]

This period, as has been mentioned above, saw the state increasingly involved in reforming the central administration, and particularly the military. New

---

118 VGMA, No. 639, 129–130.
119 Nuruosmaniye Library, Fihrist, No. 6, 206a.
120 Nuruosmaniye Library, Fihrist, No. 6, 205b–206a.
121 VGMA, No. 741, 336, and 340.

libraries were being opened and these contained Western books. That is not to say that the classical libraries were being neglected. In fact, this period sees great energy expended on inspection, control, and reorganization of libraries whenever necessary. The process of increasing central control over the library system became even more significant in the reign of Mahmud II.

In 1807, the reign of Selim III came to an abrupt and bloody end with his deposition and death at the hand of the Janissaries, the Ottoman troops who were set against any reforms which threatened their status and privileges. When Mahmud II came to the throne in 1809, he realized that the reforms would have to be postponed until he was in a position to neutralize the forces of reaction. Thus, the earlier part of his reign was marked by stealthy preparations for carrying out a broad program of reforms, which would include the education of the future elite. This would inevitably make its impression on the library system.

The classical Ottoman system essentially divided the branches of learning according to the traditional Islamic syllabus, which was taught in the colleges created as religious foundations; these, therefore, were not within the realm of the state, and their administration was generally free from direct state interference. In the reign of Selim III, a new type of library was introduced in the School of Engineering, a library which was to contain books in Western languages and translations of Western books mainly on technical subjects. This new direction was to continue in Mahmud II's reign. We see new institutions of learning with new libraries, again not stocked with the classical texts, but rather with Western studies.[122] However, in this period the trend towards Western-style institutions was constrained by the small number of people who were involved in the process of reforms. As the century progressed the intellectual elite were increasingly to look to the West, not only in the sciences, but also in literature and the social sciences. But at this stage, the overwhelming majority of library books were manuscripts dealing with traditional Islamic sciences, and they were to be found in the traditional Ottoman libraries.

In 1826, with the reform of the whole system of government, new ministries, which had not existed before, were introduced. One of these was to be the Ministry of Endowments (Evkaf Nezareti), which was responsible for the supervision of all trusts. Thus, all colleges, mosques, and other trust institutions, including libraries, were to come under the direct supervision of one single centralized authority.

---

122 For this type of library see: R. Tuba Çavdar, "Tanzimat'tan Cumhuriyet'e Kadar Osmanlı Kütüphanelerinin Gelişimi" (PhD diss., Istanbul University, 1995), 29–53.

Shortly after the establishment of the Ministry of Endowments, several libraries underwent inspections and new lists of the collections were drawn up. This suggests that there was a policy decision to take stock of what had recently come under their jurisdiction. We have evidence of inspections of several libraries, and reports of these inspections have survived.

The system of foundation libraries had for many years been expanding, and the trend was to continue throughout the reign of Mahmud II. An anonymous American traveler in Istanbul noticed that in 1833 there were libraries next to or inside almost every mosque and in many dervish convents.[123] The fact that Istanbul had become well supplied with libraries meant that the provinces continued to attract foundations, so that almost every city, and indeed many small towns, could boast a library, however small. In this period, the foundation of these libraries is well documented. For example, in 1808 Yılanlıoğlu Şeyh Ali built a library in Eğridir, in the courtyard of his college, and placed 218 of his books in it;[124] in 1811, Vahid Pasha opened a library in Kütahya; Süleyman Pasha built a library in Çay, near Samsun;[125] in 1812, Ahmed Ağa donated his books to the Kurşunlu Mosque in Harput, in eastern Anatolia.[126] Libraries were also endowed in areas further afield. Mehmed Pasha founded a library in the Grand Mosque of Jerusalem;[127] Hamza Efendi, the mufti of Athens, set aside a room in his house for the purpose of teaching and donated books for the use of students.[128] In 1813, Mehmed Ali Pasha (the future ruler of Egypt), built a library in his home town, Kavala, now in northern Greece,[129] and in 1818 Sırrı Selim Bey built a library in the Seyfullah Mosque and College in Salonica.[130]

---

123 Sketches of Turkey in 1831 and 1832 by an American (New York: J. & J. Harper, 1833), 142.
124 Fehmi Aksu, "Yazma Kitaplar," Ün 3, no. 28 (1936): 394; Süleyman Sükutî Yiğitbaşı, Eğridir-Felekâbâd Tarihi (İstanbul: Çeltüt Matbaacılık, 1972), 132; Yücel Özkaya, "Anadoludaki Büyük Hanedanlıklar," Belleten 56, no. 217 (1992): 838.
125 VGMA, No. 733, 44.
126 Süleymaniye library, Harput Section No. 127.
127 Şemim Emsem, "Osmanlı İmparatorluğu Devrinde Türkiye Kütüphanelerinin Tarihçesi," TKDB 9, no. 1–2 (1960): 35.
128 VGMA, No. 987, 129–132.
129 VGMA, No. 580, 275; Ekrem Hakkı Ayverdi, Avrupa'da Osmanlı Mimari Eserleri: Bulgaristan, Yunanistan, Arnavutluk (İstanbul: İstanbul Fetih Cemiyeti, 1982), 236–237.
130 VGMA, No. 987, 115–120. These are just some of the libraries opened in this period. We know that following libraries were also opened: Müftü Mosque Library in İzmir (1819); Şeyh Ahmed Gazzi Library in Bursa (1819); Osman Ağa Library in Arapgir (1820); Hayatizade Library in Elbistan (1823); Şeyh Mustafa Efendi Library in Burdur (1824); Halil Ağa Library in Silistra (1823); Necip Paşa Library in Tire (1827); Şakir Efendi Library in Çankırı (1828); Merdiyye and Münire College Libraries in Kastamonu (1828, 1835); Çaşnigir Library in Manisa (1832); Saçlı Mahmud Efendi Library in Amasya (1833); Ragıbiyye Library in Diyarbakır (1833); İbrahim Paşa Library in Elazığ (1834); Cennetzade Abdullah Efendi Library in Erzurum (1834); Abdullah b. Süleyman Paşa Library in Samsun, and Mustafa Ağa Library in Medina.

Vahid Pasha Library in Kütahya provides us with an insight into how provincial towns attracted libraries. Vahid Pasha was exiled to the city and during his residence there he noted that the students complained of a lack of a library.[131] When he had the opportunity, at some later date, in 1811, he donated 210 books to the Yıldırım Beyazıt Mosque in Kütahya.[132] The books were at first kept in a cabinet in the mosque, and as he added to the collection, a year later (1812), he had a special room built in the courtyard.[133] Thereafter, he continued to send books whenever the opportunity arose.[134]

There is also evidence to suggest that provincial libraries were used for other activities besides reading. When Grand Vizier Dervish Mehmed Pasha founded an independent library in the provincial town of Burdur, he stipulated that each day a portion of Buhari's collection of prophetic traditions was to be read aloud by one of the librarians as a spiritual exercise. On Thursdays and Sundays, after the noon and afternoon prayer, and on holy days, after the evening prayer a dervish ritual, according to the rite of the Nakşibendi dervish order, was to be performed. On the birthday of the Prophet, a *Mevlid* poem was to be recited after the evening prayer. After all these rituals, sweets were to be distributed to all attendees.[135]

Of particular note, in Istanbul is the remarkable number of new libraries donated to dervish convents. In the reign of Mahmud II, at least seven new dervish convent libraries were inaugurated. These collections were of course different from college library collections, in that they tended to contain works of a mystical and poetic nature. Of these libraries the Galata Mevlevihane and Said Pertev Pasha's library are of particular interest for the extent of their collections. For the Galata Mevlevihane, Halet Efendi, a statesman, poet and Mevlevi dervish, built a library building within the garden of the convent. In 1820, he donated 266 books[136] and two years later he donated a further 547 books.[137] The library reflected the founder's interest in history, literature, and mystical works. Being a dervish convent library, he stipulated that it was not the trust administrator who was to appoint the librarian, as would normally be expected, but the spiritual master of the dervish convent. The first librarian should be a bachelor and be resident in the dervish convent, while the imam should act as

---

131 Uzunçarşılıoğlu İsmail Hakkı, *Kütahya Şehri* (İstanbul: Devlet Matbaası, 1932), 133.
132 VGMA, No. 579, 706.
133 Hamza Güner, *Kütahya Camileri* (Kütahya: n.p., 1964), 21. For the detailed list of expenses entailed in the building and furnishing of the library see: BOA, DBŞM, No. 7965.
134 VGMA, No. 579, 627, 680, 684, 688, 695–699.
135 Istanbul Court Registers, İstanbul Kadılığı, No. 122, 37a–38a.
136 Süleymaniye Library, Halet Efendi Section No. 837, No. 1, 1b–21b.
137 Süleymaniye Library, Halet Efendi Section No. 837, No. 1, 22b–38a; Istanbul Court Registers, Evkaf-ı Hümayun Müfettişliği, No. 375, 1b–7b.

second librarian.[138] Said Pertev Pasha's dervish convent library was set up in the garden of the Çiçekçi Mosque in Üsküdar, where the Nakşibendi convent was situated. The library building was endowed with a large collection and two full-time librarians were appointed, with appropriately adequate salaries.[139]

As for Sultan Mahmud II himself, he chose to make his imperial foundation not in Istanbul, but in Medina. He built a college and a library and accommodation for the librarians.[140] Although we do not know how many books were initially donated by Mahmud II, we know that in 1839 he sent a bookbinder from Istanbul to the library and that the binder repaired 646 books.[141] Sixty years later a yearbook for the province noted that there were 4,569 books in the library.[142] A document from 1835 notes that the sultan intended to build a similar library in Mecca:

> As there is no independent library in Mecca, books having been donated by worthy benefactors, but with the death of their keepers books having gone missing, it is my intention to build a library in Mecca, just as I did in Medina.[143]

The sultan went on to say that he had ordered that all books in existing collections should be brought together and a list drawn up. He would then make up any deficiency in the collection. We do not know whether his wish was realized or not, but his successor Abdülmecid (1839–1861) would found a library in the city[144] and it is likely that the books which Mahmud II had ordered to be collected became the nucleus of Mecidiye Library, Abdülmecid's own foundation.

Increasingly, library collections were inspected during Mahmud II's reign. Even before the institution of the Ministry of Endowments, noted above, the process of inspecting collections had got underway. With the coming of the ministry, the process gained momentum. As a result of these inspections, new

---

138 Süleymaniye Library, Halet Efendi Section No. 837, No. 1, 8a–b.
139 VGMA, No. Kasa 108, 6–9.
140 BOA, Hatt-ı Hümayun 26, 913. See also O. Spies, "Die Bibliotheken des Hidschas," *ZDMG* 40 (1936): 96–98 and Hammadî Ali Muhammed et-Tunisî, "el-Mektebatü'l-amme bi'l-Medineti'l-Münevvere, madiha ve haziriha" (MA thesis, King Abdülaziz University, Jiddah, 1981): 1–7.
141 İşki Mustafa b. Ömer Kilisî, *Ta'tirü Ercai'd-Devleti'l-Mecdiyye*, Istanbul University Library, T. Y. 1490, 166a–b.
142 *Hicaz Vilayeti Salnamesi* (Mekke-i Mükerreme: [Vilayet Matbaası?], 1309H), 307.
143 BOA, Mühimme-i Mısır, No. 13, 82.
144 BOA, Mühimme-i Mısır, No. 13, 168.

catalogues were frequently prepared, deficiencies in collections made good, and when deemed appropriate the location of the library would be changed. One of the most important functions of the inspection was to establish that the trusts' administrators were carrying out their duties in accordance with the wishes of the founder, as laid down in the endowment deed.[145]

In 1815, Çorlulu Ali Pasha's collection in his Darü'l-Hadis in Istanbul was checked and a new list of books was prepared.[146] In 1816, certain collections which had been endowed to the Fatih Mosque were removed to the independent library at Beyazıd, which had been built some fifty years previously by Veliyüddin Efendi. A new catalogue was prepared for these books.[147] In 1820, both Damad İbrahim Pasha's and the Nuruosmaniye collections, which had been in existence for some one hundred and seventy years, respectively, were inspected "because for a considerable time their condition was unknown," and new catalogues were drawn up.[148] In 1827, the library of the Valide Sultan Mosque in Bahçekapı was inspected and a new catalogue prepared.[149] The books which Chief Mufti Damadzade Ahmed Efendi had endowed to the mosque of Selim I were inspected in May 1828 and transferred to a dervish convent in the same district, and most importantly, a librarian was appointed to look after the books.[150]

In Cyprus, there were several collections which had been endowed over the centuries to the Ayasofya Mosque (not to be confused with the Ayasofya in Istanbul; there were several churches named after the Holy Wisdom which were converted to mosques). In the courtyard of the mosque, Mahmud II erected a building to house these collections, to which he added other collections which had been endowed to other institutions; he also provided for the future running of the library.[151]

In a memorandum written by Mahmud II to his vizier, Mehmed Emin Rauf Pasha, in November 1830, we see the sultan providing for the repair of the college library built by his father, Abdülhamid I, in Medina. He ordered the five hundred books, which were scattered in various locations, to be brought

---

145 Nazif Öztürk, *Türk Yenileşme Tarihi Çerçevesinde Vakıf Müessesesi* (Ankara: Türkiye Diyanet Vakfı, 1995), 393.
146 BOA, Bab-ı Defteri, Baş Muhallefat Halifesi, No. 13 242.
147 Beyazıd Umumi Library, Veliyüddin Section No. 3291, 4b.
148 Nuruosmaniye Library, Fihrist, No. 3, 1b.
149 University Library, İbnülemin Section No. 2485.
150 BOA, Cevdet-Maarif, No. 2821.
151 İ. Parmaksızoğlu, *Kıbrıs Sultan İkinci Mahmud Kütüphanesi* (Ankara: Türk Kütüphaneciler Derneği, 1964); Beria Remzi Özoran, "Kıbrıs'ta Sultan Mahmut Kütüphanesi," *Türk Kültürü* 8, no. 92 (1970): 513–515; Mustafa Haşim Altan, "Die Bibliotheken im türkisch-zypriotischen Bundesstaat," *Biblos* 28 (1979): 306–309.

together and placed in newly built cabinets in the college.[152] In the following year, it was stipulated that books were not to be lent out, but to be read within the confines of the college.[153]

In January 1831, Mahmud II had a collection of books removed from the palace and placed in Laleli College Library, which had been built by Mustafa III. These books were not from the endowed collection of Ahmed III, but were a collection of books established by Mustafa III and placed in Bostancılar Ocağı Library, which had fallen into disuse. Mahmud II gave the reason for moving the collection: Firstly, he noted that the collection had ceased to be used, especially with the opening of Ahmed III's library at the Topkapı Palace and, consequently, the books were not being cared for and might fall into disrepair. Furthermore, Mustafa III's library at Laleli College had gaps in its collection, which would be made good by the transfer. Finally, he wanted the books to be used by those people who could benefit from them.[154]

Several other collections were inspected at this time: Ayasofya Library in 1831,[155] while in 1833 inspections were carried out at Merzifonlu Mustafa Pasha College Library, Veliyüddin Library and Abdülhamid I's library in Medina.[156] In 1837, the Galata Palace College Library collection, which had been transferred to Ayasofya Library, was inspected by a commission who drew up a list of the works and split the collection into two, one part going to Fatih Library and the other remaining at Ayasofya,[157] both libraries and the Galata Palace collection having been endowed by Mahmud I.

With the abolition of the Janissary corps in 1826, the Bektashi convents, closely associated with the corps, were also shut down. When they were closed, lists were made of the books in the convents, two of which have survived, that of books at the Elmalı and the Demirci Baba convents.[158]

In 1838, Mahmud II sent binders to Medina to repair and rebind the books in various locations in this city. The judge of Medina at the time noted in his history of Medina that the binders had rebound and repaired 521 books in the Prophet's Mosque, 646 in the Mahmudiye College, 432 in Hamidiye Library,

---

152 BOA, Mühimme-i Mısır, No. 13, 41–42.
153 BOA, Mühimme-i Mısır, No. 13, 54.
154 VGMA, No. 642, 103–104.
155 Süleymaniye Library, Fihrist, No. 3.
156 Beyazıt Umumi Library, No. 21, 346; Beyazıt Umumi Library, Veliyüddin Efendi Section No. 3290; BOA, Cevdet-Maarif, 8613, Cevdet-Maarif, No. 1870 and İbrahim Ateş, "Mescid-i Nebevî'nin Yapıldığı Günden Bu Yana Geçirdiği Genişletme Girişimleri," VD 24 (1994): 14, respectively.
157 Süleymaniye Library, Ayasofya, Fihrist, No. 6, 1b–11b.
158 BOA, MAD. 9771, 10, and 56.

922 in the Karabaş College, twenty in the Özbek College, and 961 in the Beşir Ağa College.[159]

Mahmud II's reign is characterized by the rationalizing of all trusts and religious foundations under the jurisdiction of one ministry. Whenever the opportunity arose, collections were split up, brought together, or transferred to strengthen existing collections. At the same time as Mahmud II organized and surveyed the classical Ottoman libraries, changes were coming about which would bring with them a new type of library. By Mahmud II's death three institutions had libraries which contained printed books in European languages dealing with medicine, science, and technology. Soon, these works were to be translated into Turkish and printed. These were to become the bases of the new Ottoman library collections. The new libraries were set up by the government to serve the needs of the reforms. While the classical Ottoman libraries would continue to exist until the coming of the Republic in 1920s, the new, European-style libraries eventually made the classical library obsolete in the educational system.

---

159 Işkî Mustafa b. Ömer Kilisî, *Ta'tirü Ercai'd-Devleti'l-Mecdiyye*, Istanbul University Library, T. Y. 1490, 177a.

Chapter Five

Foundation Libraries in the Age of Reforms (1839–1922)

By the end of the eighteenth century, the Ottoman library system had matured into a sophisticated network of manuscript collections, adequate to meet all the needs of the educational system. Paradoxically, this came at precisely the moment when a series of political crises and disastrous wars had convinced Ottoman statesmen to embrace modernization. Western institutions were to be set up throughout the empire in the next century, and whilst the empire was sustained, albeit within increasingly reduced borders, until the First World War, older institutions, including foundation libraries, were rendered redundant. The earlier reforms, beginning in the late eighteenth century, failed due to the intransigence of the Janissary corps, at that time the corrupt and ineffective backbone of the army. Modernization had to wait until 1826 when Mahmud II destroyed the corps and then proceeded to introduce institutions based on Western models. The process of modernization effected all institutions in the empire, not least of all the library system.

It should, however, be emphasized that the Westernizing elite was still a very small minority of the reading public and for the vast majority foundation libraries continued to flourish. Unlike the destruction of the Janissary corps, the dysfunctionality within the library system crept in slowly, almost imperceptibly. Even after the announcement of the program of reforms within the empire in 1839, foundation libraries continued to be established, even up to the beginning of the twentieth century. Among these, the most important were the Hüsrev Pasha Library in Eyüp (1839), the Esad Efendi Library in Sultanahmet (1846), the Şeyh Mehmed Murad Library in Darü'l-mesnevi in Fatih (1844), the Nafiz Pasha Library in Yenikapı Mevlevihane (1851), the Chief Mufti Arif Hikmet Bey Library in Medina (1855), the Pertevniyal Sultan Library in the Valide Mosque (1871), the Hasan Hüsnü Pasha Library in Eyüp (1895), and the Hacı Mahmud Efendi Library in the dervish convent of Yahya Efendi in Beşiktaş (1901).[1] Of course, there were also many other libraries with small collections established in Istanbul and throughout the empire. However, the number of donations to existing libraries and the foundation of new libraries declined markedly in this period, reflecting to some extent the increasing obsolescence of the system.

FIGURE 9. Hüsrev Pasha Library, Istanbul, est. 1854.

One of the basic causes of the decline of foundation libraries was that it had not been possible to introduce the new knowledge into these libraries, as they were essentially alienated from the state by their status as charities governed by Islamic law. What is more, the scholars and librarians who were familiar with the libraries would not have been able to deal with the new subject headings, least of

---

1   For other libraries founded in this period see Tuba Çavdar's thesis: "Tanzimat'tan Cumhuriyete Kadar Osmanlı Kütüphanelerinin Gelişimi" (PhD diss., Istanbul University, 1995), 4–26.

all the foreign books in Western languages. There was no way that the classical Ottoman library could be modernized. Instead, it was cast aside as new libraries with librarians acquainted with Western languages and culture were founded to serve the requirements of the state. The state, however, did not wish to ignore the old library system. It recognized that this was a rich cultural treasury which had to be preserved. Various attempts to safeguard the collections were made throughout the remaining years of the Ottoman Empire.[2]

In 1826, all charitable institutions, libraries included, were brought together under the administration of a Ministry of Endowments.[3] After the announcement, in 1839, of the intention of the government to introduce wide-sweeping reforms throughout the empire, the responsibility for administering the libraries, appointing and supervising the staff was handed to the newly established Ministry of Education.[4] However, as charitable foundations, foundation libraries still received their budget from the Ministry of Endowments, which meant that they were under the twin responsibility of both the Ministries of Endowments and Education. This situation was to last for the rest of the century, so that we see in a report, dated 1904, that this twin responsibility was seen as a fundamental problem for the well-being of the system of foundation libraries:

> The main reason for the foundation libraries being in a pitiful condition is the system of shared responsibility. On the one hand, being foundations, the salary of the librarians, the cost of repairs to the library buildings, the repair of books and bindings is the responsibility of the Ministry of Endowments. On the other hand, the responsibility for supervising and inspecting the running of the library, belongs to the Ministry of Education. It is this twin responsibility which causes the problem. For instance, when a library is closed by the Ministry of Endowments to carry out repair work, it becomes impossible for the Ministry of Education to inspect it, and thus it effectively loses control of the library.[5]

---

2   Throughout this period several attempts were made. See, for instance, BOA, MF, KTV, 1/2; 3/90; 4/68; 5/15; 5/57; 5/71; 6/31; 6/58; 7/8; 8/10.
3   Nazif Öztürk, *Türk Yenileşme Tarihi Çerçevesinde Vakıf Müessesesi* (Ankara: Türkiye Diyanet Vakfı, 1995), 393.
4   BOA, Ayniyat Defteri, No. 421, 19.
5   İsmail E. Erünsal, *Kütüphanecilikle İlgili Osmanlıca Metinler ve Belgeler*, vol. 2 (İstanbul: Edebiyat Fakültesi Matbaası, 1990), 446. See also: BOA, ŞD, Evkaf, 126/4: BOA, MF, KTV, 3/11, and 3/12.

To overcome this problem, the day-to-day running and decision making was handed to the Ministry of Education, which would be responsible for all aspects of administration, except for finance, which was to be provided by the Ministry of Endowments.[6] Thus, in the budget discussion of 1907, the minister of education was able to summarize the situation: "We are entirely responsible for the running of the foundation libraries; the Ministry of Endowments provides the income."[7]

However, this transfer of responsibility did not create the desired effect and the condition of the foundation libraries continued to deteriorate. A minister of endowments, in 1911, proposed that responsibility for foundation libraries should be transferred back to the minister of endowments:

> It is understood that the responsibility for running foundation libraries was recently given to the Ministry of Education. In my humble opinion, if the responsibility were to be transferred to the Ministry of Endowments where the responsibility used to be in the past, we will not only be acting in accordance with the wills of the founders, but we will thus ensure their survival.[8]

In 1912, responsibility for the foundation libraries was given back to Ministry of Endowments,[9] but this time the government allocated two hundred thousand Turkish piastres to the ministry's budget to help cover the shortfall between income and expenditure.[10] Although a special office, entitled the Directorship of Educational Endowments (Müessesat-ı İlmiyye Müdüriyyeti), was established to administer foundation libraries, it appears that neither the change of responsibility, nor the creation or activities of this new department actually benefited them.[11]

---

6 Nazif Öztürk, *Türk Yenileşme Tarihi Çerçevesinde Vakıf Müessesesi* (Ankara: Türkiye Diyanet Vakfı, 1995), 396–397.

7 *Meclis-i Meb'usanın Yüzsekizinci İctima Zabıtnamesi, Takvim-i Vekayi'*, year 2, no. 544 (18 May 1326R), 2137.

8 *Evkaf Nazırı Hammâdezâde Halil Hamdi Paşa Tarafından Evkaf Hakkında Sadarete Takdim Edilen Layiha Suretidir* (İstanbul, n.d.), 37.

9 Özer Soysal, *Türk Kütüphaneciliği, Geleneksel Yapıdan Yeniden Yapılanışa*, vol. 1 (Ankara: T.C. Kültür Bakanlığı, Kütüphaneler Genel Müdürlüğü, 1988), 93; *Düstûr*, Tertib-i sanî, vol. 6 (İstanbul: Matbaa-i Amire, 1331H), 575.

10 *Takvîm-i Vekayi'*, no. 2556.

11 İsmail E. Erünsal, *Kütüphanecilikle İlgili Osmanlıca Metinler ve Belgeler*, vol. 2 (İstanbul: Edebiyat Fakültesi Matbaası, 1990), 488–489.

In 1912 and 1913, Turkey was involved in the two Balkan wars which were followed by the First World War and the War of Independence (1919–1922). By 1923, when the republic was declared, Turkey had been at war for ten years and Istanbul was still under foreign occupation. In the first years of the republic, it was noted that the foundation libraries were in a disastrous state, some being no more than storage rooms for unread books. It was recommended that these libraries be re-opened and made available to scholars.[12]

It seems that from the turn of the century the decline in the condition of libraries began to accelerate. The criticism levelled at the deteriorated state of the libraries, be it in newspapers, official documents, reports or noted by foreign travelers, dwelled on the irregular and unannounced opening times, the poor salaries allocated to librarians who were often incompetent, the poor condition of the books and the scattered nature of the collections.

The problem of the opening times of foundation libraries had existed for some years in the previous century. As early as 1861, Ahmad Faris al-Shidyaq, a scholar of Arabic language and literature and an eminent publisher, noted that when he attempted to work in Istanbul libraries:

> Some [libraries] were also shut for several months a year, the people of Istanbul seldom frequent these libraries, so their closure does not much matter to them: what is important is the closing time of the coffeehouses.[13]

In 1870, an anonymous correspondent in the *Hadika* newspaper complained:

> The aforementioned libraries close when the teaching term of the lessons given in the mosques comes to an end. During the term-time they are shut on Tuesdays and Fridays anyway, on the other days they are only open for one or two hours after six o' clock [i.e. 12:00 noon according to Western time keeping] if they open at all. Thus, they are open when the normal reader is

---

12 The introduction by Hamit Zübeyir Koşar to the translation of Paul Guyaş's Book: *Halk Kütüphanelerinin Suret-i Te'sisi ve Usul-i İdaresi* (İstanbul, 1925), 3; reprinted in Erünsal's *Kütüphanecilikle İlgili Osmanlıca Metinler ve Belgeler*, vol. 1 (İstanbul: Edebiyat Fakültesi Matbaası, 1982), 411.

13 Quoted in Geoffrey Roper's article: "Ahmad Faris al-Shidyaq and the Libraries of Europe and the Ottoman Empire," *Libraries & Culture* 33, no. 3 (Summer 1998): 242 and footnote 65.

busy working in his occupation, so they are in fact only of any practical use to college students.[14]

To rectify this problem, the Ministry of Education published a set of instructions in 1879 concerning the running of foundation libraries. The very first article addresses itself to this precise problem: "Article one: Libraries will open one hour before noon and close three hours after noon and during these four hours the librarian will be on duty."[15]

From complaints made in the following years it is clear that these instructions were being largely ignored. This is confirmed by the Indian scholar Shiblî Nu'manî, who complains in 1892 that the libraries were open less than three hours a day and closed for up to four months in the year.[16] In a report dated 1904, it was noted that apart from famous libraries, there were many libraries in mosques and mausoleums where it was not possible to know if they were ever open to the public.[17] In 1908, H. G. Dwight, a British journalist, visited Feyzullah Efendi's Library, where he noted:

> I also saw a finely bound catalogue to which nothing has been added for two hundred years. For that matter the library does not look as if anyone had consulted it for two hundred years, though the librarian is supposed to be there every day except Tuesday and Friday. He accordingly spends most of his time in his bookshop in the Fatih Mosque yard.[18]

The authorities were not complacent, and more attempts were made, although ineffectual, to rectify the situation. An Egyptian scholar, Ahmed Zeki Pasha, was invited by the grand vizier to survey Istanbul libraries and produce a report with recommendations. In his report, dated 1909, he also refers to opening times of foundation libraries as the main problem:

---

14 *Hadika*, no. 40, 320 (İstanbul: n.p., T. Sani 1286R).
15 Mahmud Cevad, *Maarif-i Umumiye Nezareti, Tarihçe-i Teşkilat ve İcraatı* (İstanbul: Matbaa-i Amire, 1338H), 207.
16 Şibli Numani, *Anadolu, Suriye ve Mısır Seyahatnamesi*, trans. Yusuf Karaca (İstanbul: Risale, 2002), 95.
17 Quoted in Erünsal's *Kütüphanecilikle İlgili Osmanlıca Metinler ve Belgeler*, vol. 2 (İstanbul, 1990), 447.
18 H. G. Dwight, *Constantinople Old and New* (London: C. Scribner's Sons, 1915), 70–71.

A more important problem is that the librarian only opens after noon and closes the library before the afternoon prayer if he wants [effectively less than two hours]. The days on which libraries are open are quite rare. The librarians open the library whenever they feel like it so that the libraries are of very little use to potential readers.[19]

By 1912, little had been done to ameliorate the position. In the budget debate held in parliament (Meclis-i Meb'usan), a member complained that "as we pay these librarians in Istanbul a mere fifty, sixty, or one hundred piastres a month they do not feel that they are required to attend to their duties more than once a week or twice a month or even once a month."[20]

At the very beginning of the twentieth century, a writer witnessed this problem thus:

> One day I visited a library surviving from our ancestors [i. e. a foundation library]. This was my third visit before I could find it open. By luck I could also find the librarian. However, the time was approaching noon and the librarian wanted to make his ablutions for the noon prayer, so I waited until he was finished. After a while the book I requested was made available to me. I was shown to a small narrow room where I set myself on a cushion and began to read.[21]

The whimsical behavior of librarians in opening the libraries to the public even inspired poems. A certain poet called Seracettin wrote some verses in imitation of La Fontaine, entitled "The Librarian Mouse":

> If the librarian was ever there, for he was always missed,
> Maybe he was a grocer or a herbalist
>
> In a foundation library, so the story goes
> For such a long time that nobody knows

19 Quoted in Erünsal's *Kütüphanecilikle İlgili Osmanlıca Metinler ve Belgeler*, vol. 1 (İstanbul: Edebiyat Fakültesi Matbaası, 1982), 330–331.
20 *Takvim-i Vekayi'*, year 2, no. 544 (18 May 1326R), 2128. For the documents concerning this problem see: BOA, MF, KTV, 3/91; 4/44; 4/120; 7/71; 7/77; 7/85; 8/104.
21 Tüccarzade İbrahim Hilmi, *Maarifimiz ve Servet-i Milliyemiz Felâketlerimizin Esbâbı* (İstanbul: Kitabhane-yi İslâm ve Askerî, 1329H), 63.

I cannot say, for it was always shut
And everyone said this cannot go on, but

There is nobody responsible and nobody cares
And then the mice too saw the state of affairs[22]

The point of the poem is that the poet was treating a topic that must have been a bone of contention among the reading public.

Many accounts, documents,[23] travelers' reports, and other sources note that librarians were paid a derisory amount of money and had to perform other duties in order to survive, and that their work elsewhere did not permit them to work as librarians for more than a few hours a week. The reason for the librarians' salaries being so low is explained by the inflexible nature of a foundation. The salaries specified in the foundation deed could not be changed (except in the case of imperial foundations). As inflation ravaged the Ottoman Empire, just as in the rest of Europe, the value of the asper and piastre dropped until they were a mere fraction of their former value.[24] When the families of the founder were able to, they could create another foundation deed in which they specified which employees were to receive increases in their salary, and of course they would donate some source of income to cover the increased salary, but this was not a very common occurrence.[25] The older a foundation deed was the less people there were with a familial or other interest to insure that it was viable and working as intended.

The Ministry of Endowments in 1826 was set up partly with the intention of solving the financial problems most of the foundations faced, but most of the resources of the state were going to the modernization of the army, setting up new educational institutions and the attempt to quell the rebellion in Greece, which later led to Greek independence. In the face of all the demands being put on the Ottoman treasury, libraries held a low priority.

Ahmad Faris al-Shidyaq noted the injustice of paying salaries that had not been adjusted for inflation:

So, the librarians have an excuse for their failure to remain at their posts, since it is unjust to expect people to give up all the

---

22 "Hafız-ı Kütüb Fare," *Muallimler Mecmuası*, year 2, no. 22 (1924), 742.
23 BOA, MF, KTV, 7/22; 7/44.
24 Ş. Pamuk, *A Monetary History of the Ottoman Empire* (Cambridge: Cambridge University Press, 2000), 193.
25 *TKT*, 145–148.

hours of the day in order to earn an amount insufficient to buy a single loaf of bread.[26]

Shiblî Nu'manî also noted that although the librarians in the foundation libraries were payed extremely low salaries, consisting of basic food items and the equivalent of a mere two rupees a month, they nevertheless remained, for the best part, men of high religious scruple and honesty. When visiting Aşir Efendi's Library, Nu'manî suggested to the head librarian that he should sell the abundant grapes which hung from the vines climbing up the outer wall. The answer was that it was impossible because the grapes were part of the foundation and were only for the benefit of readers in the library. Nu'manî adds that the head librarian was too poor to get married and was forced to spend his nights in the library.[27]

While in 1909 complaints were made that librarians could not be expected to work for between twenty-five and 120 piastres a month, we see a member of the parliament making the following suggestion in the 1911 budget debate:

> As far as I know the salary for the head librarian at the Public Library is 1000 piastres, and the other librarians receive 800 while the porter receives 400 piastres, while on the other hand the salaries of the famous foundation libraries is a mere 150 piastres. Since a porter at the Public Library receives 400 piastres how can we justify the salaries given to the librarians at the Rüstem Pasha and Selim Ağa Libraries. I propose that they receive a 300 piastres increase in their salaries.[28]

The salaries at the Beyazıt Public Library were relatively high because it was established and maintained by the state; it was not a foundation library. From this, we see that the state recognized the importance of libraries and paid their staff reasonable salaries; it was the foundation libraries that could not do so, and this was a matter for public concern.

The fundamental problem underlying the foundation library system was a lack of money to keep it running. However, there were other problems too. In the foundation system, positions could be inherited or sold by their holder. This may not have created problems for some of the institutions, but for

---

26 G. Roper, "Ahmad Fâris al-Shidyaq and the Libraries of Europe and the Ottoman Empire," *Libraries & Culture* 33, no. 3 (Summer, 1998): 243.

27 Şibli Numani, *Anadolu, Suriye ve Mısır Seyahatnamesi*, trans. Yusuf Karaca (İstanbul: Risale, 2002), 91–92.

28 *Takvim-i Vekayi'*, year 2, no. 544 (18 May 1326R), 2136.

libraries this was not an acceptable practice. Sometimes a child would inherit the librarianship and sometimes posts could be sold as useful extra sources of income to persons who were not competent to carry out the duties of librarian. In these cases, deputies were appointed and were paid even less than the derisory official salary. We cannot expect these deputies to have been either enthusiastic about their work or indeed even competent to perform it. Originally, founders would intend that their son or grandson administer the foundation, but as the administration was handed down through succeeding generations, there was increasingly less enthusiasm to ensure that the founder's intentions were carried out. The posts of librarians and junior librarians, doormen, cleaners, and sweepers were sometimes inherited or bought. From the eighteenth century onwards, certain library founders had noted the practice and had stated that the position of librarian was not to be sold. However, as the inheritance of positions in the foundation system was an old established tradition, it was not possible to ban it categorically. Therefore, library founders permitted this practice under certain conditions.[29]

After the introduction of the program of reforms, the Ministry of Education attempted to stop this practice in the libraries. In a document from the Ministry of Education to the Grand Vizierate, dated 1882, we see this concern for the libraries expressed quite frankly:[30]

Your Servant's Humble Submission:

Since the positions of some of the libraries in Istanbul are held by some persons who are either government employees, tradesmen or menial workers, then they cannot perform the duties themselves, so they appoint certain deputies who are ignorant and incompetent and since these deputies receive a pittance from the holders of the posts, they do not open the libraries regularly at the proper times and take no precaution to look after the books, so that some of the precious and rare books donated by benefactors suffer harm and sometimes are lost.

---

29 Erünsal, *Kütüphanecilikle İlgili Osmanlıca Metinler ve Belgeler*, vol. 1 (İstanbul: Edebiyat Fakültesi Matbaası, 1982), 180–181.
30 BOA, Şura-yı Devlet, 209/9.

Later in the document, it is noted that a committee of the Ministry of Education reached certain conclusions and made the following recommendations: Firstly, to ban the practice of allowing deputies to perform the work of the librarians. If the actual holder of the post of librarian is competent and willing, he himself may continue in the post, otherwise he is to resign. Secondly, holders of posts who are either not competent or unwilling to perform the duty of librarian may, if they have bought their post, sell it on to someone who is both willing and competent, provided that the person buying the post is approved by the Ministry of Education. In order to establish the competence of librarians, the following criteria were established:

> To know whether a person can be a librarian he should be examined to find out whether he can determine what language a book is written in and what the subject of the book is. He should be able to identify the catalogue number. He therefore should have familiarity with the basis of Arabic and Persian grammar and should be able to write and read Turkish. Those librarians who are considered to have those qualities should remain in their posts and those who have not should be educated to acquire these qualities.

It was recommended that as there were often several positions in a library, such as sweepers, doormen, and second librarians, where the incumbents never appeared at their posts, such positions should be abolished and amalgamated into a single post, and likewise the salaries be amalgamated, creating a sum large enough to ensure that the personnel who attended the library were adequately paid.

From correspondence between the Ministry of Education and the Grand Vizierate it seems that these recommendations were adopted and promulgated in a codex of regulations. The codex to which the correspondence refers is probably codex no. 568, entitled "Codex concerning the positions of primary school teachers and assistants, librarians, sweepers and doormen."[31] In this codex, the qualifications, procedure for selection and appointment of librarians and other library personnel are given, but it also addresses the problems of eliminating deputy librarians and unqualified holders of librarian posts. We do not know how effectively the codex was applied, but from the criticism

---

31 BOA, Şura-yı Devlet, 568.

of librarians and libraries that continued through to the end of the Ottoman Empire, it would not be unfair to presume that its effect was minimal.

Another problem of the foundation library system was the location of small collections. Many of the smaller donations were located in mosques and dervish convents scattered throughout Istanbul, and even if there was a librarian in attendance it often meant a long walk to consult a single work and often no possibility of comparing two manuscripts. Smaller collections located in buildings that were not purpose-built libraries often deteriorated due to unsuitable storage conditions.[32] Several scholars and some reports complained of the deteriorating condition of the books in these collections. For example, a certain scholar, Nuri Efendi, in a report dated 1900, noted:

> Our libraries are in a pitiful condition. Some collections have been transferred to other locations and are no longer accessible while the doors of some libraries have been locked and are sealed. As for those that are open to the public, they are so filthy that you are hard pressed to find somewhere to sit. When a book arrives your heart sinks seeing its condition: it is covered in years of dust and looks as if it is about to fall apart.[33]

In 1861, al-Shidyaq noted that many scholars were wasting time and energy walking throughout the city from one collection to another. He recommended that all the small collections should be transferred to a single location in the centrally located Nuruosmaniye district of Istanbul and that a librarian be appointed and paid five hundred piastres a month, but on condition that he be present in the library from morning to evening on those days when the library was to be open to the public.[34] Münif Pasha also pointed out to the same problem in his report submitted to the Grand Vizier Ali Pasha, in 1870.[35]

In a document dated 1904, it was noted that if immediate action was not taken there were some fifty thousand to sixty thousand books at risk of being damaged, among which were rare and valuable works. The document ends with the following suggestion:

---

32 BOA, MF, KTV, 3/91.
33 BOA, Yıldız Evrakı, 14/2045/126/10.
34 Roper, "Ahmad Faris al-Shidyaq and the Libraries of Europe and the Ottoman Empire," 243.
35 Müjgan Cunbur, "Münif Paşa Layihası ve Değerlendirilmesi," *TAD* 2, nos. 2–3 (1964): 226.

To sum up [one solution would be] to gather all collections to one location but to store the books in separate rooms, each room bearing the name of the donor. If it is not possible to bring the great libraries to this central location, then at least the smaller collections which are rotting away in cabinets and chests in mosques and mausoleums should be centralized.[36]

The Egyptian scholar Ahmed Zeki Pasha echoes these ideas and he too recommended centralization of smaller collections, both to preserve the books and to facilitate scholarship.[37]

In a parliamentary debate (session 107), some members referred to this problem and the minister of education replied thus:

As I have previously mentioned, the Ministry intends to build a central public library and funds for the building will be allocated in next year's budget. We are in the planning stage of this project. This belongs to the future. This library is absolutely essential for us. We [the ministry] have a [public] library in Bayezid. The others belong to foundations. They are run according to the law governing foundations. If I can obtain a favorable legal opinion, I shall gather these libraries to one location.[38]

From the debate, we realize that the members of parliament understood and accepted that as the foundations were governed by religious law it was necessary to obtain an opinion from the committee of the chief mufti as to whether the law permitted the transfer of a collection to a central location when this had not been envisaged by the founder.[39] In fact, in no case was this explicitly provided for in a foundation deed.

This issue had arisen previously in 1909. The Ministry of Endowments had requested the chief mufti to issue an opinion to allow the minister to gather libraries to a central location. On that occasion the chief mufti could not issue an opinion allowing the books to be moved. In a letter to the mufti's office, the minister of endowments, Hammade-zade Halil Pasha, explained to the chief mufti that there was a precedent for this. Apparently, exactly the same

---

36 BOA, H, HMD, 1322 (9.1).
37 İsmail E. Erünsal, *Kütüphanecilikle İlgili Osmanlıca Metinler ve Belgeler*, vol. 2 (İstanbul: Edebiyat Fakültesi Matbaası, 1982), 324, 329–330.
38 *Takvim-i Vekayi'*, year 2, no. 544 (18 May 1326R), 2126- 2127.
39 *Takvim-i Vekayi'*, year 2, no. 544 (18 May 1326R), 2127

problem had existed in Egypt, so they had sought the opinion of the scholars who had issued a favorable opinion. With this opinion, the smaller collections were gathered to one location and the religious establishment then realized the benefits of centralization. The chief mufti replied that the Committee for Issuing Legal Opinion had decided that books could not be removed from the location to which the founder had donated them. He added, however, that they could be temporarily removed to a suitable location while the storage place or building in which the books had been stored was being repaired.[40]

Whatever the intention of the mufti's office was, the minister of education interpreted it as the official go-ahead to centralize the smaller collections. In the parliamentary debate, the minister noted that the chief mufti had in the past "found a way to enable them to centralize the books which were deteriorating and scattered here and there in a newly prepared place."[41] He was referring to an earlier request made by his ministry from the mufti's office for an opinion on this exact question, and the opinion issued at that time was identical: the books could be moved while the designated repository was being repaired.[42]

The situation looked as if it could be resolved in the following year when a new minister of endowments, Hayri Efendi, was appointed. Faced with the problem of administering the foundations himself, he shed some of his scruples and planned to build a large central library to house four hundred thousand books. However, he realized that while the library was being built, steps would have to be taken to preserve the existing collections, so he embarked on a program of repairing the existing buildings and installing electricity where practicable. He then moved some of the smaller collections to the renovated libraries.[43]

During his term in office, Hayri Efendi tried to rationalize the foundation libraries by designating some of the larger ones as specialist libraries, to where, presumably, the books from small collections would be moved. But we do not

---

40 Meşihat Archive, Defter No. 5. This document published by the author: İsmail E. Erünsal, "Evkaf Nazırı Hammade-zade Halil Paşa'nın İstanbul'da mevcut Vakıf Kütüphanelerinin Islahı ve Bir Mekanda Toplanması Konusundaki Çalışmaları," in *Türk Kütüphaneciliğinden İzdüşümler: Nail Bayraktar'a Armağan I (Hatıra ve Bilimsel Makaleler)*, ed. İrfan Dağdelen, Hüseyin Türkmen, and Nergis Ulu (İstanbul: Büyükşehir Belediye Başkanlığı, 2005), 90–98.

41 *Meclis-i Meb'usan Zabıt Ceridesi*, Devre 1, İctima Senesi 2, vol. 6 (Ankara: TBMM Basımevi, 1986), 67–68, 87.

42 The abovementioned document mentions that sometime earlier the Ministry of Education requested their opinion about the same issue and received the same answer.

43 *Evkaf-ı Hümâyun Nezâreti'nin Tarihçe-i Teşkilatı ve Nüzzârın Terâcim-i Ahvâli*. (İstanbul: Evkaf-ı İslâmiye Matbaası, 1335H), 238–239; BOA, MF, KTV, 5/36/47; 6/20/25; 6/31/35/51; 8/10.

know to what extent this plan was implemented. However, an article in the journal *Türk Yurdu* reports that four thousand books on history and geography were removed from twenty-one libraries and housed in the Nuruosmaniye Library.[44] Apparently, the process of rehousing collections continued during the First World War. A letter from the Directorate of Endowments in Istanbul informs us that the Kılıç Ali Pasha Library and some collections from the district of Fındıklı were rehoused in a new library building, completed a year earlier, in the Sultan Selim district.[45] But no matter how desperate the need for a central foundation library was, the series of crises that befell the Ottoman Empire in its last years precluded the possibility of this being achieved.

Yet another problem for the user of foundation libraries was the lack of any union catalogue.[46] Foundation libraries did have catalogues, but like their predecessors from the sixteenth century, they were drawn up primarily to audit the contents of a library, rather than to facilitate the reader in his search for a book. Even in the nineteenth century the catalogue was still an inventory of books rather than a modern catalogue. The only innovation was created in the last quarter of the century, when the catalogues of all of the Istanbul libraries were printed with location numbers, indicating that they were intended as aids for the reader to search for a book, rather than as an inventory. The scattered nature of the collections in Istanbul created a need for a union catalogue of all the Istanbul libraries. As we have seen, two attempts were made, but neither was completed, the third promising attempt floundering in the course of the First World War.[47]

All attempts to rationalize, modernize, or develop the foundation libraries in the second half of the nineteenth century and at the beginning of the twentieth century bore little fruit. This was for a number of reasons, the first being paradoxically that the legal framework which protected foundations from government interference also prevented them from being modernized.[48] The most vexing problem was the lack of funding. While the larger libraries, which had been founded by the Ottoman sultans or rich statesmen, usually managed to survive on the funds allocated to it, the smaller collections could not. The second half of the nineteenth century witnessed a series of economic and

---

44 *Türk Yurdu*, 9/94 (İstanbul, 1331H), 46–47.
45 Turgut Kut's private archive, library files.
46 For the various attempts to prepare a union catalogue of Istanbul libraries, see Tuba Çavdar's thesis.
47 For a survey of cataloguing in this period, see chapter 8, "Catalogues and Cataloguing."
48 Maya Shatzmiller, "Islamic Institutions and Property Rights: The Case of the Public Waqf," *JESHO* 44, no.1 (2001): 70.

political crises in which the preservation of books, no matter how rare, was not a priority. However, we see attempts in the first decade of the twentieth century by the Ministry of Education to control all foundation libraries within the empire. Questionnaires were sent to all provincial governors to attempt to discover how many libraries existed and the size of the collections and whether the libraries were staffed or not. The information gathered by these questionnaires gives us an extremely useful statistical survey of the libraries throughout the empire.[49]

As the Ottoman state embraced Westernization, it gradually began to develop alternative schools based on models for the teaching of Western sciences. The elite were no longer to be educated in the traditional colleges, but in state schools where French was the foreign language rather than Arabic. The foundation libraries had been established mainly to provide the students at these colleges with books which were mainly in Arabic. Gradually, as the importance of the classical medrese disappeared, so did the need for this type of library. By the end of the Ottoman Empire, the foundation library had become the preserve of only the students or scholars of Islam and history.

A report written by the supervisor of education in Bursa noted the redundant state of the foundation libraries in 1916 in precisely these terms: The libraries which contained many valuable manuscripts were more like museums than places of learning, housing collections of Arabic books of use only to students of religion and the few books of science gave information which was in conflict with modern empirical sciences. Leaving aside the independent libraries, he reports that the collections endowed to mosques, which were for the benefit of the layman, were mostly written in Arabic, which he could not read.[50]

The upheaval of the First World War, followed by the War of Independence, caused many libraries to close down. With the coming of the republic after 1923, the existing legal and educational systems were abolished and replaced with Western models. This marked the end of the foundation library as an information resource for the public. With the alphabet reforms of 1928, children entering school could not even recognize the alphabet, never mind read the books. The foundation library was now merely a source of knowledge for a very small minority of students and scholars studying Islamic culture. In 1927, on the eve of the adoption of the Latin alphabet, a Turkish scholar Ali Canib wrote an article entitled "The Need for Modern Libraries," in which he observed the state of the Ottoman foundation library and explained succinctly how they had metamorphosed from public libraries to research libraries:

49 Turgut Kut's private archive, libraries file.
50 BOA, MF, KTV, No. 9/27.

There are at present, especially in Istanbul, libraries, which have very rich collections. But they only serve scholars; they are not for the common people. The fact that readers come even from as far as Europe demonstrates their importance. However, we should not forget that the readers coming from Europe are involved in scholarly and historical research. When you enter the Nuruosmaniye, Ragıb Pasha, Köprülü or Ayasofya Libraries you will find them empty, save for perhaps two or three people in some corner reading quietly and taking notes. Even the Bayezid Public Library and the Millet Library, which are the busiest, are not very frequented. Why? Because these libraries are the repositories of works which belong to our life before the reforms, the period when we formed a part of Eastern Civilization. They are very rich for the study of this period.[51]

The plan to centralize the smaller collections into one central location was finally realized from 1918 onwards. The books from the smaller collections and some of the large collections are currently located in the Süleymaniye Library, which has the world's largest collection of Islamic manuscripts to which scholars from all over the world regularly have resource. Together with some independent libraries housing larger collections, the Süleymaniye is staffed by trained librarians who, in the spirit of the Turkish Republic and conscious of the rich heritage they have inherited from their ancestors, are at the service of the readers from nine o'clock to five o'clock, five days a week. Furthermore, the books are well conserved and are being restored to their former conditions.

---

51 *Hayat*, vol. 2, no. 46 (1927): 2.

Part 2

ORGANIZATION

FIGURE 10. The interior of the Ragıb Pasha Library, Istanbul, est. 1763. As depicted in Mouradgea D'ohsson, *Tableau général de l'Empire Othoman*, vol. 1 (Paris: Imprimerie de monsieur [Firmin Didot], 1787).

Chapter Six

Personnel

In the early years of the Ottoman Empire, as the libraries did not have a separate building, being part of a mosque or a college or a larger complex surrounding these, there was no particular establishment allocated for a body of library staff.[1] Indeed, in some cases there was no librarian appointed for the care of the books which were placed within these institutions and his duties were performed by a member of staff of the institution in which the library was located. For example, there was no allowance made for a librarian for the libraries in the college founded by Umur Bey in Bergama (1440),[2] in the college founded by Sultan Murad II in Edirne (1435),[3] or in the college founded by Saruca Pasha in Gelibolu (1442).[4] However, Umur Bey had allowed an extra stipend of one asper per day for the muezzin of the mosque he built in Bursa to care for the books.[5] In this early period the only member of staff for the library tended to be a single librarian appointed on a stipend of between one and three aspers per day. The other duties associated with libraries, such as supervision, cleaning,

---

1   In the account books governing the establishment of these religious foundations, the post of librarian is listed among the staff of mosques, colleges, or the complexes. See for example, BOA, MAD 22, 5; MAD 626, 72; MAD 5455, 18; Ruus 94, 674.
2   VGMA, No. 591, 181.
3   TSA, No. D. 7081.
4   M. Tayyib Gökbilgin, *XV-XVI. Asırlarda Edirne ve Paşa Livası* (İstanbul: Üçler Basımevi, 1952), 248–252.
5   VGMA, No. 591, 182.

maintenance, and financial control were carried out by the staff of the institution in which the library was located.

Although the Ottoman libraries after the conquest of Istanbul (1453) continued to form part of larger institutions and were administered by them, there is a discernible increase in the number of librarians and the appointment, for the first time, of assistant librarians. The daily stipend, however, with a few exceptions, was not increased. Only with the inflation of the second half of the sixteenth century do we see any significant rise in stipends for library personnel; and towards the end of the seventeenth century, with the endowment of rich foundations and appearance of libraries independent of colleges or mosques, we find a further increase in the number of library personnel allocated to a library.

While at first the staff appointed to the independent libraries consisted, as for example in the Köprülü Library, of personnel whose duties encompassed those of librarians, later, in the eighteenth and nineteenth centuries, the staff of the independent libraries proliferated to such an extent that they included teachers, who taught part of the college syllabus. Thus, as outlined in the previous section, over four centuries the Ottoman library evolved from its humble beginnings as an ancillary function of the mosque and college to an independent institution to itself performing the functions of mosque and college. The difference between libraries in the early period and to a certain extent up to the sixteenth and seventeenth centuries and those founded after the seventeenth century is one of emphasis. While in the first period the library was an extension of the functions of prayer and learning, in the second period prayer and learning became incidental functions of the library.

Thus, while the staff of the Köprülü Library consisted of three librarians, a binder, and a doorkeeper, the libraries of Sultan Ahmed III and Ayasofya acquired teachers in Koran, prophetic tradition, and law. In this period, the complement of library personnel greatly increased. Apart from the teaching staff, the library at Ayasofya was able to boast of no less than six librarians, one assistant librarian, one cataloguer, two *noktacıs* (employees who verified the progress of Buhari recitation),[6] two keepers charged with the security and cleaning of the books, two doorkeepers, three floor-sweepers, one painter/decorator to keep the walls clean, two building maintenance personnel, one plumber for maintenance of the lead roof, and one thurifer (*buhurcu*), who was

---

6 Some endowments for mosque complexes made allowance for daily salaries to be paid to persons who were required to read Buhari's book of Islamic Traditions. In order to check that the conditions of the endowment were fulfilled by those persons in receipt of the salaries, *noktacıs* were appointed to note the progress of each reader of Buhari.

charged with ensuring that incense was burnt throughout the library to keep the air pleasantly scented.[7]

On the staff of those libraries endowed in the sixteenth and seventeenth centuries, which were not established as independent entities, were a number of librarians, one binder, and sometimes a doorkeeper. Other duties, such as administration, repairs, and maintenance were performed by the staff of the complex in which the library was situated. With the emergence of libraries with their own independent buildings, it followed that the staff should be enlarged to include a separate corps of maintenance personnel, but administratively the library tended to be treated as an annex of the larger complex.

Staff and Salaries

Selection and Appointment

The deed of endowment governing the establishment of a library usually avoided describing the qualifications, duties and selection of the staff in general terms, but tended to specify, at some considerable length, the governing criteria for each individual post. This section will therefore deal with the general practices governing the appointment and dismissal of staff, and the particular qualifications and duties of each member of the staff will be dealt with in their relevant sections.

According to the documents and deeds of endowments the following procedure seems to have been adhered to in the employment of library staff: whenever a position became vacant, the administrator of the endowment chose a candidate who met the conditions of the foundation deed and submitted his name to the supervisor (*nazır*).[8] The supervisor, in turn, would forward the proposal to the Imperial Council. In the deed for Hacı Selim Ağa Library this process is neatly summarized:

> The administrator of the endowment will select a person possessed of knowledge and virtue and recommend him to the

---

7   The *buhurcu* was charged with ensuring that incense was burnt throughout the library to keep the air scented.
8   Each endowment was under the ultimate control of a supervisor (*nazır*), usually a high-ranking member of the government who was entrusted with ensuring that the endowment was properly administered.

supervisor, who upon appending his signature of approval, the person will be appointed.[9]

The process for appointing a new member of staff to a library was painstaking. Having reached the Imperial Council, the document of application for the appointment of a member of staff would be sent to the appropriate offices of government, a note to the effect of "append records" or "search records" being attached to the application. Firstly, the seal on the application would be checked for authenticity; if authentic a marginal note of "seal corresponds" would be made on the document. Meanwhile, the registry copy of the deed would be brought from the store and the clerks would check that the post did in fact exist and that the procedure for appointment had been followed correctly. On finding everything in order, a note would be made on the top left corner, and this would be initialed by the head of the office. Thereafter, the application would be checked against the current register of posts, to discover whether the post was vacant. Only then was it returned to the Imperial Council for final approval. If approval was given, it was appended to the document of application, and the decision was registered in the registry of appointments. The divan retained the document of application and issued a warrant to the appointee.

This system of appointments, with the supervisor of a trust communicating directly with the Imperial Council, must have been regarded as unsatisfactory, because after the abolition of the Janissary corps the first ministry to be introduced in the program of reforms was a Ministry of Foundations (1826). With the introduction of this ministry, a hierarchy was established whereby the appointment no longer went to the supervisor, who was usually a high-ranking statesman, but to the ministry where the minister would be ultimately responsible for attaching, literally, his seal of approval to the appointment paper. With the establishment of a Ministry of Education in 1857, the appointment of librarians became the responsibility of the Ministry of Education.

The reason for this painstaking process becomes clear when examining the correspondence and records surrounding such appointments. The forging of documents and applications for unvacated posts were common offences.[10] According to one registry of appointments, the post of librarian at Balıkesir was given when it was falsely claimed that its holder had died.[11] A similar case can be

---

9 VGMA, No. 579, 122.
10 See for some examples: BOA, Mühimme Register 6, 177 and 458; Mühimme Register 14, 1080; Mühimme Register 16, 181; Ruus 30, 357; Ruus 35, 56, 294, and 353; Ruus 37, 179; Cevdet-Evkaf 10, 344.
11 BOA, Ruus 64, 295.

found in an account book dealing with the Süleymaniye endowment. When the irregularity was discovered, it was immediately rectified.[12]

Another document reveals that a certain Musa, who was working as a second librarian in the Merzifonlu Mustafa Pasha Library in Istanbul, had applied for a copy of his warrant which had been lost. The document notes tersely: "No record of a Musa appointed as second librarian can be found."[13] When the librarian of Fazlullah Pasha Mosque in Edirne died, the judge of this city, who was also supervisor of this endowment, submitted the name of Sunullah Efendi for the post. However, on checking the application against the current register of posts, it was discovered that the post had already been given to a certain Ali without the knowledge of the judge of the city, whose recommendation was a necessary condition of appointment for this endowment.[14]

Library personnel, therefore, carefully guarded their warrants of appointment against loss, lest fraudulent claims be made to the post. Should a warrant be lost, the same procedure was followed as in the original appointment, in order to avoid any possibility of fraud. It often happened that all posts were reviewed on the accession of a new sultan and renewed warrants were issued.[15] In the Hacı Beşir Ağa endowment register there is a fresh entry for every member of the library staff on the accession of a sultan, indicating that warrants were renewed with a change of sultan.[16] Dismissals from positions happened essentially in the same way.

Salaries

The salaries allocated for the staff of the library was specified by the founder in the endowment deed. In the early period when libraries were located within a mosque or dervish convent the payment for the staff servicing the library was usually an additional payment and, consequently, very small. For example, while the preacher at the Umur Bey Mosque in Bursa was given four aspers a day, the muezzin, who received two aspers, was given one additional asper for performing extra duties as the librarian.[17] In the college of Sultan Murad II in Edirne the professor received fifty aspers per day, the preacher four, and the

---

12 BOA, Müteferrik 89, 114a.
13 TSA, E. 474, No. 7.
14 BOA, Ruus 13.
15 BOA, Mühimme Register 27, 50; İbnülemin-Evkaf, 3109 and 3194.
16 VGMA, No. 29, 57.
17 BOA, MAD 22, 5; MAD 626, 72.

librarian two.[18] In the Fatih complex in Istanbul, fifty aspers a day were allocated for the professors, ten for a preacher, and five for a librarian. In the Eyüp Complex, the preacher's salary was five aspers while the librarian's was one.[19]

During the seventeenth and eighteenth centuries, the salaries of college librarians increased and the gap between their salaries and those of other staff of the colleges somewhat decreased—at least in some instances. In Hekimoğlu Pasha's college in the Davud Pasha district of Istanbul, a certain Mehmed Efendi who was a teacher at the college was also appointed as supervisor of the library with an extra daily stipend of thirty aspers. At the same time, librarians were receiving ten aspers a day.[20] The teacher at Nevşehirli İbrahim Pasha's college in the Şehzadebaşı district of Istanbul was in receipt of a daily stipend of one hundred aspers, while the Koran teacher received thirty aspers and the librarians fifteen aspers.[21] The teacher of the Hacı Besir Ağa's college in Eyüp was given twenty-five aspers, the teacher of Prophetic traditions twenty, and the librarian fifteen.[22]

With the emergence of the independent libraries, we can observe that provision was made for the appointment of librarians in receipt of relatively high salaries. While the librarians of the colleges were receiving between fifteen and twenty aspers, the librarians in independent libraries were receiving between twenty and 140 aspers. Inflation continued to erode the value of the salaries of librarians. The Ministry of Foundations, established in 1826 to address this problem, encouraged the administrators of foundations to pay their staff a living wage, but could not supply the necessary funds to do so. Foundations were expected to find the money themselves, which they were usually unable to do.

The salaries of the library personnel were paid by the administrators. If the administrator did not reside in the same city, he would appoint a deputy to carry out his duties, including the payment of salaries. Although library personnel were usually paid monthly, some libraries situated in distant provinces made allowance for the librarians to be paid twice yearly, such as Yusuf Ağa Library in Konya[23] and the Raşid Efendi in Kayseri.[24]

---

18 Ömer L. Barkan, "Edirne ve Civarındaki Bazı İmaret Tesislerinin Yıllık Muhasebe Bilançoları," *Belgeler* 1, no. 2 (1965): 322.

19 Ömer L. Barkan, "Fatih Camii ve İmareti Tesislerinin 1489–1490 Yıllarına Ait Muhasebe Bilançoları," *İktisat Fakültesi Mecmuası* 23, nos. 1–2 (1962): 311–312.

20 Millet Library, Feyzullah Efendi Section, 2197.

21 VGMA, Defter 38, 90.

22 VGMA, No. 736, 4.

23 Müjgan Cunbur, "Yusuf Ağa Kütüphanesi ve Kütüphane Vakfiyesi," *TAD* 1, no. 1 (1963): 216.

24 VGMA, No. 579, 68.

Towards the end of the nineteenth century, the old system of calculating wages on a daily basis in aspers (which had long ceased to exist as a coin) and paying them on a monthly or quarterly basis was gradually phased out and salaries were generally calculated and paid in piastres on a monthly basis.

Increases in Salaries

Because salaries were specified by the foundation deeds of the endowment libraries, the conditions of which were strictly upheld by law, there was no way in which salaries could be increased to counteract the ravages of inflation. Any increase had to be awarded by extraordinary measures. An exception to this principle were the imperial endowments founded by the sultans themselves; the terms of these could often be reviewed by succeeding sultans.[25] In the account books of the Mehmed II's mosque at Fatih, we can clearly observe the mechanism for reviewing salaries: While the salaries for the librarian had been set at six aspers in a deed prepared during the reign of Bayezid II (1481–1512) it was revised upwards to eight aspers in March 1592 after a petition had been submitted by the judge of Istanbul for the approval of the sultan, who gave his consent.[26] This salary was again revised to twelve aspers in August 1593 after a petition had been submitted by the director of the Imperial Chancery (reisülküttab).[27]

However, the endowments founded by statesmen, scholars, merchants, and others, invariably provided for fixed salaries which could not be revised with the passage of time. For example, the librarian at the complex of Çoban Mustafa Pasha in Gebze was in receipt of a daily stipend of three aspers in 1522,[28] and his salary remained unaltered almost a century later, as can be seen in the account book for the period 1602–1606.[29] However, in some account books, we observe that the librarian was given irregular supplements to his salary out of those moneys that remained unallocated at the end of the fiscal year. We can therefore assume that this practice of making up the fixed salaries from the yearly financial surplus was not an uncommon practice.[30]

---

25 These imperial endowments were considered inheritable endowments (irsadî vakıfs) and the law provided means whereby alteration could be made to their original conditions.

26 BOA, MAD 5103, 108.

27 BOA, MAD 5305, 79.

28 BOA, MAD 626, 244.

29 BOA, MAD 5070, 4, 24, 40, 114, and 126.

30 For example, Vahid Pasha, in his endowment deed, specifies that the librarians at his mosque should receive not only their fixed salary, but also the revenue from a certain flour mill, VGMA, No. 579, 702.

There were also other extraordinary measures for increasing the salaries of library personnel, of which the most common was for the descendants of the founder to make a supplemental foundation to the original endowment, precisely for the purpose of increasing salaries. We observe this phenomenon in the endowments of the Köprülü,[31] Atıf Efendi,[32] Aşir Efendi,[33] Süleymaniye,[34] and Abdullah Münzevî[35] Libraries.

Another method for keeping incomes abreast of inflation was to allocate extra duties to the incumbent of a post, thus providing him with a further source of income: for example, in an account book dated 1766, we observe that the second librarian of the library of Ahmed III also acted as a factor for the foundation of the Valide Sultan endowment.[36] This multiple tenure of posts can be seen in some other cases, such as in the Mihrimah Valide Sultan Mosque. On the death of the librarian in 1595, the librarian's post salaried at three aspers was given to the preacher of the mosque who earned ten aspers.[37] In the same mosque the post of librarian was held by the master of the dervish convent situated in the complex according to the accounts of 1629.[38] Records on Mehmed IV's mosque in Crete from 1630 show that a certain Hasan Efendi, who was the librarian, also occupied the posts of preacher and teacher of the mosque.[39]

Two entries in the account book of the Turhan Valide Sultan endowment at Bahçekapı in Istanbul give us a clearer idea of the extra duties performed by librarians. According to these accounts, which were for the year 1727, the monthly stipend of Mustafa Efendi, a librarian, was 450 aspers, but this was supplemented by the salaries from three other duties, boosting his salary to a total of 730 aspers. The second entry in this account book shows that although the assistant librarian's monthly stipend was fixed at three hundred aspers a month, he performed four additional duties, leaving him with a total monthly salary of 1,290 aspers.[40]

31 VGMA, No. 580, 13–14; VGMA, No. 76, 42–43 and 46–47.
32 Istanbul Court Registers, Evkaf-ı Hümayun Müfettişliği 164, 383b; Atıf Efendi Library 2858, 133b and 2859, 2, 6.
33 Süleymaniye Library, Aşir Efendi Section 473, 8b; Hafid Efendi Section 486, 6b–9b.
34 Istanbul Court Registers, Evkaf-ı Hümayun Müfettişliği 233, 82b; Kısmet-i Askeriyye 533, 91b–92a.
35 Bursa Eski Eserler Library, Abdullah Münzevi Vakfiyesi 17–26.
36 BOA, Süleymaniye 26, 23.
37 BOA, MAD 5455, 85, 91.
38 BOA, MAD 6483, 5.
39 BOA, Süleymaniye 2918, 2a.
40 BOA, Süleymaniye 2874, 1b.

This system of supplementing fixed incomes of personnel by appointing them to extra salaried duties was the method most favored for combating inflation in those endowments founded in the fifteenth and sixteenth centuries, where the stipends are likely to have become inadequate. Thus, we see in a record from 1761 that Mehmed Efendi, a librarian in the mosque founded by Süleyman the Magnificent's mother Hafsa Sultan in Manisa, had eleven extra duties.[41] In a library in Balat in Istanbul, founded by Ferruh Kethüda also during the reign of Sultan Süleyman, the librarian received ten aspers a day from extra duties over and above his fixed stipend of five aspers.[42] The assistant librarian of the Fatih Mosque Library in Istanbul had four extra duties according to a record from 1818.[43]

These extraordinary measures necessary to combat inflation continued up to the time of the foundation of the Ministry of Endowments in 1826. Shortly after this date, the minister of endowments began to adjust salaries to realistic levels. Correspondence concerning the salaries of librarians in the Atıf Efendi and Aşir Efendi libraries shows that the ministry made considerable changes to the stipends of personnel, especially after 1834.[44] With the centralization of all the separate account offices under the control of the Ministry of Endowments in 1838, the state was for the first time in a position to direct policy concerning all foundations.

Endowment Administrators

Although there were many personnel who performed a supervisory role in the administration of an endowment, there were only two offices directly concerned with the running of libraries: the supervisor of the endowment and the administrator.

The Supervisor (Nazır)

The supervisor represented the state in its role of overseeing the endowment and in particular to ensure that the administrator was running the endowment properly and in accordance with the conditions specified in the foundation deeds. The founders of the endowments usually specified that the holders of a particular post were to act as supervisor. Before the creation of the Ministry

---

41 BOA, Cevdet-Maarif 360.
42 BOA, Cevdet-Evkaf 711.
43 BOA, Cevdet-Maarif 7991.
44 C. Türkay, "İstanbul Kütüphaneleri," *Belgelerle Türk Tarihi Dergisi* 12, no. 69 (1973): 31–32.

of Endowments in 1826, the supervisors were usually chosen from among the highest ranks of the state, for example the grand vizier, the chief mufti, the chief eunuch, and the military judges of Rumelia and Anatolia. Some endowments were under the supervision of the sultan himself.

Besides overseeing the endowment, the supervisors also played a part in the appointment and dismissal of library personnel. The recommendations for appointments and dismissals forwarded by the administrator required the approval of the supervisor. It was also his duty to inspect the yearly accounts of all the endowments under his charge, which he did by appointing his own auditors.[45] Furthermore, in some library deeds, it is specified that the supervisor should count the books at specific intervals, either himself or by means of his auditor.[46]

The most influential of the supervisors were the chief eunuchs. Koçi Bey, an early seventeenth-century critique of governmental maladministration, states that the number of endowments under the control of the chief eunuch was at one time 360. The chief eunuch would in fact set aside Wednesdays as his day to convene meetings to discuss matters pertaining to the endowments in his charge and to approve or veto appointments and dismissals.[47] The grand vizier, on the other hand, was too busy to supervise the endowments in his charge, and the supervision was carried on his behalf by the director of the Imperial Chancery.[48]

The founders of an endowment would allocate a stipend to the supervisor. At one point it was claimed that the chief eunuch was making 38,280,000 piastres a year from the endowments. Some founders made no provision for a stipend for the supervisor, wishing the supervisor to perform his duties for free.[49]

The supervisors, as we have observed, were usually high-ranking statesmen, such as the grand vizier, the chief mufti, or the chief eunuch. Following the government reforms of the 1820 and 1830s, it was realized that statesmen were often too busy to supervise the endowments efficiently and the role of supervisor was taken over by the newly created Ministry of Foundations.

With the creation of the large library collections, which became more numerous particularly from the middle of eighteenth century onwards, we observe that library founders appointed an additional supervisor to the library besides the usual supervisor of the endowment. Founders in this period

---

45 BOA, Mühimme Register 55, 151.
46 VGMA, No. 82, 8; Istanbul Court Registers, Evkaf-ı Hümayun Müfettişliği 171, 10b.
47 İsmail Hakkı Uzunçarşılı, *Osmanlı Devletinin Saray Teşkilatı* (Ankara: Türk Tarih Kurumu Basımevi, 1945), 179.
48 İsmail Hakkı Uzunçarşılı, *Osmanlı Devletinin Merkez ve Bahriye Teşkilatı* (Ankara: Türk Tarih Kurumu Basımevi, 1948), 176.
49 VGMA, No. 579, 69 and 704; VGMA, No. 730, 86.

recognized that the statesmen from whose ranks the supervisors were chosen were usually too concerned with affairs of state to occupy themselves with the necessary intricacies of supervising the running of a library. It can be seen from this trend that the founders considered that close supervision by a secondary supervisor, who was to be chosen from among the employees of the endowment, was essential for preserving the libraries which they had endowed.

Thus, the Grand Vizier Hekimoğlu Ali Pasha appointed the chief eunuch as supervisor for his endowment at Davudpaşa in Istanbul, and chose a teacher from his college to act as supervisor of books.[50] In Hüseyin Ağa's library in Bursa there was also, in 1760, a supervisor of books.[51] According to some endowment records the supervisor of the library of Ayasofya founded by Mahmud I, was in 1747, the palace preacher Mehmed Efendi, who had a stipend of twenty aspers a day[52] and in 1786 it was the librarian Süleyman Efendi.[53] Other examples from this period were the appointments of supervisors to the libraries of Nuruosmaniye (1755),[54] Bostancılar Ocağı (1768),[55] Galata Palace (1754),[56] Kılıç Ali Pasha (1801),[57] and Raşid Efendi (1797).[58]

We can see from foundation deeds that the supervisors of the libraries were expected to oversee the counting of the books at a specified time to ensure that the library hours were carefully kept and generally to safeguard the books. In his foundation deed of 1559, Bedreddin Mahmud stipulated that one of the two keys to the book store should be given to the supervisor of the library and that the store should not be opened unless he was present.[59]

Some founders specified that the people of the quarter in which the library was found were to act communally, and without payment, as supervisor. Thus we see in the libraries of the Üsküplü Mosque at Cibali in Istanbul[60] and in the İplikçi Mosque Library in Konya[61] and in the dervish convent library in the

50 VGMA, No. 736, 68.
51 VGMA, No. 578, 41.
52 VGMA, Defter 87, 1b.
53 BOA, Süleymaniye, Sultan Mahmud I's File.
54 TSA, D. 3311; VGMA, 98, 10–12.
55 VGMA, Kasa 187, 356–358.
56 VGMA, Defter 87, 9.
57 Süleymaniye Library, Kılıç Ali Paşa Section 1050, 9a.
58 VGMA, No. 579, 67.
59 VGMA, No. 582, 33.
60 Istanbul Court Registers, Ahi Çelebi 19, 36b.
61 Istanbul Court Registers, Ahi Çelebi 29, 23a.

Temenye quarter of Bursa[62] no individual supervisor, but rather the communal supervision of the local population.

Administrator (Mütevelli)

Because the administrator was the person most directly involved in the running of an endowment, founders tended to make provisions for the post to be kept within his or her family. Thus, many endowments remained within the control of a single family over several centuries. In cases where the founder did not nominate a person to the post, he would usually specify necessary qualities for the position; it would be left to the local judge to select a suitable candidate.

The administrators were usually required not only to be scholarly, pious, and virtuous, but also to have the necessary experience for administration. Founders often went to great lengths to ensure that the administrator was a religious person. For instance, in 1681 the preacher of Ayasofya, Şeyh Ali, when donating his books to this mosque, demanded that the administrator should be a supporter of the Kadızade movement, a puritanical group renowned for their overzealous propagation of strict orthodoxy.[63]

The administrator's main function was to ensure that the endowment was run in a way that rendered it financially viable. To this end, he employed collectors (câbi) for gathering the revenues. He would ensure that all the expenses and salaries of the endowment were met and render accounts for auditing at the end of every financial year. The administrator was also involved in many aspects of the running of the library. As mentioned above, he recommended the appointment and dismissals of all library personnel. We presume that he was also responsible for granting permission for personnel to leave their posts for any pressing reason. Thus, we see Raşid Efendi, when founding his library, making the administrator responsible for granting leave for the librarians to go on pilgrimage or to visit their families.[64]

Another aspect of the administrator's function was to supervise the regular count of books in the library. In some endowment deeds, it was a requirement that whenever a librarian left his post all the books were to be counted again, whereupon they became the responsibility of the administrator until the appointment of a new librarian. The administrator was ultimately responsible

---

62 Bursa Court Registers, B. 41, No. 235, 160a.
63 Istanbul Court Registers, Rumeli Sadareti 129, 81b.
64 VGMA, 579, 68.

for the care of the books. He was responsible for ensuring that all broken bindings or loose fascicles brought to his attention were repaired by the binder. According to some endowment deeds, the administrator was responsible for replacing missing books using general funds of the endowment.[65]

As with the supervisor, the administrator was usually provided with a stipend, but in some cases the founder would lay down that the duties be performed without financial reward.

Most administrators appointed to libraries in the provinces chose to remain resident in Istanbul, in which case they would appoint a deputy (*kaimmakam-ı mütevelli*).[66] Although the deputy had the authority of the administrator, he still required his superior's approval for many decisions.

Personnel Working in the Library

The number of personnel in a library would vary according to the period, size, and status of the library, namely, whether it was housed within another building or was independent. In the early Ottoman period, library personnel often consisted of a single librarian while by the mid-eighteenth century Ayasofya Library could boast of no fewer than twenty-nine members on its staff, although some of them were appointed as teachers. From the end of the sixteenth century onwards, a steady proliferation of library personnel can be observed. In the seventeenth century, with the enlargement of collections belonging to the libraries that were housed in the colleges and mosque complexes, we see the addition of binders to the library personnel. With the appearance of the independent library building, provision was made for the library to employ its own cleaners, repairmen, doormen and other functionaries.

The Librarian (*Hafız-ı kütüb*)

When the founder of a library drew up his deed of foundation, he specified the qualities sought in all members of the staff. While many posts were described in a couple of lines, the founder was often at great pains to describe in some

---

65 VGMA, No. 82, 8; VGMA, No. 571, 119; VGMA, No. 579, 67–68; VGMA, No. 731, 150; VGMA, No. 735, 169; VGMA, No. 737, 213; Istanbul Court Registers, Evkaf-ı Hümayun 171, 10b; Galata Mahkemesi 17, 187; Ahi Çelebi Mahkemesi 19, 36b.
66 Deputies were even appointed for libraries in Istanbul as when Ragıb Pasha, having no sons, appointed his daughter to the post of administrator, and then appointed a deputy to assist her in administration.

detail the qualifications of candidates for the post of librarian. Similarly, the circumstances surrounding his appointment and dismissal, his duties and the conditions of his employment were often specified in considerable detail.

The librarian was usually referred to by the title *hafız-ı kütüb*, namely, the "keeper of books." More rarely he was referred to as *emin-i kütüb*, the "custodian of books," or by the term more popular in the Arabic-speaking provinces, *hazin*, "guardian," or *hazin-i kütüb*, "guardian of books."

The scanty information concerning librarians in the early period give us very little idea of the qualities sought in the candidates for the post. The earliest foundation deed to give any substantive information about the qualities of librarians is the deed for the library in the Fatih Complex (1470). According to a clause in the deed, the librarian should be a person with a good grasp of bibliography and should be very familiar with the textbooks used by teachers, assistant teachers, and students at the college.[67] The deeds of other libraries founded in the reign of Mehmed II (1451–1481) do not, however, make any requirements as to the qualities of the librarian.

In the foundation deed of the library founded by Bayezid II in Edirne in 1488, it is specified that the librarian should be pious, a believer and trustworthy.[68] When Süleyman the Magnificent (1520–1566) endowed a complex in the name of his daughter, Mihrimah, he specified the conditions noted above for the Fatih Mosque deed and those in the deed of Bayezid II.[69] In the deed of Bedreddin Mahmud at Kayseri (dated 1559), we find further qualities, namely that the librarian should be able to protect the books.[70]

When Feridun Bey, a well-known statesman, founded a library in his school in Istanbul (1560) he summarized in his elegant Ottoman style those qualities we find above, to which he adds some of his own:

> A person should be appointed who is trustworthy, religious and
> upright, a man of dignity and good faith, ... a man of knowledge
> and wisdom, ... a man by nature suited to the protection of
> books ... nor should he be [as in the words of the holy Koran]
> as the likeness of an ass carrying books ... nor should he be an

---

67 *Fatih Mehmet II Vakfiyeleri* (Ankara: Vakıflar Umum Müdürlüğü Neşriyatı, 1938), facsimile 268–269.
68 Belediye Library (now Atatürk Kitaplığı), Mc. O. 61, 43b.
69 Süleymaniye Library, Esad Efendi Section 3752, No. 2, 22b.
70 VGMA, No. 582/1, 33.

ignorant evil-doer who would scatter books to the winds like autumn leaves.[71]

The deed for the Selimiye Complex Library (1575) in Edirne adds two further conditions: the second librarian should be possessed of a good scribal hand and the third librarian should be a good artist capable of decorating books.[72]

In the seventeenth century, the conditions found are essentially the same as in previous deeds, except in one deed that requires that the librarian should know the procedure for issuing and recalling books.[73] Although in the eighteenth and nineteenth centuries the qualifications of the librarian remain, on the whole, the same as previously, we observe in some cases particular stipulations laid down according both to the nature of the library and the particular wishes of the founder. When the library was attached to a larger institution such as a mosque, college, or dervish convent, it was sometimes required that the duties of the librarian be carried out by one of the officers of that institution, a preacher of a mosque, a teacher or student of a college, or the master of a dervish convent. Thus, we see that while Beşir Ağa demanded that the first librarian in his college library at Eyüp (1735) should be appointed from outside, the second and third librarians should be students at the college.[74] The purpose of this was to ensure that, when the first librarian went home, the second and third librarians, being resident students, would be able to extend the opening hours of the library for the convenience of their colleagues. Şerif Halil Efendi, envisaging that the first librarian in his mosque in Cerrahpaşa (1744) would also be the timekeeper at the mosque, specified that he should be a man qualified in the science of astronomy.[75]

While many founders considered scholarship a useful additional quality for their librarians, when librarians became teachers this trait became essential. Thus, we see in some endowments careful provisions to ensure the possession of a certain level of scholarship by their librarians. Selim Ağa, for instance, specified that two of the three librarians of his library in Üsküdar (1782) should be good scholars, and to this end he provided for an examination of the candidates for

---

71 VGMA, No. 570, 198. We see, two centuries later, that the same clauses with the same wording are repeated in the deed of Seyyid Ahmed Efendi who founded a library in the Yakup Bey Mosque in İzmir in 1775. See: VGMA, No. 744, 59.
72 Müjgan Cunbur, "Osmanlı Çağı Türk Vakıf Kütüphanelerinde Personel Düzenini Geliştirme Çabaları," *VII. Türk Tarih Kongresi* (Ankara: Türk Tarih Kurumu Basımevi, 1973): 679.
73 Süleymaniye Library, Yeni Cami Section 150, 45a–b.
74 VGMA, No. 736, 4.
75 It was the duty of the timekeeper to calculate the exact times of the five daily prayers.

the post to be conducted by the chief mufti.[76] Similarly, Dervish Mehmed Pasha also believed it to be essential that his librarians be good scholars, but does not, however, indicate how they were to be chosen.[77]

In the eighteenth century, we see measures taken to prevent the abuse of multiple tenures by which several posts were held by one person, particularly in independent libraries and college libraries with large collections where the regular presence of a librarian was essential to its proper functioning. Thus, we see Veliyüddin Efendi specify that no judge, teacher, preacher, or Sufi master should be appointed librarian.[78] A century later, we see this same clause in more comprehensive versions in the library deeds of Raşid Efendi (1797)[79] and Yusuf Ağa (1794),[80] who among other categories excludes candidates who were occupied in crafts, industry or trade.

We occasionally come across unusual stipulations in deeds governing the choice of librarians as, for instance, in the endowment of Halet Efendi (1820), where it was required that the first librarian be a man free of the contagion of lethargy and that he should be a bachelor.[81]

The administrator of an endowment was ultimately responsible for the appointment of librarians and the criteria for selecting a suitable candidate were often laid down in the foundation deeds. While these criteria were usually in the form of some remarks noting the qualities desirable in a librarian, as we have seen above, in some cases the choice was restricted by other considerations. Morevi el-Hac Hüseyin Ağa had his son, Mustafa Efendi, appointed to the post of librarian in his college in İzmir (1740) and stipulated that his successors in the post were to be the eldest, most knowledgeable, and most upright member of his family in the succeeding generations.[82] When founding his library (1801) in the Kılıç Ali Pasha Mosque in Istanbul, Debbağzade İbrahim Efendi nominated four individuals to the posts of librarian, and, thereafter, it was left to the administrator to select and appoint successors.[83] Şeyh Mustafa Ali Efendi appointed his son as first librarian and his son-in-law as second librarian in the library he founded in Balat (1798).[84] In 1824, when endowing the college of the Chief Mufti Cedide Mehmed Efendi with a library, Nişastacı el-Hac Hasan

---

76 VGMA, No. 579, 122.
77 Istanbul Court Registers, İstanbul Kadılığı 122, 37b.
78 VGMA, No. 745, 80.
79 VGMA, No. 579, 68.
80 Müjgan Cunbur, "Yusuf Ağa Kütüphanesi ve Kütüphane Vakfiyesi," TAD 1, no.1 (1964): 214.
81 Süleymaniye Library, Halet Efendi Section 837, No. 1, 8b–9a.
82 VGMA, No. 736, 217.
83 Süleymaniye Library, Kılıç Ali Paşa Section 1049, No. 2, 44b.
84 Istanbul Court Registers, Kasımpaşa Mahkemesi 107, 90.

Efendi nominated one of the students to the post of librarian and provided that after his death a successor was to be elected by the students of the college.[85] Vahid Pasha envisaged that the librarian would be chosen by the consensus of the judge, teachers, and scholars of Kütahya, the city in which the library was situated.[86]

In situations where a founder had endowed a library, but failed to provide for librarians, we see the administrator appointing personnel on an *ad hoc* basis. Thus we see that the administrators of the Mehmed Pasha library in Erkilet in Kayseri and Keyvan Bey's library in Bosnia appointed two librarians to each library in order to preserve the collections.[87] We see from a petition to the Imperial Council that Şeyh Hacı Ahmed Efendi endowed books to an unnamed institution in Amasya. Claiming that the library thus founded had no income to provide for a librarian, he requested that the state allocate funds from properties in Amasya to make good this deficiency. He also nominated himself as librarian.[88]

With the transfer of responsibility of the running of libraries to the Ministry of Education, the urge to make practices uniform and free from abuse gathered apace, so that by 1884 personnel were appointed only after sitting an examination. How the examination was conducted may have remained the subject of conjecture, but for the fortunate discovery of an examination paper in the Ottoman archives.[89] The examination attempts to determine whether the candidate for job of librarian could read Persian and Arabic and had a basic level of numeracy. The candidate was required to vocalize and translate short Persian and Arabic texts and to do simple addition and subtraction. While the numeracy questions are fairly simple, the language questions require a fairly high competence in both languages.

Like all posts in endowment institutions, there was a tendency, as we shall see below, for the librarian's posts to be handed down from father to son. As a result of this, a position as librarian was in some cases held by several people, the most common example being when a librarian passed the position to his sons who were all suitable candidates and therefore shared the stipend and duties. This situation was termed a "shared post." When the second librarian of the Köprülü

---

85 Istanbul Court Registers, Davudpaşa Mahkemesi 95, 85.
86 VGMA, No. 579, 702.
87 BOA, Cevdet-Maarif 8093; BOA, Cevdet-Maarif 141, respectively.
88 BOA, Cevdet-Maarif 2342.
89 BOA, MF, KTV 5, No. 100.

Library died in 1783, his three sons were appointed to the post.[90] We see this happening also in other libraries.[91]

The basic duty of the librarian was the conservation of the collection in his care. However, as the role of librarian became established, his duties became more specific and varied. Because the information we have from early period is fragmentary, we can only assume that the role of the librarian in this period was that of custodian. We see, for example, that the librarian in Umur Bey Mosque at Bursa (1440) was simply required to issue books to the faithful in the mosque, and to prevent them from taking the books outside.[92]

After the conquest of Istanbul (1453), the first college library was established at Eyüp by Mehmed II. The deed for this library describes the role of librarian in the most basic terms: "A person will be appointed to protect the books which are to be placed there."[93] However, only a little later we see in a deed for the Fatih Complex that the librarian was forbidden from denying books to the students and staff and was required to direct all his efforts to conserving the collection and supervising the lending of books.[94]

Some twenty years later, when Bayezid II founded a library in his complex in Edirne (1490), the deed had become comparatively specific in describing the role of the librarian. Apart from protecting the books, he is required to follow a set procedure for lending books, namely he should always lend a book in front of witnesses, he should then count the fascicles and the folios and note these, together with the condition of the binding, the size of the book, and the names of witnesses, in his register. It is further specified that students not be allowed to take the books out of the college.[95]

In the deed of Süleyman the Magnificent's foundation (1549), made in the name of his daughter Mihrimah Sultan, it is added that the librarian should not keep readers waiting for books, which should be presented free of dust.[96] Thereafter, in later deeds, we notice that cleaning the books becomes one of the specific duties of the librarian. The deed of the Bedreddin Mahmud Library in Kayseri (1559) stipulates that the cleaning of books should be done annually during the month of Ramazan, at which time the annual checking of books was

90 BOA, Cevdet-Maarif 103.
91 See for some examples: BOA, Cevdet-Maarif 5825; BOA, Ruus 33, 40; Ruus 35, 294; Cevdet-Evkaf 13, 507; BOA, Müteferrik 89, 114a.
92 VGMA, No. 591, 183.
93 Istanbul Court Registers, Evkaf-ı Hümayun Müfettişliği 46, 83.
94 T. Öz, Zwei Stiftungsurkunden des Sultan Mehmed II, Fatih (İstanbul: n.p., 1935), 14–15.
95 Belediye Library (now Atatürk Library), Mc. O. 61, 44a.
96 Süleymaniye Library, Esad Efendi Section 3752, No. 2, 22b.

to take place and their replacement in the same order as that of the inventory. It was also specified that the librarian was to keep one of the keys to the storeroom.[97]

In the sixteenth century, further duties were added; for example, Sinan Pasha, conqueror of Yemen, required his librarian to survey the state of repair of the books in his charge and to inform the administrator when book bindings needed repair or renewal.[98] Mehmed Ağa, the chief eunuch, in his library (1591) also provided for repair and renewal, but stipulated that the librarian should attend to any broken binding that very day, without delay.[99]

In the deed of the collection endowed to the Cihangir Mosque by Mahmud Bey (1593), the master of the guild of Bosphorus boatmen, the duties of the librarian are described thus:

> The librarian is to lend books to those who are able to read and those who wish to read that they may benefit from the books that they have asked for. The books should be lent on the deposit of a sizable pledge. The librarian is to register the name of the book, the name of the borrower and his physical description, and below this he is to enter details of the pledge and the date of lending. No book is to be lent for more than a month.[100]

We see little change in the terms concerning the duties of librarians during the second half of the seventeenth century. I have found only one deed that adds any further requirement to the previous conditions such as the taking of pledges and cleaning of books. In his endowment in Balat in Istanbul (1677), Reisülküttab Mustafa Efendi demands that his librarian perform his duties with a cheerful disposition, that he should always be well spoken and polite, and that he should refrain from rudeness and severity.[101]

Towards the end of the seventeenth century, we find in the foundation deed of the Feyzullah Efendi Library (1699) that, besides the emphasis being placed on the cleanliness of the books in the collection, for which purpose an extra stipend was allocated to the librarian, there is the somewhat unusual stipulation that the doors of the library should be sealed every night by the librarian.[102]

---

97 VGMA, No. 582/1, 33.
98 BOA, Süleymaniye, Haremeyn File 1.
99 TSA, EH 3028, 96a.
100 Istanbul Court Registers, Galata Mahkemesi 17, 187.
101 Istanbul Court Registers, Bab Mahkemesi 29, 130b.
102 VGMA, No. 571, 118.

In the eighteenth century, we find a gradual proliferation of conditions in the foundation deeds of the libraries. In the independent library founded by Atıf Efendi, there is the provision for the first librarian to lead noon and afternoon prayers in the library and the second librarian was to recite the call to prayer in the reading room.[103] We also see that the third librarian was required to light the lamps in the library.[104] This provision for the librarians to act as functionaries in the recital of the daily prayers also occurs in the deed of Ragıb Pasha (1762).[105] Of course, these were obligatory daily prayers. In the nineteenth century, we see the addition of supererogatory prayers and religious ceremonies to the list of requirements for the librarian and his assistants. Thus, it was specified in the foundation deed of Kılıç Ali Pasha (1801) that the librarian should open the doors of the library with a prayer consisting of the "Ya-Sin" chapter of the Koran and that after the noon prayer each of the four librarians should silently read a section of the Koran, so that every week the whole Koran would be read between them for the soul of the founder.[106] When endowing his library (1805), Hafid Efendi, for his part, demanded that the whole Koran should be recited over a period of one year, by a librarian whose competence in recitation was recognized by the others.[107] In the deed of Dervish Mehmed Pasha (1818), it was specified that the librarians should read Buhari, the renowned collection of prophetic traditions, and should participate in the Sufi ceremonies of the Nakşibendi order of dervishes, which would take place once a week in the library.[108]

The attitude and behavior of the librarian towards the readers seems to have been a prime concern of the founders. Hüseyin Ağa, founding his library in Bursa (1760), describes the relationship between librarian and readers thus:

> When a student or scribe requests a book, the librarian should
> issue the book in a professional manner and not embarrass the
> reader by reminding him that he had already fetched the book
> for him several times before.[109]

---

103 VGMA, No. 735, 257.
104 The son of Atıf Efendi made an additional endowment (1752) in which he stipulates that the third librarian was to recite the first chapter of the Koran, which is a short prayer, in return for which he was to receive an extra daily stipend of one asper. Atıf Efendi Library 2858, 134a. This condition was also added to the endowments of Yusuf Ağa (1794) and Raşid Efendi (1797).
105 VGMA, No. 82, 6.
106 Süleymaniye Library, Kılıç Ali Paşa Section 1049, No. 1, 10a.
107 Süleymaniye Library, Hafid Efendi Section 487, 6b–7a.
108 Istanbul Court Registers, İstanbul Kadılığı 122, 37b.
109 VGMA, No. 578, 41.

In the foundation deeds drawn up by Tırnovalı Ali Ağa (1762), Ragıb Pasha (1762), and Veliyüddin Efendi (1769), we find that the three founders have felt the necessity to prescribe the correct attitude of the librarian to his readers, all three employing virtually the same words: "The librarians should not be of a forbidding disposition and they should be encouraging and cheerful, welcoming and respectful."[110] This stipulation also appears in a different form in the imperial endowment of Abdülhamid I (1781): "He should avoid treating the reader harshly nor should he refuse his request or reprimand him."[111]

When Es-Seyyid Ahmed Efendi endowed a library to the Yakup Bey Mosque in İzmir (1782), he forbade his librarian to refuse issuing books for some spurious excuse: "Whoever it may be, should he wish to read or copy a book, they are not to use a pretext, such as the time of day or some other excuse to avoid issuing a book."[112] Requirements governing the behavior of librarians is not restricted to the tasks of issuing and recalling books. From the eighteenth century onwards, we observe an increasing interest by the founders in the way that the reading room was supervised. Thus we see, for example, Yusuf Ağa in his foundation in Konya (1794), specifying that the librarian or his junior assistant should observe the conduct of readers out of the corner of his eye to insure against the loss of books or folios.[113] Raşid Efendi, in his endowment (1797), stipulated that the librarian should prevent the disfigurement of books with ink or other means, and should supervise the reader carefully, but politely.[114]

As mentioned previously, it became increasingly common in the eighteenth century for the larger libraries to do some teaching. This teaching was carried out by a qualified teacher who was on the establishment of the library staff. However, in exceptional cases the librarian was required to teach, as, for example, in the foundation of Selim Ağa (1782), who wanted two of his three librarians to offer classes in the library and allocated extra stipends for this duty.[115]

Another of the librarian's duties was the regular inspection of books. Although it is not regularly specified in the foundation deeds, we can see that in practice the librarian always participated in the periodic inspection of books. After checking the contents of the collection, a new catalogue was often drawn up. We

---

110 Istanbul Court Registers, Evkaf-ı Hümayun 171, 10a-b; VGMA, No. 82, 5; VGMA, No. 745, 80.
111 VGMA, Kasa 159, 11.
112 VGMA, No. 742, 7
113 Müjgan Cunbur, "Yusuf Ağa Kütüphanesi ve Kütüphane Vakfiyesi," *TAD* 1, no.1 (1964): 215.
114 VGMA, No. 579, 67–68.
115 VGMA, No. 579, 122.

do not know, however, to what extent the librarian was involved in preparing the book lists.

Up to the eighteenth century, there is no particular provision stating how long a librarian was expected to be on duty nor prohibitions against deputizing his duties to others. But, from the beginning of the eighteenth century, we observe founders requiring that the librarian should be personally on duty for the entire period that the library was open. Mustafa III (1757–1774) even issued an imperial decree to proscribe these abuses in his own endowment.[116] In the libraries endowed by Köprülü, Feyzullah Efendi, Ragıb Pasha, Veliyüddin Efendi, Hacı Selim Ağa, Yusuf Ağa, Raşid Efendi, and Vahid Pasha, we see stipulations that the librarian himself should perform his duties personally and should work all day. In some of the libraries which employed many librarians, we often find established in the foundation deeds a rota specifying the days on which the librarians were to work. In the foundation deeds of Nevşehirli İbrahim Pasha (1729) and Kılıç Ali Pasha (1801), there were four librarians, of which two were always to be on duty.[117] In the deed for the Nuruosmaniye Library, there is a provision for the librarians to perform their duties in rota. In Toderini's account of the Nuruosmaniye Library, he describes the rota, thus:

> There are six librarians, two of whom are constantly on duty every day, so their turn comes twice a week; because the libraries are closed on Friday, which is always a holiday for Muslims.[118]

In order to ensure that the collections housed in the libraries did not suffer losses, the deeds often made the librarians responsible for paying for the loss of a book out of their own pocket. Although there is no provision for reimbursement to be paid by librarians in the deeds of the Mehmed II's library, we see from a sixteenth-century inventory of the books that the librarian actually made good the loss of a book or obtained from the reader a replacement copy. The following entries from this inventory are instances where books have been replaced:

> *Kitabu'l-Lemha*: This book was lost while in the hands of the late Mevlana Nureddin, and the librarian Muhyiddin accepted in its place a book that has a decorated binding and contains several essays on mysticism.

---

116 VGMA, Kasa 187, 352–353.
117 VGMA, No. 38, 90; Süleymaniye Library, Kılıç Ali Paşa Section 1049, No. 1, 10a.
118 G. Toderini, *De la litterature des Turcs, traduit de l'Italien par l'Abbe de Cournand*, vol. 2 (Paris: Chez Poinçot, 1789), 95–96.

Kitabu Biharu'z-Zahire. This book was lost during the term of librarian Muhyiddin. When the aforementioned librarian was departing for Baghdad, the books were checked, and it was found that this book was not in the storeroom. A replacement was given by the aforementioned librarian. The name of the replacement is also *Bihar-ı Zahire.*[119]

To further insure against loss of books, a provision in many deeds called for the dismissal of a librarian whose behavior was likely to lead to losses. In 1881, the state introduced a book of regulations for the administration of libraries. This contained a uniform set of rules mainly drawn up from the wishes of the founders as expressed in the foundation deeds. The theft (or collusion in the theft) of a book by a librarian now became subject to article 82 of the newly drafted criminal code.[120]

The deeds provide for the dismissal of a librarian should he lend a book without first taking a pledge as deposit, lend a book where the deeds forbade the practice, fail to turn up on three consecutive days without an excuse, or fail to meet other stipulations in the deeds. He was also to be dismissed if he left his post while on duty, employed a deputy, attempted to work on rota where it was not provided for in the deeds, took outside employment such as that of a teacher or a judge, extended his period of leave without permission, or was lazy.

Stipends allocated to librarians differed to a great extent, depending not only on the period when the endowment was made, but also on the size of the library and on whether the post was full-time. In the early period the stipend allocated to the librarians was one or two aspers a day. This sum was not increased for a period of time with the sole exceptions of the librarians of the Fatih Complex, who were allocated six aspers,[121] and the librarian of Mahmud Pasha College (1474), who was given five.[122]

There is little evidence for increases in stipends during the reign of Bayezid II (1481–1512), the son of Mehmed II. In his foundations, he allocated a stipend of two aspers for the librarian in Amasya,[123] two aspers for the librarian in Edirne,[124] and three aspers for the librarian in Istanbul.[125] By the reign of Süleyman the Magnificent there are small increases, so that the librarian's stipend varied from one to six aspers.

119 TSA, D. 9559, 38b, 23a.
120 Mahmud Cevad, *Maarif-i Umumiye Nezareti, Tarihçe-i Teşkilat ve İcraatı* (İstanbul: Matbaa-i Amire, 1338H.), 207–209.
121 BOA, MAD 5103, 108.
122 İVTD, 43.
123 BOA, MAD 5455, 76.
124 Belediye Library (now Atatürk Library), Mc. O. 91, 298 and 321.
125 BOA, MAD 5103, 273.

During the latter part of the sixteenth century and early part of the seventeenth century, the Ottoman Empire suffered the ravages of inflation.[126] Although stipends were increased, they only went up to an average of between three and eight aspers and lagged behind the rate of inflation to a significant extent. In order to counteract the erosion of the value of the asper, Sokollu Mehmed Pasha in a foundation deed dated 981/1574 included the following clause:

> Let it be known that whenever the asper is mentioned we refer to the Ottoman asper. At the time of compilation of this book [i.e., the foundation deed] one dinar is equivalent to 60 Ottoman dirhems. If, with time, changes occur to the values of the dirhem and dinar, then changes are to be made to re-establish the former parity.[127]

It is only toward the end of the seventeenth century, with the foundation of independent libraries and the large college libraries, that we find any significant increase in stipends. The first librarian of the Köprülü Library (1678) had a stipend of twenty aspers, the second and third librarians receiving ten aspers each.[128] The first librarian of Merzifonlu Koca Mustafa Pasha College Library (1681) received twenty aspers and the second ten aspers.[129] The three librarians of Amcazade Hüseyin Pasha Library (1700) each received twenty aspers,[130] and three librarians at the Feyzullah Efendi Library each received fifteen.[131] These last two cases are rare examples where the founders chose to pay the various grades of librarians the same stipend.

Up to the foundation of the Ayasofya Library in 1740, stipends in the libraries of Istanbul and Anatolia generally varied between five and twenty-five aspers. However, in the first endowment deed for Ayasofya, we see salaries set at forty-five aspers for the first librarian and thirty-five aspers each for the second, third, and fourth librarians.[132] In the second endowment, twelve years later, a further two librarians were added to the establishment and their stipends raised to ninety for the first librarian, eighty for the second, seventy for the third, and fifty for the fourth, while the two new posts had a stipend of forty aspers each.[133] When Atıf Efendi

---

126 Ömer L. Barkan, "XVI. Asrın İkinci Yarısında Türkiye'de Fiat Hareketleri," *Belleten* 34, no. 136 (1970): 568.
127 VGMA, No. 572, 62.
128 Köprülü Library, Vakfiye 4, 60b.
129 BOA, Ruus 42, 303; Cevdet-Maarif 8213.
130 BOA, İbnülemin-Tevcihat 890.
131 VGMA, No. 571, 119; BOA, Cevdet-Maarif 583.
132 VGMA, No. 47, 15; VGMA, 639, 3.
133 VGMA, No. 639, 62b; TSA, E. 1767.

founded an independent library in 1741, he stipulated that he wished to ensure that the librarians would devote themselves to their duties and was therefore allocating them generous stipends, which were eighty aspers for the first librarian, seventy-five for the second librarian, and seventy for the third.[134] In this period, the librarians in the other large libraries were in receipt of stipends around thirty to sixty aspers. The smaller libraries, however, offered stipends of between two and fifteen aspers.

In the second half of the eighteenth century, two more large libraries were founded. The founder of the first of these, Ragıb Pasha stipulated that as the librarians were forbidden to do any other work, 120 aspers were to be given to the first librarian and 110 aspers to the second.[135] The second of these large libraries was the imperial foundation of Abdülhamid I, where the librarians had stipends similar to those at Ragıb Pasha's library.

There was little significant increase during the last quarter of the eighteenth and first quarter of nineteenth centuries, so that by the time of the establishment of the Ministry of Endowments in 1826, the larger libraries tended to offer between eighty and 120 aspers to the first librarian and slightly less for the second and third librarians.[136]

Throughout the whole Ottoman period, we find instances where libraries were endowed without any provision for a paid librarian. In these cases, it was usually stipulated that the work of librarians would be carried out without remuneration by a specified member of staff in the institution to which library was endowed.

Besides their salaries, librarians also benefited from benefits that went with the post. As it was the custom for the imperial complexes in which teaching was carried out to provide accommodation and meals from the kitchens, the librarians were often provided with free meals and a ration of bread. We see in a document concerning the Fatih Complex that the librarian was included in a list of those members of the staff who were entitled to eat in the kitchens.[137] The account book for Bayezid II's complex is even more specific, as we see that the librarian was included among "the 87 persons who were to be given at each meal, one piece of meat, two loaves of bread and one ladle of vegetable or rice soup."[138]

We see instances where other arrangements were made for providing the librarians with food. In Süleyman the Magnificent's college at Rhodes, the

---

134 VGMA, No. 735, 257.

135 VGMA, No. 82, 6.

136 *TKT*, 175.

137 Süheyl Ünver, *Fatih Aşhanesi Tevzi'namesi* (İstanbul: İstanbul Fetih Derneği, 1953), 10.

138 Ömer L. Barkan, "Edirne ve Civarındaki Bazı İmaret Te'sislerinin Yıllık Muhasebe Bilançoları," *Belgeler* 1, no. 2 (1965): 287–288.

librarian was supplied with loaves of bread,[139] but his counterpart in Istanbul was given meals.[140] We see from the foundation deed of Ayasofya Library that the librarian was provided with food thus: "Every day after the morning prayer there should be bread and soup, and before noon soup, but on Friday rice, and this should be offered to the staff of the library."[141] In the libraries of the Mahmud Pasha College and the Kasım Pasha Mosque, the librarians were given money with which to buy food.[142]

Accommodation was also provided by some foundations. In the deeds of the libraries of Atıf Efendi (1741),[143] Ragıb Pasha (1763),[144] Veliyüddin Efendi (1768),[145] Karavezir Mehmed Pasha (1780),[146] Abdülhamid I (1781),[147] Halil Hamid Pasha (1783),[148] Çelebi Mehmed Said Efendi (1789),[149] and Ahmed Ağa of Rhodes (1793),[150] the librarian was to be housed in a residence belonging to the foundation.

Like stipends, the number of librarians employed in the library evolved over time. It was only in the seventeenth century, with the emergence of the independent library, that we see the employment of more than one. The odd instance of libraries with more than one librarian before this period was very much the exception.

With the foundation of the Köprülü Library (1678), we see the establishment of a library staff consisting of three librarians. Thereafter, it became increasingly common for the larger college libraries to employ two or three librarians. This would seem to be due to two factors, firstly, the example of Köprülü Library, and secondly, the large number of rich endowments made at this time, which so enlarged the collections that it became necessary to provide for more librarians. The three college libraries founded between 1699 and 1701 by Amcazade

---

139 BOA, Cevdet-Maarif 6585.
140 BOA, MAD 19, 342.
141 VGMA, Kasa 47.
142 BOA, MAD 5102, 79, 150, 463 and BOA, Ruus 1, 145, respectively.
143 VGMA, No. 735, 257.
144 VGMA, No. 82, 6.
145 VGMA, No. 745, 79.
146 VGMA, No. 742, 72.
147 VGMA, Kasa 159, 115.
148 VGMA, No. 628, 547.
149 VGMA, No. 743, 501.
150 VGMA, No. 743, 80.

Hüseyin Pasha,[151] Merzifonlu Kara Mustafa Pasha[152] and Feyzullah Efendi,[153] respectively, were instructed to appoint more than one librarian.

In the first half of the eighteenth century, we see the larger Istanbul libraries employing between two and four librarians, while the provincial libraries continued to employ a single librarian. In Istanbul this trend remained fairly stable throughout the second half of the eighteenth century and the whole of the nineteenth century, with a few exceptions where we may observe up to six librarians employed in the largest libraries, as for example in the Ayasofya Library and the Nuruosmaniye Library. In the provinces, however, there was an increase in the number of librarians during this period, as, for example, in the Halil Hamid Pasha Library in Isparta, the Yusuf Ağa Library in Konya and Vahid Pasha Library in Kütahya, each of which employed two librarians, the Raşid Efendi Library in Kayseri, and the Dervish Mehmed Pasha Library in Burdur, each of which had three librarians.

When more than one librarian was appointed, it was usual to refer to them as the first, second, or third librarian. However, there are instances where the first is termed the "head librarian." It was usually the case that promotion came with the death, retirement, or dismissal of a senior librarian, so that when the post of first librarian became vacant, it was filled by that of the second librarian, whose post was, in turn, filled by the third, and so on, the most junior post being filled by an appointment from outside the library.

It was also a common practice in foundations for a holder of a post to transfer it to another person. Although spurious reasons may have been given for the transfer, it is known that these posts were actually sold. The mechanism for transferring a post was to apply to a judge for permission to transfer, and then to go through the normal procedures for appointments.[154] This type of transfer was known in the Ottoman Empire as cession (*ferağ*) and renunciation (*kasr-ı yed*). It is clear from some documents that this practice was, for a time, also prevalent in libraries. In order to avoid situations where librarians may have transferred their post to a person who was not qualified, many founders began, from the beginning of the eighteenth century, to insert clauses in deeds that expressly forbade this practice.[155] Furthermore, any attempt to transfer a post was made grounds for dismissal.

---

151 Süleymaniye Library, Yazma Bağışlar Section 2272, 3b.

152 BOA, Cevdet-Maarif 8213.

153 VGMA, No. 571, 119.

154 Ali Haydar, *Tertîbü's-Sunuf fî Ahkami'l-Vukuf* (İstanbul: Şirket-i Mürettebiyye Matbaası, 1337H), 542–545.

155 Exceptions to this tendency can be seen in two deeds drawn up in this period. The first belonging to Aşir Efendi's library in Istanbul, states that under certain conditions a post

Posts were also inherited by the sons of the holders, the practice becoming so common that it came to be accepted as legitimate. Although it was recognized that this practice was not in the interest of the libraries, the founders knew that they were powerless to prevent it and therefore attempted, starting at the beginning of the eighteenth century, to regulate it as much as possible. Hence, we see many examples of founders attempting to prevent the inheritance of a post by a son who was too young or unsuitable. In the deed of the Veliyüddin Efendi Library, the harmful effects of this practice are clearly described:

> Since this above [the librarian's] post requires a mature and capable person, if it be given to a child, there is no doubt that since he himself will be unable to perform the duties, he will be forced to use a deputy who may be a stranger whose circumstances are unknown, and it is clear that there will be deficiencies in the conservation of the collection. When a librarian dies, his post should not therefore, be given to his son, if he be a child, or if he be a man who is unqualified or inappropriate, on the sole grounds that the post was his father's. Let the post be given to a person who deserves it and is suitably qualified.[156]

The practice of deputizing the duties of librarian had through the ages become so customary as to be impervious to abolition so that it continued throughout the nineteenth-century period of reforms despite the many attempts to put a stop to the practice.

Aide to the Librarian (Hafız-ı Kütüb Yamağı)

In a few libraries, we come across the position of auxiliary librarian, who functioned as an aide to the librarian. They are variously termed *yamak, muavin, mülazım* in Ottoman Turkish, which all mean "helper" or "aide" in English. It is clear that their function is more or less identical. The only mention of this post in the sixteenth and seventeenth centuries occurs in the deed for Ferruh Kethüda's library (1566), where provision is made for two aspers a day to be given to a

---

may be transferred (Süleymaniye Library, Aşir Efendi Section 473, 10a). The second can be found in Ahmed Ağa's library in Rhodes, where we see that posts may be transferred with the consent of the people of the town, who, in turn are to ensure that the transfer is for a good reason (VGMA, No. 734, 93).

156 VGMA, No. 745, 80.

person who would aid the librarian.[157] However, here the post is referred to by the term *muavin* (helper) rather than *yamak* (aide). It is not until almost two centuries later that we see this post again; in the deed for Ragıb Pasha's library (1762), his duties are described thus:

> There should be appointed two persons of capability and aptitude to act as aides to the first and second librarians. Every day they should be present at the library and generally help the librarians and, in particular, fetch books for them and replace them with perfect diligence and attention.[158]

Just as in Ragıb Pasha's library, as in Hacı Selim Ağa's library (1782), two aides were provided for.[159] In the former library, the daily stipend for these assistants was set at fifteen aspers, while in the latter it was only ten. In Yusuf Ağa's library in Konya (1794), the two posts of aides carried the extraordinarily high stipend of fifty aspers, and furthermore the aides were graded as first and second aide.[160] In Aşir Efendi's library (1800), provision was made for two aides (here termed *mülazım*), who were graded and paid differentially, thirty-five aspers for the first, and thirty for the second.[161]

This post is peculiar to the earlier and later parts of our survey. The reason that we do not see this post during the latter part of the sixteenth and all of the seventeenth and the early part of the eighteenth century is that his duties were performed by the assistant librarian, whose post was abolished about the middle of the eighteenth century, for reasons that will be given below.

Assistant Librarian (Katib-i Kütüb)

The assistant librarian is invariably, with a single exception, referred to as *katib-i kütüb*. While the librarian's title, *hafız-ı kütüb* (keeper of books) suggests that he functions as the person responsible for the books, the assistant's title of *katib-i kütüb*, literally the "clerk of books," implies that his function is primarily secretarial.

---

157 VGMA, No. 570, 60.
158 VGMA, No. 82, 6.
159 VGMA, No. 579, 122.
160 Müjgan Cunbur, "Yusuf Ağa Kütüphanesi ve Kütüphane Vakfiyesi," *TAD* 1, no. 1 (1964): 214.
161 Süleymaniye Library, Aşir Efendi Section 473, 8b–9a.

The earliest record of this post is found in an account book for Murad II's imperial foundation at Edirne. According to these accounts, the assistant librarian was paid two aspers a day.[162] In the imperial foundation of Mehmed II (1451–1481) in Istanbul, the duties of the assistant librarian is described thus:

> He has appointed an assistant who is comprehensive in his knowledge in order that he may keep the number and the names of the books in his register and whenever a book is lent it should be registered by him that he may know it. And whenever a request for a book is made, it should be lent with the help of the assistant.[163]

In the imperial foundation of Süleyman the Magnificent, we see that no provision is made in the deed for the appointment of librarians, except that on the endowment of books to the foundation a librarian and assistant librarian were to be appointed.[164] In an account book for this complex for the years 1583–1593, we observe that a certain Mustafa Efendi was holding the post of assistant librarian on a daily stipend of four aspers.[165] In Selim II's library in the complex he founded in Edirne, we can see that the duties of assistant librarian were given to the third librarian.[166] In the foundation deed (1662) of Turhan Valide Sultan, the sultan's mother, it is stipulated that the assistant librarian will keep the receipts for books lent out and will register their names.[167] In a further deed she made in 1666, new duties were added to the post of assistant librarian: "When lending books the assistant librarian is to establish the branch of science to which it belongs and he is also to establish its title and count the folios and fascicles. He is also required to consult with the librarian as to whether the book should be lent and should make inquiries as to the character of the borrower before the book is lent."[168]

---

162 BOA, MAD 5455, 18.

163 *Fatih Mehmed II Vakfiyeleri* (Ankara: Vakıflar Umum Müdürlüğü Neşriyatı, 1938), facsimile 269–270.

164 Kemal Edib Kürkçüoğlu, *Süleymaniye Vakfiyesi* (Ankara: Vakıflar Umum Müdürlüğü, 1962), facsimile 151–152.

165 BOA, MAD 5103, 4.

166 Müjgan Cunbur, "Osmanlı Çağı Türk Vakıf Kütüphanelerinde Personel Düzenini Geliştirme Çabaları," *VII. Türk Tarih Kongresi* (Ankara: Türk Tarih Kurumu Basımevi, 1973), 679.

167 Süleymaniye Library, Yeni Cami Section 150, 45a-b.

168 VGMA, No. 744, 28.

As we have seen from the above examples taken from the fifteenth to the seventeenth centuries, the most important duty of the assistant librarian was to register books lent out. But with the trend against the practice of lending books from the end of the seventeenth century and its complete abolition during the eighteenth century, the duties of the assistant librarian gradually switched to the cataloguing of books and the preparation of inventories. The deeds of the libraries of Amcazade Hüseyin Pasha, Yeni Cami, and Damad İbrahim Pasha note that the assistant librarian should draw up catalogues.[169] In Beşir Ağa's college library in Eyüp, we see a student being appointed as assistant librarian to prepare a catalogue of the books.[170]

In the libraries in the Fatih and Ayasofya Complexes, endowed by Mahmud I, an assistant librarian was appointed to draw up a catalogue which would be used to check losses whenever an inventory of books was made.[171]

In the libraries founded at the end of eighteenth century and the beginning of the nineteenth century, we do not see the post of assistant librarian either in Istanbul or in the provinces. It seems as if the post had become redundant due, most probably, to the fact that other personnel, such as the inspectors of foundations or librarians, increasingly became involved in the task of cataloguing the collection and making regular inventories.

When comparing the salary of an assistant librarian to that of librarian, we see that as time went on the assistant librarian received increasingly less. In Murad II's foundation (1435), both the librarian and the assistant received two aspers, while in the Fatih (1470) and Süleymaniye Complexes (1557) the librarian received six aspers and the assistant librarian four. From this period to that of the endowment of the library at Ayasofya (1740), the assistant librarian seems to have generally received half of the stipend allocated to the librarian. Thereafter, there is a marked decrease in the stipend of the assistant compared to that of the first librarian. According to the endowment document of Ayasofya the assistant librarian received a mere ten aspers compared to the ninety aspers allocated to the first librarian, while in the endowment of Mahmud I at Fatih (1742), the assistant librarian received a fifth of the stipend given to the first librarian.

---

169 Süleymaniye Library, Yazma Bağışlar Section 2272, 4a, Yeni Cami Section 1200, 22a and VGMA, No. 38, 90 respectively.
170 VGMA, No. 736, 4.
171 VGMA, No. 47, 16, 25 and VGMA, Defter 87, 6 respectively.

Bookbinders (Mücellid)

The earliest reference to bookbinders is in the fifteenth century where we find a provision for a binder to be paid two aspers daily so that he may see to the repair and maintenance of separately bound sections of the Koran and the law books pertaining to the imperial foundation of Mehmed I in Amasya (1417).[172] This, however, strictly speaking, was not a library position, as the binder was responsible to the complex as a whole, and was not employed exclusively in the library. During the reign of Mehmed II (1451–1481), the only reference to binders is in an account book for the Eyüp Mosque, where again he is responsible to the complex rather than the library.[173] What is surprising is that no provision is made for a binder to maintain the rich collection in the college library founded by Mehmed II. We can only presume that the books were looked after by the binder in the Palace Library.[174]

Throughout the next hundred years references to binders are sparse and uninformative.[175] Although there is no mention of a binder among the personnel of the Süleymaniye Complex in its deed, we learn from a record that at a later date a binder was appointed.[176] It is only in the foundation deed of İsmihan Sultan, daughter of Selim II, that we begin to have any information on the role of the binder:

> It is a condition that if it becomes necessary to renew the bindings of the scriptures and the books listed below, which have become worn with the passage of days and months, they are to be bound with bindings identical to the originals to prevent fraud, deception and substitution.[177]

---

172 Belediye Library (now Atatürk Library), Mc. O. 70, 335.

173 BOA, MAD 4792, 31.

174 An account book from 1478, mentions that the palace employed two binders one of whom received twelve aspers and the other five aspers. See: A. Refik, "Fatih Devrine Ait Vesikalar," *TOEM*, nos. 49–62 (1337H): 7.

175 In an account book of Şehzade Mehmed's complex in Istanbul, for instance, for the year 1584 it is mentioned that a certain Mehmed is receiving two aspers per day for repairing books (BOA, MAD 5103, 397).

176 BOA, Ruus 66, 233.

177 The point of this condition was that as books were generally described by their bindings, as well as their contents, so that the substitution of a book by another copy required that the binding be changed too.

In the deed for Selim II's own complex in Edirne, it is stipulated that "an upright person who was skilled in his craft" should be appointed as bookbinder.[178] Sinan Pasha, in the deed of his foundation (1586), did not provide for a binder, but required that the administrator see to the repair and maintenance of books, presumably by sending the books out to a binder.[179]

No libraries founded in the seventeenth century employed their own binders, with the exception of the Turhan Valide Sultan's library in Yeni Cami, the Köprülü Library,[180] and the college library founded by Feyzullah Efendi, who stipulated that a binder was to be employed and that he should not take the books off the premises, probably a precaution against possible abuse.

However, in the larger libraries founded in the first half of the eighteenth century we generally see provision for a binder to be appointed. The following libraries all employed a binder: the college library of Amcazade Hüseyin Pasha, Ahmed III's Palace Library built for the use of the palace staff, and his library at Yeni Cami, the college library founded by Nevşehirli İbrahim Pasha, the college libraries of Hacı Beşir Ağa in Eyüp and Cağaloğlu, Mahmud I's library in Ayasofya, the Atıf Efendi Library, and the Hekimoğlu Ali Pasha Library. In the Nuruosmaniye Library, the binder was also required to ornament and gild the books.[181]

Towards the end of the eighteenth and the beginning of the nineteenth century, we see a reversal in the trend, so that with the exception of the Selim Ağa and Halet Efendi Libraries, the post of binder ceases to exist, and the maintenance of bindings is left to outside craftsmen. The library founders in this period usually allocated a special fund for binding and repairs. Hüseyin Ağa, for example, allocated the sum of 2,880 aspers a year for binding.[182] Vahid Pasha and Ahmed Ağa specified in their foundation deeds that bindings should be repaired when required, from the general fund of surplus revenue.[183] In the foundation deed of the mosque library founded by Mehmed Ali Pasha in Kavala, provision is made for repairs to bindings to be paid for out of the general fund of the foundation.[184] In the Raşid Efendi

---

178 Müjgan Cunbur, "Osmanlı Çağı Türk Vakıf Kütüphanelerinde Personel Düzenini Geliştirme Çabaları," *VII. Türk Tarih Kongresi* (Ankara: Türk Tarih Kurumu Basımevi, 1973), 679.

179 Süleymaniye Library, Haremeyn File I.

180 In the Köprülü Library we see the post of a second binder endowed in 1764.

181 VGMA, Dolap 49, 23.

182 VGMA, No. 578, 75.

183 VGMA, No. 579, 703 and VGMA, No. 743, 94 respectively.

184 VGMA, No. 580, 275.

library in Kayseri, the deed allows for income from the endowments to be allocated to the repair and renewal of binding when the need arose, and we see in a financial summary for the year 1827 that forty-seven piastres were spent on binding.[185]

The stipends offered to binders were comparatively low, never exceeding ten aspers a day, which would suggest that the post of binder was part time. Despite the comparatively low sum allocated to the binder's stipend, it seems that, towards the end of the period under discussion, the founders still considered it more economical to have books bound by self-employed binders.

Doorkeeper (Bevvab)

In almost all complexes and colleges, there was a doorkeeper who opened and closed the main gate at the prescribed hours. As one would expect, it was only with the emergence of the independent library that we see the post of doorkeeper on the staff of libraries.

In the foundation deeds, we see that doorkeepers were required to be trustworthy, reliable, and upright. His duties, apart from attending to the main gate, are very rarely described, and then only in the vaguest terms. In the college library attached to the palace at Galata (1754), it was stipulated by Mahmud I, the founder, that the door keeper should hand over the key to the ağa of the palace, after shutting up for the night.[186] The doorkeeper in Aşir Efendi's library was required to act as sweeper, to fetch water and light the charcoal stoves in the reading room during winter.[187] In the libraries that Mahmud I endowed at Ayasofya and Fatih, the doorkeeper was required to act as watchman and his title was expanded to "watchman-doorkeeper."[188] However, in the libraries of Yeni Cami, the Nuruosmaniye and Veliyüddin Efendi, there were two distinct posts, watchman and doorkeeper.

While the vast majority of libraries had only one doorkeeper, the richly endowed libraries could boast more than one, as in the foundations at Ayasofya and Fatih, which had two "watchmen-doorkeepers," and the Nuruosmaniye Library, which had six watchmen and three doorkeepers.

---

185 VGMA, No. 579, 68.
186 VGMA, No. 87, 9.
187 Süleymaniye Library, Aşir Efendi Section 473, 9a–b.
188 TSA, E. 1767.

The daily stipend of the doorkeepers varied between five and fifteen aspers. In the Hamidiye Library, however, the post of doorkeeper was combined with that of sweeper and his stipend was fifty aspers daily.[189]

Sweepers (Ferraş)

It was the responsibility of the sweeper to keep the building clean. It is only with the emergence of the independent library that the library staff acquired its own sweeper. Not surprisingly, there are no particular qualifications expected of the sweeper, except in those libraries where the post is amalgamated with that of the more responsible position of doorkeeper, in which case he is expected to be trustworthy, reliable, and upright.

In very few deeds do we see any description of his duties. When the Süleymaniye Mosque Library was reorganized by Mahmud I and his vizier, Köse Mustafa Bahir Pasha, it was stipulated that:

> In the glorious library the sweeper is to present himself in the library every day from morning time until the time of the afternoon prayer. He is to attend the librarian and sweep and dust the library and lay the cushions and then to stand at the door of the library and check the books on the persons entering and leaving the library.[190]

This is the only reference we have to any personnel acting as a security check on people entering and leaving a library. In the Vahid Pasha Library in Kütahya, the sweeper was expected to clean and sweep the library, while in the library of Raşid Efendi he was also required to roll up and re-lay the carpets and rush matting.[191] Although in some cases it was a full-time position, this post, which carried its own daily stipend, was often given as an extra duty to a functionary of some nearby institution or was given to the doorkeeper. Most libraries employed a single sweeper, but in the following larger libraries there was more than one sweeper: Topkapı Palace Library, Ayasofya Library, Fatih Library, Süleymaniye Library, Nuruosmaniye Library, and the Bostancılar Ocağı Library.

---

189 VGMA, Kasa 159, 115.
190 BOA, Müteferrik 89, 114b.
191 VGMA, No. 579, 703 and VGMA, No. 579, 67.

Personnel for the Maintenance of the Library Building

In the independent libraries, it was necessary to make provision for the maintenance of the building. Some founders therefore created posts for maintenance men. Atıf Efendi allocated a daily stipend of eight aspers for a plumber to maintain the lead drains and water conduits, and four aspers for a carpenter.[192] In Mahmud I's foundation deed for the Ayasofya Library, provision was made for the posts of "repairer," a worker in lead for the roof, a worker in mother-of-pearl to repair the inlaid wood furnishings, and a cleaner to remove marks and stains from the walls.[193] In the Fatih foundation, there was only one maintenance man.[194] In the deeds of other independent libraries, provision is made for one or more maintenance personnel.

We have, in the above few pages, surveyed the general trends in the staffing of Ottoman libraries, from their humble beginnings when there was likely to have been just a single member of staff to the later period where a library could boast of an establishment of more than twenty personnel. Together with this increase in the number of personnel, we also have, as one would expect, specialization in the job descriptions of the staff, so that personnel were assigned particular tasks, including maintenance of the fabric, cleaning and security of the building, care, repair, lending, and cataloguing of books, as well as the administration of the whole establishment.

---

192 TSA, D. 3306.
193 TSA, D. 1767.
194 TSA, D. 1767.

Chapter Seven

The Establishment and Maintenance of Collections

Numerous documents and account books pertaining to the libraries and their collections help historians trace the foundation and enlargement of Ottoman library collections. From these, we have been able to draw a clearer picture of the general state of the collections housed in the Ottoman libraries as they evolved from their humble origins to large and valuable collections in the later centuries. It should be noted that throughout this period the library collections consisted either entirely, or almost entirely, of manuscripts. It was not until 1727 that the first Turkish publishing house was established and even by 1802 only forty-five books had been printed.[1] Thereafter, printing increased apace, but even to the end of the period under discussion few printed books had entered foundation libraries.

The Establishment of the Collections

The Ottoman library finds its origins in the practice of benefactors endowing books to colleges and mosques, for the benefit of the students or the public. By

---

1   Jale Baysal, "Turkish Publishing Activities Before and After the New Alphabet," *Anatolica* 8 (1981): 121–122.

the sixteenth century it was common for the founder of a college to endow, at the same time, a collection of books, the majority of which were the textbooks taught in that institution.

The members of the *ulema*, that is, the learned professions of the Ottoman Empire, who were unable to found libraries, often donated their books to existing colleges, mosques, and dervish convents or bequeathed their books and their house to be used as a library by the people of the district in which they lived.[2] The foundation of an independent library entailed not only the erection of a building and the establishment of the collection to be housed therein, but also required the endowment of lands and other properties to generate the revenues needed for the maintenance and running of the library. As it was only wealthy individuals who could afford to found a library, we find that the founders were generally members of the royal family and statesmen. The scholars and members of the learned professions usually donated their books to an existing institution.

When donating a single volume or a small number of books, it was usually the custom to inscribe on each volume the donor's name and the institution to which the books were donated, and sometimes the date. This was enough to establish that the book was an endowment and therefore governed by the principles of Islamic law. However, when donating a sizeable collection, founders typically drew up an endowment deed (*vakfiye*), which described the conditions under which the books were to be used including an inventory of the books or, at least, the number of books endowed. Towards the end of the deeds, we always come across a "withdrawal clause" in which the benefactor discusses the legality of endowing the books, and quotes the arguments of some authorities supporting the legality of the endowment.[3] While there was some room for argument in Islamic law as to whether it was permitted to endow moveable property, such as furniture, money, books, and so on, the majority view among Islamic scholars was that it was permitted.[4] The purpose of dealing with the question of legality

---

2 BOA, Tapu-Tahrir Deteri, No. 1070, 53, 211, 220, 239–241, 27 272; Istanbul Court Registers, Evkaf-ı Hümayun Muhasibliği, No. 102, 150a–151b; İVTD 172, 338; BOA, MAD, 557, 11–12; Istanbul Court Registers, Balat Mahkemesi No. 2, 5a; Galata Mahkemesi No. 17, 187–188; VGMA, No. 572, 13; BOA, Sül. No. 2918, 12a.

3 For some examples see: VGMA, No. 582l1, 35; Istanbul Court Registers, Evkaf-ı Hümayun Müfettişliği No. 25, 11–12; VGMA, No. 736, 207; Istanbul Court Registers, Evkaf-ı Hümayun Müfettişliği No. 63, 20; VGMA, No. 628, 54 549.

4 For an analysis of the views of Islamic scholars on this question see: Youssef Eché, *Les Bibliotheques Arabes* (Damascus: n.p., 1967), 68–74. Ebu's-Su'ud, the famous *şeyhülislam* in Süleyman the Magnificent's reign, in his defence of this practice, which was under attack by Birgili Mehmed Efendi, argued that as the practice had become common usage, a status accepted by Islamic law, then it was permissable. He went on to list several authorities who considered it permissable (Süleymaniye Library, Bağdadlı Vehbi Section 477/1, 3a).

within the deeds was to prevent future generations of the benefactor raising the question again and perhaps ruling against its legality, thereby allowing the endowment to be dissolved.[5]

It was not, however, always necessary to draw up deeds of endowment when founding a library or donating books, it being sufficient to enter a clause in one's will. Indeed, there are cases where the verbal endowment in front of two witnesses was considered sufficient to found a library.[6]

We find that the basic collections of books endowed at the time of founding of the institutions varied considerably in size. Before the conquest of Istanbul (1453), no library was founded with more than a hundred volumes, but after the conquest we see foundations in which the libraries had increasingly larger collections, as for example in the college of Mahmud Pasha which had a library of 195 books,[7] the dervish convent of Şeyh Vefa with 381,[8] and in the complex of Mehmed II 839 books.[9] In the provinces, we see İshak Bey's library in Skopje housing 331 volumes,[10] while the collections in the libraries of Edirne varied from nineteen to 99 books.[11] However, in the deed of Molla Yegan dated 1461, it is mentioned that he endowed 2,900 books to his mosque in Bursa upon his death.[12] This is the richest collection provided for a library in the sixteenth and seventeenth centuries.

Mehmed II was succeeded by his son Bayezid II. Although he was a renowned bibliophile and amassed a large collection, the libraries he founded and the other libraries founded during his reign had fairly small collections, varying considerably in size. In the complex founded by Bayezid II himself in Edirne, the library consisted of a mere forty-two books,[13] while the richest collection founded in his reign was endowed to the village mosque of Çavlı in the district of Kandıra, in 1496; it consisted of 210 works.[14]

Up to the last quarter of the seventeenth century there was no appreciable trend towards an increase in the size of the founder collections; libraries

---

5 Istanbul Court Registers, Ahi Çelebi Mahkemesi No. 19, 36b; Evkaf-ı Hümayun Müfettişliği No. 213, 15a–b.
6 Istanbul Court Registers, Kısmet-i Askeriyye No. 8, 62a.
7 İVTD. 43.
8 Istanbul Court Registers, Evkaf-ı Hümayun Muhasibliği No. 102, 151a.
9 TSA, D. 9559.
10 Hasan Kaleşi, "Yugoslavya'da İlk Türk Kütüphaneleri," Türk Kültürü 4/38 (1965): 41 2.
11 BOA, Tapu-Tahrir Defteri No. 1070, 19, 220, 434–435.
12 Bursa Court Registers, A. 156/208, 204b.
13 M. Tayyib Gökbilgin, XV-XVI. Asırlarda Edirne ve Paşa Livası (İstanbul: Üçler Basımevi, 1952), appendix p. 42.
14 VGMA, No. 579, 224–227.

generally consisted of between forty and 150 books with the exception of two large foundations, the Selimiye Library (1579)[15] in Edirne and Bedreddin Mahmud Library (1559)[16] in Kayseri consisting of up to four hundred books each. With the foundation of the independent Köprülü Library in 1678, we see the endowment of a collection of two thousand volumes.[17] Two statesmen from the famous Köprülü family, Merzifonlu Kara Mustafa Pasha and Amcazade Hüseyin Pasha, each endowed college libraries of about five hundred volumes, in 1681 and 1700 respectively.[18]

During the reign of Ahmed III the collections generally varied in size between three hundred and five hundred books,[19] with the exception of three large libraries: the independent library founded by Şehid Ali Pasha (1715), the college library of Damad İbrahim Pasha (1720) and the mosque library of Ahmed III (Yeni Cami, 1725) which contained between one thousand and two thousand books.[20] The library founded by Ahmed III in Topkapı Palace for the use of the Palace staff contained around five thousand books.[21]

In the reign of Mahmud I, the richest public library was that at Ayasofya, which is said, by the historian Subhi, to have housed four thousand volumes.[22] Other large libraries, such as Atıf Efendi's library (1741), the Fatih Library (1742), and Reisülküttab Mustafa Efendi's library (1747) contained between one thousand and two thousand books.[23]

In the Nuruosmaniye Library (1755), which was endowed by Mahmud I's brother, Osman III, we find the richest collection of the eighteenth century with over five thousand books,[24] a figure which was to remain unsurpassed for a century. For the remainder of the period under discussion the mosque and college libraries were usually endowed with a founder collection of between three hundred to five hundred books, while the independent libraries were usually founded with a collection of rarely more than two thousand books.

---

15 Vakıtlar Genel Müdürlüğü Archive No. 1395, 87–114.

16 VGMA, No. 581/1, 31–33.

17 M. Gökman, *Kütüphanelerimizden Notlar* (İstanbul: Kardeşler Basımevi, 1952), 36.

18 Beyazıt Umumi Library No. 21, 346.

19 Şemin Emsem, "Osmanlı Imparatorluğu Devrinde Türkiye Kütüphanelerinin Tarihçesi," *TKDB* 9, nos. 1–2 (1960): 26–35.

20 Halit Dener, *Süleymaniye Umumi Kütüphanesi* (İstanbul: İstanbul Maarif Basımevi, 1957), 52–53; Süleymaniye Library, Yazma Bağışlar 2269 and 2742.

21 Şükrü Yenal, "Topkapı Sarayı Müzesi Enderun Kitaplığı," *Güzel Sanatlar* 6 (1949): 90; İsmail E. Erünsal, "The Establishment and Maintenance of Collections in the Ottoman Libraries: 1400–1839," *Libri* 39, no. 1 (1989): 4.

22 Subhi, *Tarih* (İstanbul: Raşid Mehmed Efendi Matbaası, 1198H), 174.

23 TSA, D. 3306; Süleymaniye Library, Yazma Bağışlar 2738, 244 .

24 Nuruosmaniye Library No. 3, 161a.

In these libraries, we see the accession of one or two printed books during the reign of Ahmed III, and up to the end of the eighteenth century there were never more than forty printed books in any one library.[25] According to Professor Stajnova, the library founded by Pazvantoğlu Osman Pasha in Vidin at the beginning of the nineteenth century contained an almost complete collection of the forty-five books published by the Müteferrika Press.[26] This collection may have reflected the founder's eagerness to acquire books on every subject. This was unusual, for printed books did not generally find their way into library collections for a number of reasons. The Müteferrika Press did not publish the type of book in demand by college students and the libraries did not generally have budgets for buying books. However, exceptionally, we see Mahmud II issuing a decree in 1816 to the effect that a number of copies of Asım Efendi's translation of the *Kamus*, an Arabic-Turkish dictionary, should be purchased and one copy each should be deposited in the most important libraries.[27]

By the middle of the nineteenth century, we begin to see a few printed books coming onto the shelves of foundation libraries. This came about for two reasons. Firstly, the printing presses realized that money could be made from printing college text books, as well as histories and translations, and an increasing number of printed college texts became available on the market. Secondly, and more importantly, with the responsibility for running libraries coming under the Ministry of Education, funds were now available for the purchase of books. Thus, we see in 1910 requests for a number of printed books from the librarians of foundation libraries to the department of libraries in the Ministry of Education. These requests seem to have been granted.[28]

The Expansion of the Main Collections

The primary collection of a library was expanded in various ways, one of the most common being for the founder himself or someone from his family to make additional endowments. For instance, Hafız Mustafa Pasha founded a library at Arapgir with a collection of 164 volumes[29] to which he added a further

---

25 Halit Dener, *Süleymaniye Umumi Kütüphanesi* (İstanbul: İstanbul Maarif Basımevi, 1957), 37, 46, 65.
26 Mihaila Stajnova, "Ottoman Libraries in Vidin," *Etudes Balkaniques* 2 (1979), 57.
27 BOA, Hatt-ı Hümayun No. 18713.
28 BOA, MF. KTV. File. 8, No. 153 and 157.
29 TSA, E.137/45.

thirty-four in 1773 and 38 in 1774.[30] Similarly, Vahid Pasha founded a library in Kütahya (1811) with 217 books, to which he added whenever the opportunity arose as he was posted to the various provincial cities in the empire.[31] Halet Efendi, the famous Ottoman poet and statesman, endowed his books in two instalments.[32]

Almost all independent libraries received large additional endowments from the relatives and descendants of the founder. The collections in the Köprülü (1678), Atıf Efendi (1741), Aşir Efendi (1747), and Veliyüddin Efendi (1769) libraries were enlarged significantly through endowments of this kind.[33]

While these additional endowments tended to be fairly sizeable, there were also many smaller endowments made by the public. These small endowments were extremely important for the expansion of the libraries, as, for example, in the case of Fatih Mosque Library which began with a founder collection of 839 books, but could, within a hundred years of its foundation, boast almost 1,800[34] and at the beginning of nineteenth century a survey of this library recorded that there were more than 5,500 works in this collection.[35]

It was common for a person working in a complex to provide for his books to be left on his death to the institution where he had worked,[36] or to leave them to the local mosque, college or library.[37] On the other hand, many people preferred to leave their books to a library in the province where they were born and brought up.[38] These smaller endowments usually represented the complete collection of a scholar, teacher, judge, or minor statesman, consisting of from a handful of books to a relatively large collection of about three hundred.

Much smaller, but nevertheless significant, were casual donations of one, two, or more books by the public. These donations were so small that they often

---

30 TSA, E.137/46.
31 VGMA, No. 579, 626–27, 684–685, 688,695, 699, 713–717.
32 Istanbul Court Registers, Evkaf-ı Hümayun Müfettişliği No. 375, 6b.
33 VGMA, No. 580, 17-18, No. 76, 43; Istanbul Court Registers, Ahi Çelebi Mahkemesi no 163, 57e; Atıf Efendi Library No. 2858/9–12; *Vâsıf Tarihi*, vol. 1 (Cairo: Bulak, 1246H), 206–207; Süleymaniye Library, Aşir Efendi 473; Halid Efendi 486, 487.
34 TSA, D.9559.
35 Süleymaniye Library, Yazma Bağışlar No. 252; TSA, D. 3310.
36 Istanbul Court Registers, Üsküdar Mahkemesi No. 383, 58b–59a; Eyüp Mahkemesi No. 212, 19a; Rumeli Sadareti No. 8, 55a. Uzunçarşılı notes that the famous scholar Mevlana Musannifek (d.1470), who held a teaching post at the Sahn College, left a will in which his books were bequeathed to that college: *İlmiye Teşkilatı* (Ankara: Türk Tarih Kurumu Basımevi, 1965), 6.
37 Istanbul Court Registers, Üsküdar Mahkemesi No. 148, 48b, No. 287, 89b; Ahi Çelebi Mahkemesi No. 19, 36b–37a; Galata Mahkemesi No. 584, 63b–64a.
38 Istanbul Court Registers, Eyüp Mahkemesi No. 287, 30a–31b; Bab Mahkemesi No. 57, 169b–170a; VGMA, No. 735, 97.

did not warrant the drawing up of an endowment deed. Sometimes the name of donator was recorded on the flyleaf of the book, sometimes merely the word *vakf* (endowment). In Durud Dede's collection, which was housed in the Durud Dede College in Ankara, there are 251 books of which there is no record of the donor.[39] This suggests that these books were made up of numerous small donations.

While it can be claimed that the collections in libraries in the Ottoman Empire were created by the direct endowment of books, it should be noted that there were exceptional cases where provision was made for libraries to purchase books. We find that in the deeds of libraries created by Murad II in 1435,[40] Bayezid II in 1488,[41] İsmihan Sultan in 1568,[42] and Peremeciler Kethüdası Mahmud Bey in 1593,[43] provision was made for funds to be made available to purchase replacement copies of books that were worn out or had been lost.

Although few Ottoman libraries had funds to purchase books requested by readers, there is evidence to suggest that in some cases books were bought and donated by benefactors to meet the demand of the readers. The historian Vasıf Efendi recounts that the son of Veliyüddin Efendi used to buy the books that students needed in the library endowed by his father.[44] Mehmed Asım Bey, an administrator of the Köprülü Library, mentions in the deed of an endowment he made to the library that he had purchased and donated many books as they were required by students. As part of the endowment, he left a sum of money specifically for the purchase of books required by readers.[45] However, there seems to be no evidence that many books were bought from this fund; on the contrary, we find from accounts for 1835–1838, that only three books were purchased out of these funds, one, the *Haşiye-i Fenari*, being listed as among the "extraordinary expenditures." On the same page in the account book, we notice that the library took out a subscription to the official Ottoman gazette, the *Takvim-i Vekayi*, which had begun publication shortly before.[46]

It should be borne in mind that, as mentioned above, these books were almost all manuscripts and consequently expensive. We have some examples of the costs involved in commissioning a scribe to copy a book, and the costs

---

39 Turgut Kut's Private Archive, Libraries File.
40 TSA, D.7081.
41 M. Tayyib Gökbilgin, *XV-XVI. Asırlarda Edirne ve Paşa Livası* (İstanbul: Üçler Basımevi, 1952), appendix p. 54.
42 VGMA, No. 572, 147.
43 Istanbul Court Registers, Galata Mahkemesi No. 17, 187.
44 *Vâsıf Tarihi*, vol. 1 (Cairo: Bulak, 1246H), 206.
45 VGMA, No. 580, 1–14.
46 Köprülü Library No. 2491/16, 2a.

are not inconsiderable.[47] It is understandable therefore that we do not observe Ottoman libraries embarking on a policy of commissioning copies of books to expand their collection. We may presume that the prices of second-hand books were somewhat less than the cost of commissioning new copies.[48]

The one institution that consistently commissioned the copying of books was the imperial palace. While a detailed study of the palace library does not fall within the bounds of this study, it is nevertheless important in that it provided the source of the many rich imperial endowments made by successive sultans and members of their family. In the production of these books, a large staff was employed and we find in a register which lists the personnel of the palace during the reign of Bayezid II (1481–1512) that there were eight copyists (katiban-ı kütüb-i hassa), nine binders (mücellid), and twenty-two ornamentors (nakkaş) working.[49] According to the historian Ali, there were employed at the palace at the end of sixteenth century a large number of artisans occupied solely with the production of books.[50] In a register of salaries from 1651, we notice that the palace employed, in that year, forty-nine copyists, eleven binders, and many other craftsmen, such as illuminators, margin-decorators, gilders, and so on.[51]

The palace also purchased books,[52] but by far the greatest number of books entered the imperial collection as gifts to the sultan. In a register of gifts from the reign of Bayezid II, we discover that the presentation of books to the sovereign was commonplace.[53] In a document covering the years 1748–1753, we see that Mahmud I was presented with no less than five thousand books.[54] When he endowed the mosque at Ayasofya with a library, many of the statesmen and

---

47 İsmail E. Erünsal, Kütüphanecilikle İlgili Osmanlıca Metinler ve Belgeler, vol. 1 (İstanbul: Edebiyat Fakültesi Matbaası, 1982), 78.

48 Volney, a traveler in the Ottoman Empire towards the end of the eighteenth century notes the great expense involved in copying: "From this state of facts, we are certainly authorized to affirm, not only that there is a scarcity of good books in the East, but that books of any kind are very rare. The reason of this is evident. In these countries every book is a manuscript; the writing of which is necessarily slow, difficult, and expensive. The labor of many months produces but one copy," C. Volney, Travels Through Syria and Egypt, in the Years 1783, 1784 and 1785, vol 2 (London: G. G. J. and J. Robinson, 1788), 450.

49 Ö. Lütfi Barkan, "H.933–934 (M.1527–1528) Mali Yılına ait Bir Bütçe Örneği," İktisat Fakültesi Mecmuası 15 (1953): 309–310.

50 A. Tietze, Mustafa Ali's Counsel for Sultans of 1581 (Vienna: Verlag der Oesterreichischen Akademie der Wissenschaften, 1979), 155–156.

51 TSA, D.486, 1–2.

52 BOA, Mühimme Register No. 64, 11; MAD, 4973, 13; MAD, 19432; TSA, D. 21, 56a–b.

53 Belediye Library, Mc.0.71. For the contents of this register see: İsmail E. Erünsal," II. Bayezid Devrine Ait Bir In'amat Defteri," TAD 10–11 (1981): 303–309.

54 TSA, D.10524.

scholars who attended the opening ceremony presented books to the sultan for the palace library.[55]

A particularly valued means of enriching the palace collections came by way of gifts from ambassadors from Islamic countries to the east of the Ottoman territories. These would be books prized not only for their originality, but also for their rich decoration which would befit a present for the sultan.[56] A further source of books from the same territories would come from statesmen and princes who had fallen foul of the Safavid rulers of Persia and sought asylum in Ottoman territories.[57]

Another way in which the Palace Library was able to expand its collection was through the common practice of confiscating the goods of individuals who died or had been executed. We have, for example, a list of books, dated 1589, belonging to Mehmed Pasha, which came to the palace library following his execution.[58] When Şehid Ali Pasha died on campaign, we know that a major part of his rich library was confiscated.[59] There are many further examples of the confiscation of books during the reign of the bibliophile Sultan Mahmud I.[60]

Periodic Inspections and Inventories

In the foundation deeds of libraries, provision was generally made for the periodic inspection of books. The first extant record (written in 1453) in which this provision can be found is an endowment clause referring to the library of Umur Bey in Bursa in which he specifies: "Whoever is appointed the şeyh of this institution should conserve and oversee the books and should, once every six months, count them."[61]

---

55 Subhi, *Tarih* (İstanbul: Raşid Mehmed Efendi Matbaası, 1198H), 174a–b. See also Ayasofya file in Süheyl Ünver's Archive, in Süleymaniye Library.

56 Lale Uluç, "Ottoman Book Collectors and Illustrated Sixteenth Century Shiraz Manuscripts," *Revue des Mondes Musulmans et de la Méditerranée*, no. 87–88 (1999): 91–96.

57 Ebulfez Rahimov, "Safevîlerin Türkiye'ye Hediye Gönderdiği Kitaplar," *Türk Kültürü*, 33, no. 386 (1995): 344–352.

58 TSA, D. 4057.

59 İsmail E. Erünsal, "Şehid Ali Paşa'nın İstanbul'da Kurduğu Kütüphaneler ve Müsadere Edilen Kitaplar," *Kütüphanecilik Dergisi* 1 (1987): 84–85.

60 BOA, Cevdet-Dahiliye 6615, Cevdet-Belediye 4479, Cevdet-Maliye 24,548; BOA, Bab-ı Defteri, Baş Muhasebe 12,435 and 12,651; MAD, 665, 3–6; MAD, 5456, 324; MAD, 10,177, 230–231; MAD, 9950, 313–320; MAD, 10,346, 361 and 371 TSA, D. 21, 5b–6b; D. 23, 36a–b, 37a, 89b–90a; D. 4057; D. 3228/4 and 8.

61 Bursa Eski Eserler Library, Ulu Cami No. 436, 329b.

Some twenty years later we see that regular inspection were also required in the Fatih Library founded by Mehmed II (1451–1481), in the deed of which it was stipulated that the supervisor of the foundation should inspect the books every three months.[62] This was later changed to every month.[63] In the deed of the Bayezid II's foundation, the inspection was to take place once a year, but no particular time of the year was specified.[64]

In the libraries founded later, the time for the annual inspection was often specified. Bedreddin Mahmud (1559) called for an annual inspection during Ramazan, the ninth month of the year in the Islamic calendar.[65] Hacı Beşir Ağa (1735), Arpa Emini Ali Ağa (1762), Ragıb Pasha (1762), Veliyüddin Efendi (1769), Ahmed Ağa of Rhodes (1793), Debbağzade İbrahim Efendi (1804), Vahid Pasha (1811), and Halet Efendi (1822) all specified the month of Muharrem, the first month of the year, for the annual inspection.[66] In a deed dated 1786, we see Abdullah Münzevi establishing a library in the famous Ulu Cami in Bursa and rather curiously specifying that the inspection should take place in the middle of the month of Şaban, the eighth month of the year.[67] The only reason one could put forward for this choice of date was that he intended to have the library in good order before the start of the holy month of Ramazan (the ninth month of the year), in which one would expect the library to be put to greater use by the congregation using the books for devotional reading.

After responsibility for the running of libraries was transferred to the Ministry of Education in the nineteenth century, the ministry increasingly extended its control over all aspects of libraries. In the 1881 publication of the administrative regulations governing foundation libraries, we see that the ministry provided for the inspection of libraries every three months when the entire inventory of each library was to be checked.[68]

These clauses demanding periodic inspections were a precaution against the loss of books. However, we should not presume that the inspections were carried out scrupulously as stipulated in the deeds. In fact, there is evidence

---

62 Süleymaniye Library, Nuri Arlases Section 242, 67b.

63 *Fatih Mehmed II Vakfiyeleri* (Ankara: Vakıflar Umum Müdürlüğü Neşriyatı, 1938), facsimile 270.

64 BOA, MAD, 7706, 315.

65 VGMA, No. 582/1, 33.

66 VGMA, No. 736, 4; Istanbul Court Registers, Evkaf-ı Hümayun Müfettişliği No. 171, 10b; No. 82, 8, No. 745, 81, No. 743, 93; Süleymaniye Library, Kılıç Ali Paşa No. 1049/1, 9a; VGMA, No. 579, 703; Süleymaniye Library, Halet Efendi No. 837, 9a.

67 Bursa Eski Eserler Library, Abdullah Münzevi's foundation deed, 1–15.

68 Mahmud Cevad, *Maarif-i Umumiye Nezareti, Tarihçe-i Teşkilat ve İcraatı* (İstanbul: Matbaa-i Amire, 1338H.), 209.

to suggest that the inspections were carried out in some libraries somewhat less than regularly. In a document, dated 1584, it is noted that inspection had not been carried out in the Fatih Library for more than ten years.[69] In 1720, it was noted that the library of Mahmud Pasha had no inventory made for over fifty years.[70] Similarly there are remarks made over the length of time since inventories had been drawn up for the libraries of Damad İbrahim Pasha (1720),[71] Ayasofya (1740),[72] Veliyüddin Efendi (1769),[73] Merzifonlu Kara Mustafa Pasha (1681),[74] and Nuruosmaniye (1755).[75] It was probably in order to ensure that inventories would be made regularly that Mehmed Ali Pasha required that inventories be drawn up only every three years (1813).[76]

There was little uniformity in the manner in which the periodic inspections were to be supervised. In the library of the Fatih Complex, the inspection was to be overseen by the supervisor of the foundation,[77] while in the library of Bedreddin Mahmud (1559) it was stipulated that the supervisor, administrator, and accountant (katib) of the foundation should attend the inspection, together with the librarians.[78] In the foundation deed of Abbas Ağa b. Abdüsselam (1670), it is mentioned that the inspection was to be supervised by the Inspector of the Holy Cities of Mecca and Medina (Evkaf-ı Haremeyn Müfettişi),[79] in the library founded by Mehmed Ağa (1634), it was to be supervised by the administrator of the foundation;[80] in the deed of Beşir Ağa (1735) it was stipulated that the assistant librarian, supervisor, and administrator of the foundation should carry out the inspection,[81] while in Ayasofya Library (1740) it was to be conducted by "some upright men from among the senior scholars."[82] According to the deed for the Turhan Valide Sultan foundation (1666), the inspection was to be conducted by the inspector (müfettiş) of the foundation in the presence of the administrator,

---

69 Ahmed Refik, Onuncu Asr-ı Hicride İstanbul Hayatı (İstanbul: Matbaa-i Orhaniye, 1333H), 54.
70 VGMA, No. 741, 336.
71 Süleymaniye Library, Yazma Bağışlar Section 2269, lb.
72 Süleymaniye Library, Ayasofya Section 3, 1b.
73 Beyazıt Umumi Library, Veliyüddin Efendi Section 3290, 1b.
74 Beyazıt Umumi Library Section 21,346.
75 Nuruosmaniye Library No. 3, lb; BOA, İbnülemin-Hatt-ı Hümayun No. 586.
76 VGMA, No. 580, 275.
77 Fatih Mehmed II Vakfıyeleri (Ankara: Vakıflar Umum Müdürlüğü Neşriyatı, 1938), facsimile 270.
78 VGMA, No. 582/2, 33.
79 Istanbul Court Registers, Evkaf-ı Hümayun Müfettişliği No. 63, 18.
80 VGMA, No. 730.
81 VGMA, No. 736, 4.
82 VGMA, Kasa No. 47, 12.

librarian and assistant librarian, and there is a particular emphasis placed upon the manner in which pledges, which were taken when books were lent out in order to prevent loss, were to be checked:

> He who is inspector of the endowment ... should attend the library and, in the presence of the librarian, administrator and assistant librarian should check the books one by one against the list bearing the imperial signature (*tuğra*), and check also the pledges accepted and should make a list of them and sign this said list and if he is unable to find a pledge for a book lent out he should not sign this list and should accordingly inform the supervisor of the endowment.[83]

In the libraries founded in Istanbul in the second half of the eighteenth century, it was generally left to the office of supervisor to manage the periodic inspection, with the provision that he was to be aided in his task by the staff of the library.[84] In the provincial libraries founded in this period, it was usually left to the local judge, mufti or scholars to conduct the inspection.[85]

If books were missing during the inspection, they were noted, but also the opportunity was taken to thoroughly clean them[86] and send damaged ones to a binder for repair.[87]

Apart from the regular inspections carried out according to the stipulations of the foundation deeds, the chief administrator of foundations may have occasionally deemed it necessary to examine the collections as well. Furthermore, there were regular inspections of all foundations in a particular locality carried out at regular intervals in order to assess their current circumstances. Although these would be general inspections, occasionally the books belonging to a foundation were individually listed, while in some cases merely the number of books was noted.

The inspection did not merely consist of checking the titles of the books against the catalogue, but entailed a more thorough examination of the books

---

83 VGMA, No. 744, 28–29.

84 VGMA, No. 82, 8, No. 745, 81, No. 579, 122.

85 Manisa Court Registers, 113, 237–238; Istanbul Court Registers, Evkaf-ı Hümayun Müfettişliği, No. 171, 10; VGMA, No. 579, 68 and 703, No. 743, 93; Müjgan Cunbur, "Yusuf Ağa Kütüphanesi ve Kütüphane Vakfiyesi," *TAD* 1, no. 1 (1963): 216.

86 VGMA, No. 582/1, 33 and No. 730.

87 Istanbul Court Registers, Evkaf-ı Hümayun Müfettişliği, No. 63, 18, No. 171, 10b; VGMA, No. 82, 8, No. 745, 81, No. 579, 122, No. 744, 28.

in order to verify that the copy was as described in the catalogue or previous inventory. We observe from the periodic inventories and catalogues that the Ottoman libraries suffered usually from substitution of a valuable book by a less valuable copy. This fraudulent practice goes back at least to the period of Mehmed II (1451–1481). From the correspondence of Ahmed Pasha to Sultan Bayezid II, we see that Molla Lütfi, the famous scholar, was accused of abusing his position as administrator of Sinan Pasha's endowment by substituting books worth five to six thousand aspers each with copies worth about thirty to forty aspers, and was further accused of the substitution of a valuable book from a college library.[88] To counteract fraud of this nature, the inspection included the examination of each book with careful attention to the number of folios, the endowment seals, the color and nature of binding, as we can see from the following entry in a catalogue prepared after an inspection in 1560 of the books in the Fatih Library:

> The second volume of the *Koranic Commentary of Ayasuluğî*: From the beginning of the chapter Maryam until the end of Koran. In the previous catalogue it was described as an unknown commentary. However, a note inscribed on the flyleaf names it as the *Commentary of Ayasuluğî*. On the flyleaf also it is recorded in large letters that this book is endowed by Sultan Mehmed Han. The text of the whole Koran from beginning till the end is written in red ink. All Damascene [paper]. Fully bound in cardboard, covered with yellow paper. Imperial endowment. 312 folios.[89]

On the first folio of a catalogue of the Nuruosmaniye Library there is written an imperial decree: "[The inspector] should show care with [the examination of] the seals and should not pass a book which does not bear a seal."[90]

This process was termed *tatbik* (comparing). Mahmud I created a post in Ayasofya for a person who would only carry out this work of comparing books with the catalogue.[91] During inspections, irregularities were noted in the existing catalogue. It often happened that with the change of administrator or librarian, or at any time it was felt necessary by the office of supervisor, a new catalogue

---

88 İsmail E. Erünsal, "Fatih Devri Kütüphaneleri ve Molla Lütfü Hakkında Birkaç Not," *Tarih Dergisi* 33 (1982): 72–78.
89 TSA, No. 9559, 7b.
90 TSA, No. D. 3305, 1b.
91 TSA, No. E. 1767.

would be drawn up.[92] One of the most important extant catalogues of the Fatih Library was drawn up in 1560 as a result of a change of librarian.[93] The following extant catalogues were drawn up also after an inspection: Turhan Valide Sultan,[94] Feyzullah Efendi,[95] Yeni Cami,[96] Ayasofya,[97] Fatih,[98] Nuruosmaniye,[99] Veliyüddin Efendi,[100] and Murad Molla.[101]

FIGURE 11. Murad Molla Library, Istanbul, est. 1775.

The catalogue for Turhan Valide Sultan was drawn up as a result of an inspection called on the appointment, in May 1711, of the librarian to one of the highest legal posts in the empire, the position of judge of Medina. This catalogue tells us which books were lost, how they were lost, and the person held responsible for the loss. A typical entry reads thus:

---

92 VGMA, Dolap No. 1628; Nuruosmaniye Library, No. 2, lb, No. 6, 206a, No. 3, lb; Beyazıt Umumi Library, No. 21346, 1b.
93 TSA, No. 9559, 2b.
94 Türk-Islam Eserleri Museum, No. 2218.
95 Millet Library, Feyzullah Efendi No. 2196.
96 Süleymaniye Library, Yazma Bağışlar No. 2742.
97 Süleymaniye Library, Ayasofya No. 3.
98 Süleymaniye Library, Yazma Bağışlar No. 242, 243.
99 Nuruosmaniye Library, No. 2, 3, 4, 6.
100 Beyazıt Umumi Library, Veliyüddin Efendi No. 3290.
101 VGMA, Dolap No. 1628.

Bahru'd-Dürer ... during the term of appointment of Mustafa Efendi, this book was burnt in the conflagration of Mirza Efendi's residence. In its place was accepted an incomplete commentary on the Koran covering the Maryam portion from chapter Yusuf to chapter Maryam.[102]

We observe in the catalogue of the Yeni Cami Library, drawn up in 1759, that several books were registered as missing, but on a later inspection the phrase *"ba'dehu bulunmuştur"* (found afterwards) with the Arabic *"sahh"* (correct) was added to some of the entries.[103] In a catalogue for the Nuruosmaniye Library, in which was registered changes resulting from an inspection carried out in 1775, we see a system of conventional signs used to denote that further inspections had been carried out. The sign in red which looks like an upside down hollow heart shape (see. Figure 12) was placed before each book to indicate that it had been inspected and the sign م (the letter "m" in the Arabic alphabet) in black ink to indicate a later inspection. For instance, a note next to *Celaleyn Tefsiri* indicates that the book was incomplete. This note was crossed out in red ink and the words "complete copy" added together with "upside down heart" sign in red. There then follows a further correction in black ink:[104] "When this volume was inspected it was not complete. The red line crossing out the black entry is mistaken and the red entry showing 'a complete copy' is also mistaken م."

It was usual to append to a catalogue drawn up after an inspection a summary of the books in the library and those missing. This summary bore the personal seals of all those who had attended the inspection. From these summaries we can learn not only the identity and position of the personnel carrying out the inspection but, also, the way in which the inspection was carried out, as well as the long-term damage inflicted on the collection by way of substitution and theft. When an inspection of the collection at the Fatih Complex was carried out in 1742, it was found that 110 books of the original 1,800 had been lost in the previous three hundred years.[105] In an inspection carried out in 1829, it was discovered that another forty-six books had been lost.[106]

---

102 Türk-Islam Eserleri Museum, No. 2218, 2b.
103 Süleymaniye Library, Yazma Bağışlar, No. 2742, 4a, 8a, 12b, 16b.
104 Nuruosmaniye Library, No. 6, 12b, 31b.
105 Süleymaniye Library, Yazma Bağışlar No. 244.
106 Süleymaniye Library, Yazma Bağışlar No. 243, 63b.

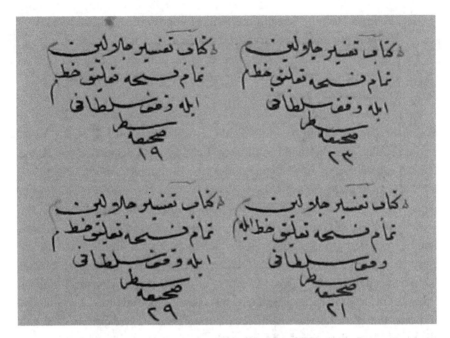

FIGURE 12. Excerpt from the Nuruosmaniye Library catalogue (1775) displaying signs of inspection before and after the titles of the books. Ms. No. 6, 12b.

In these summaries, there was also noted books which were found on the shelves of the library which were not registered in the previous inventory. In an inspection carried out in Feyzullah Efendi's library (1699) in 1741, it was found that there were forty-eight books missing and nineteen books which had not been recorded.[107] The summaries also gave the number of books for which there was a discrepancy either in the title or description. While in the summary one finds a brief note about these discrepancies, such as "and there were 87 volumes of which either the name or description did not tally,"[108] in the actual inventory there would be a more detailed description of the discrepancy:

> *The Meşariküʾl-Envar:* [original volume contained] 15 lines to a page [but] existing [volume] has 13 [lines].
> *The Meşariküʾl-Envar:* calligraphy [of original was in a] *nesh* [hand] existing [volume in a] *talik* [hand].[109]

---

107 Millet Library, Feyzullah Efendi No. 2196, 121a–124b.
108 Süleymaniye Library, Ayasofya No. 3, 151a.
109 Nuruosmaniye Library, No. 6, 31b–32a.

Some founders provided for a fee to be paid to those who were involved in the periodic inspection. In the foundation deed of Ragıb Pasha's library (1762), it was stipulated that the inspectors should receive between them 4,800 aspers at each annual inspection.[110] Veliyüddin Efendi allocated forty piastres (4,800 aspers) for an inspector.[111] Ahmed Ağa of Rhodes allocated five piastres to the assistant librarian for the task of checking the books against the catalogue and twenty-five piastres to be spent on a banquet to be given to the scholars, the notables, the great men and wealthy men of the island and the judge of the city of Rhodes who were to oversee the inspection.[112] In some documents, the cost of food is specified, as, for example, in Yusuf Ağa's foundation deed (1794) for his library in Konya in which it is stipulated that the judge of the city should carry out the inspection for which he would receive the sum of twenty piastres and that thirty piastres should be spent on coffee and a meal to be given on the completion of the inspection.[113]

From the archival documents available to us it is clear that the founders of libraries wanted to ensure that their collections remained intact and took every precaution to prevent abuses. On the whole it would seem, not only from the documents, but also from a survey of the surviving libraries with their great number of medieval books, that the Ottomans achieved a high degree of success in maintaining their libraries and ensuring their survival for posterity.

---

110 VGMA, No. 82, 8.
111 VGMA, No. 745, 81.
112 VGMA, No. 743, 94.
113 Müjgan Cunbur, "Yusuf Ağa Kütüphanesi ve Kütüphane Vakfiyesi," *TDA* 1, no. 1 (1963): 216.

Chapter Eight

Catalogues and Cataloguing

Making comprehensive lists of the books in endowed collections was an important part of the administration of Ottoman libraries. These lists were made not to facilitate the work of the librarian or to help the reader to locate a book, but rather because the legal status of foundation libraries required that inventories of endowed books were drawn up at various stages as a means of exercising control over the collection.

As a particular collection benefited from additional endowments or suffered losses through wear, theft, or fraudulent substitution, inventories were drawn up to update the original catalogue. In the early period of the Ottoman library system, these "founder inventories" were usually very brief, giving the title of the book, as well as sometimes the author and the number of volumes. These inventories may be considered the earliest examples of Ottoman library catalogues, as no other catalogue survive from this period.

There are no surviving foundation deeds or inventories for libraries founded up to the accession of Sultan Murad II in 1421. However, at the end of the foundation deed of the college he founded in Edirne in 1430, we find a list of the books endowed by him.[1]

---

1 TSA, D. 7081.

At first glance, it would seem that this is a list of books drawn up randomly. It is only when we consider the subjects of these titles that we realize that they are listed according to a classification system. Although the list bears no subject headings, we see that the books which appear first are devoted to Koranic commentary while the remaining books are on prophetic tradition. The number of volumes to each title is indicated, as is the physical condition of some of the books by the addition of the word "perfect" (*mükemmel*). After the title of some books the name of the author is listed, and when there is a second copy of a work, the word "another" (*diğer*) is added to indicate that it is a duplicate. As each book in the list bears the Arabic letters "*s-h*" (indicating *sahha*, correct), we may presume that this foundation deed had been used as an inventory at some inspection, either when the books were handed over to the librarian or at some other time.

In other libraries of this period, the lists appended to the foundation deeds are even less sophisticated. When Timurtaş Pashaoğlu Umur Bey built a mosque in Bursa, he established within it a small library. This foundation was regulated by three successive endowment documents, the first of which is dated 1440. This first endowment deed has, by ways of an appendix, a list of the books endowed, which simply gives the titles without any attempt at classification save for a division of the books into Arabic and Turkish works.[2] The only information offered apart from the titles themselves is the number of volumes for each title. The second extant document is simply a list of books contained in the library,[3] and is not classified in any way at all. The language in which the works are written is indicated after each title with the simple addition of the word Arabic (*'Arabî*) or Turkish (*Türkî*). In neither list are the names of the authors given except where the author's identity is part of the title of the book.

The third of these documents, written in Arabic and dated 1456, is a comprehensive endowment deed in which all of Umur Bey's previous endowments are brought together into one single document.[4] This lengthy scroll has by way of an appendix written on the back a list of books which had been donated by him to his mosque. While in the first and second document the books numbered a mere sixty titles, in the third and final list the number has increased to three hundred. Apart from the title, the number of volumes of each title is given, and sometimes the author's name. Many duplicate copies entered

2 VGMA, No. 591, 184.
3 Bursa Eski Eserler Library, Ulu Cami Section No. 436, 329. A list of these books is given in the Tim Stanley's article: "The Books of Umur Bey," *Muqarnas* 21 (2004): 323–331.
4 Belediye Library, Mc. Vakfiyeler No. 38.

the library, and these are indicated by the Arabic expression "again" (def'a) after the title. In the case of four books, the cataloguer is at a loss for the title of the work and has resorted to describing each of the books by their contents: "A Book Written to Condemn the Illicit Innovators" (Ehl-i bid'at ta'ni içün düzilen kitab); "An Arabic Anthology on Medicine" (Tıbdan Arabi mecmua); "A Koran with its Turkish Meaning" (Türki ma'nalu Mushaf); and "A book of Medicine Versified by Ahmedi" (Ahmedî nazmı tıb). This list also makes no attempt to classify the books either by subject or language. Similarly, there is no attempt at classification in a list of books drawn up in 1445 in the foundation deed for İshak Bey's library at Skopje.[5]

In the libraries founded after the conquest of Istanbul, the foundation deeds also have inventories. In the lists of books endowed to the four college libraries in the Fatih Complex, which were later to be united in a central library, we find inventories drawn up on the back of several of the folios of the portion of the foundation deed which has survived.[6] While the lists do not have subject headings the books are listed according to their subject: thus, the first books are Koranic commentaries, thereafter the books dealing with prophetic tradition, jurisprudence, the principles of jurisprudence, with miscellaneous books coming last. Sometime the author is given, but usually not. The number of volumes is usually noted, as well as additional descriptive information when books are incomplete. In one case, it is remarked that the book is decorated. When the four collections were united in the Fatih Mosque a new set of deeds was drawn up in which it was stipulated that the assistant librarian was to make a catalogue. However, no catalogue has survived from this period, nor is there any mention of it in the catalogue made by Hacı Hasanzade in 1561 in which two other previous catalogues are noted.

In the foundation deeds of the libraries founded by Grand Vizier Mahmud Pasha and Şeyh Vefa, we see a significant development in that books are not listed by title, but classified by subject and given a subtotal for the number of books in each classification. One must presume that there was a list of books which formed an appendix to the deeds but has been lost. These two lists are the first attempts to find subject headings in Ottoman libraries: Mahmud Pasha's deed has eleven separate headings:[7]

---

5   Hasan Kaleşi, *Najstariji vakufski dokumenti u Jugoslaviji na arapskom jeziku* (Priština: Zajednica naučnih ustanova Kosova, 1972), 99.
6   BOA, Ali Emiri Tasnifi, Fatih Devri No. 70.
7   *İVTD* 43.

Koranic commentary (*tefasir*); prophetic tradition (*ehadis*); principles of tradition (*usul-I hadis*); principles of jurisprudence (*usul-i fıkıh*); jurisprudence (*furu'-ı fıkıh*); [miscellaneous] Arabic books (*kütüb-i Arabiyye*); logic (*kütüb-i mantık*); philosophy (*kütüb-i hikmet*); astronomy (*kütüb-i hey'et*); books of narrative poetry (*kütüb-i mesnevi*); prayer books (*kütüb-i da'avat*).

Şeyh Vefa's list is somewhat more sophisticated, with nineteen headings:[8] Koran (*Kur'an-ı Kerim*); Koranic commentary (*tefasir*); Koranic recital (*kavaid-i Kur'an ve tecvid*); prophetic tradition (*hadis*); principles of jurisprudence (*usul-i fıkıh*); jurisprudence (*furu'-ı fıkıh*); mysticism *ilm-i meşayih*); semantics (*me'ani*); syntax (*nahv*); morphology (*sarf*); medicine (*tıb*); dictionaries (*lugat*); philosophy (*hikmet*); theology (*ilm-i kelam*); logic (*mantık*); astronomy (*hey'et*); poetry in Turkish and Persian (*Türkçe ve Farsça divanlar*).

The libraries founded in Edirne during the reign of Mehmed II have lists of books in the endowments register of the city, but they are merely book lists.[9]

The next example of a development towards a classified and detailed catalogue is an inventory of books in the Sadreddin Konevi dervish convent in Konya.[10] In this list, drawn in 1483, autograph manuscripts are indicated, and works of which the titles are unknown are clearly shown with the phrase "unknown" (*gayr-ı ma'lum*). In one instance, decoration is noted, with another book the calligraphic style is noted, and with another the state of binding is remarked upon.

In the foundation deed of Bayezid II's library in Edirne, we can observe, for the first time, a systematic approach to drawing up an inventory: each of the forty-two books endowed is described by its title, author, number of volumes, and number of folios, and is classified under subject headings.[11]

After the first tentative steps towards developing classified catalogues in the fifteenth century, we see sophisticated catalogues drawn up in the sixteenth century. We have three independent catalogues from this period. The earliest of these belongs to the palace library.[12] It consists of 340 folios of which the first

---

8 Istanbul Court Registers, Evkaf-ı Hümayun Muhasibliği, No. 102. 151a. For the text of this document see author's article: "Şeyh Vefa ve Vakıfları Hakkında Yeni Bir Belge," *İslam Araştırmaları Dergisi*, no. 1 (1997): 47–64.

9 BOA Tapu-Tahrir Defteri, No. 1070, 19, 220, 434–5.

10 Belediye Library, Mc. K. 116/1, 6b, 8b.

11 Belediye Library (now Atatürk Library), Mc. O. 61, 44a–b.

12 Magyar Tudomanyos Akademia Künyvtara Keleti Gyüjtment, Török F. 59. The first reference to this catalogue, that I have been able to trace, was made by E. Birnbaum in an article published in 1976: "The Ottomans and Chagatay Literature," *Central Asian Journal* 20 (1976): 165. I have made a detailed description of the catalogue in my article: "The Catalogue of Bayezid II's Palace Library," *Kütüphanecilik Dergisi, Belge Bilgi Kütüphane Araştırmaları*, no. 3 (1992): 55–66. The catalogue was the subject of an article by Miklós Maróth: "The Library of Sultan Bayezid II," in *Irano-Turkic Cultural Contacts* (2003): 111–132 and was recently published

two folios contain a list of contents followed by five folios containing a Turkish introduction which lays down the principles by which the catalogue was set out, followed by a single folio containing a preface in Arabic. There then follows the catalogue itself. On the first folio, there are two chronograms, both of which give the Islamic date as 909 [1503], the year in which the "clean copy" was completed.

Page two begins with a list of the subject headings, the first of these being a branch of Islamic Jurisprudence. It would have been far more usual to have begun with the Koran and then Koranic commentaries. However, these subjects do not appear on the content list at all. This indicates that we have one, or, more likely, two folios missing after the first page.

On page five begin the rules for the cataloguing of books in this collection, and the exceptions to these rules. It is clear that the compiler does not have access to an established tradition of cataloguing on which to fall back. We see him struggling to create a system which would not only make for some consistency, but would also serve as a guide to future librarians. The first general principle the compiler lays down is that all books dealing with a single subject should be stored together and should appear in the catalogue under the same subject heading. An exception to this is that multiple copies of books which could appear under more than one heading are to have a copy placed under each heading. The concept of cross-referencing had not yet found its way into Ottoman libraries. As an example of this problem, he cites the *Bidayetü'l-Hidaye* of el-Gazzali, which is a mystical work on Islamic law, and as such could equally be considered either a work of mysticism or a work on Islamic law. The compiler's solution is to divide the copies of this work equally between the two headings.

The compiler lays down another principle to cover the quite common case when several works are bound together. The rule he suggests is that this volume should be classified according to the work which is the most important, which he considers will be most in demand, or work that is particularly rare within its subject. An exception to this principle is the case where a single volume contains more than one work which is dominant; he leaves the classification to the arbitrary discretion of the librarian.

The rule governing the entry of the title of a book into the catalogue is based on the exact reproduction of the title as it appears on the cover of the book and/ or on the flyleaf, even though it may not be the correct or full title of the work. This rule is obviously created to facilitate the work of checking the books against

---

in its entirety: Gülru Necipoğlu, Cemal Kafadar and Cornell Fleischer (eds.), *Treasures of Knowledge: An Inventory of the Ottoman Palace Library* (1502/3-1503/4) (Leiden - Boston: Brill, 2019).

the catalogue. The importance of which the compiler attaches to this principle can be seen in the great number of examples he offers.

Books which have been catalogued are to be marked with red ink before and after the title on the flyleaf to indicate that it has been catalogued. This also serves to demarcate the title of the work as given in the catalogue from any preceding or following text.

After the rules for cataloguing are dealt with the compiler deals with the rules governing the storage of the books. Firstly, a copy of that section of the catalogue should remain in the storage depot. The valuable books should be stored separately from ordinary books, and the separate sections should be sign-posted to avoid valuable books being mixed with the ordinary books when they are taken outside to be aired and cleaned.

These rules are followed by a preface which gives a clear indication that the catalogue had been prepared in 908/1502 on the orders of Sultan Bayezid II, who had commanded the cataloguer to classify the books and to list them under separate headings according to the title written on the flyleaf and binding. The cataloguer does not give his name at the end of introduction or preface, merely referring to himself as the "one of the servants of the sultan." Fortunately, we are able to identify the cataloguer with the help of a reference made to himself in the section devoted to books on medicine.[13] He identifies three books as having been written by the humblest of the sultan's slaves, Atufî, who was also the librarian of Sultan Bayezid's library and therefore the cataloguer.[14]

In terms of the development of Ottoman librarianship and cataloguing, this catalogue is disappointing, in that it is much inferior to the catalogue of the Mehmed II's library, prepared in 1560. Under various subjects it gives only the title of the work and not always the author's name. And the cataloguer often refers to a work by its short title, which can lead to confusion with other works with the same short title, and in some cases he fails to identify the title of the work entirely and resorts to noting "a book on history" or "a book on medicine." Here it is the classification that is the overriding priority; no importance is given to the physical description of the books. The catalogue was made for the palace

---

13 My attention was drawn to this reference by Miklós Maróth's abovementioned article, 112.

14 From the catalogue we therefore learn that a scholar by the name of Atufî has been appointed to be the librarian of the Sultan Bayezid's palace library. The biographical works on the Ottoman scholars note the name of Atufî among the scholars of the period of Bayezid II's reign without making any reference to his position as librarian to the Sultan. Some archival documents, however, note that this Atufî, a librarian, was the object of the Sultan Bayezid's benificence on several occasion (Belediye Library—now Atatürk Library, Mc. O. 71, 24, 40, 449).

library, so if information was needed the right book could be found quickly. In order to ensure this, an efficient system of classification was necessary. The palace librarian's role was to identify where information could be found. This rationale is voiced in the Arabic postscript that details the aim of preparing the catalogue was to "establish the titles of the books" and to "determine the place of each book within its proper science."

However, as a list of the sultan's palace library it can offer us much useful information not only on the literary and scientific tastes of the Ottoman rulers, but also on the subsequent movement of books which were relocated from the palace library to other libraries. It also allows us to confirm the existence of certain books which no longer survive.

The second catalogue from this century belongs to the library of the mosque complex of Mehmed II, and was most probably compiled during the reign of Sultan Bayezid II by Mehemmed b. Ali Fenarî.[15] In this undated catalogue, we find an introduction which covers two folios of which the first has unfortunately become torn and the bottom half is missing. In the remaining part of the folio, the cataloguer advises the reader that it has been drawn up on the order of the reigning sultan whose specific orders were that he inspect the library which the late Sultan Mehmed II had endowed. The cataloguer has been ordered to compare the contents of the library with the existing catalogues and to establish which books were missing. After a missing section folio two begins with a discussion of how the books were to be shelved, dealing with philosophy and miscellaneous subjects. As these are the last two classifications in the catalogue, we can presume that much of the missing section on the first folio is devoted to shelving the books of the sultan on scriptural exegesis, prophetic tradition, law, and theology.

At the end of the introduction, the cataloguer advises us that he has catalogued the collection to the best of his endeavors taking care to note all the characteristics and particularities of each book. He then gives the number of books in the library as follows: 796 books donated by Mehmed II, forty-one books given as replacements by a former administrator of the endowment, Yeganoğlu, 389 books endowed by other scholars and fifteen books which were found in the library but had not been previously catalogued. The total is 1,241.

The way that entries have been drawn up suggests that the cataloguer has copied them from a previous catalogue, for whenever there is a discrepancy between the catalogue description and the cataloguer's observation it is entered as a gloss to the original entry. For example, a book on theology is

---

15 BA, D. HMH, SFTH, No. 21941/B.

entered under the section belonging to those books donated by the sultan: "*Şerh-i Metali* by Mevlana Kutbuddin, Damascene [paper], full leather binding, maroon, 222 folios." This is glossed in the same hand with the following observation: "In the previous catalogue it is written that it is a donation of the sultan but on the flyleaf of the book it is written that it is a donation of Abdülkerim."

At the end of the catalogue there are two lists, of which the first is "books which were recorded in the previous catalogue and could not be found in the library, but were recorded in the missing books list." In this list, there are fifty-seven entries, most of which are glossed with details of replacement books. The second list contains "books which were recorded in the previous catalogue, but could not be found in the library and which do not appear in the missing books list." There are eight entries in this section, two of which have a gloss added by another hand, noting that the books were found and entered into the original catalogue. Beside another entry it is recorded in the gloss that the book was lost by a certain Muhyiddin Karamani.

The method of compiling the entries in the undated catalogue is quite sophisticated. After the title of the book and the author's name, the physical description of the book is given and generally the binding is described in detail, the type of paper, sometimes the style of hand and color of inks used, the number of illuminated pages and very rarely the name of the copyist, the date of copying and whether the book was checked against other manuscripts is noted. If a book does not come within a section specifically donated by one person, then the entry will always specify who donated the book.

The third extant independent catalogue of the sixteenth century belongs also to the Fatih Mosque Library and was compiled in 1560 by a teacher of the Semaniye College within the Fatih Complex.[16] This catalogue is bound with leather spine and paper covers, measures 35x12.5 cm and consists of eighty-seven folios. The subject headings and the information pertaining to the number of folios are rubricated. In the preamble to the catalogue, the work is described in Turkish as "Register of Books" (*Kitaplar Defteri*). The Arabic introduction to the catalogue (2b–3a) which is given in full below, is in itself an important document in the history of Ottoman libraries. The compiler gives, through a progressive development, a rationale for the collection and care of books which is based on their utility as guides to man's salvation:

16 TSA, D. 9559.

In the name of God, the Merciful, the Compassionate. Praise be to God who has preserved his Great Book [the Koran] from corruption and deviation.

For as long as books smile with the tears of the pen and paper is beautified by the splendour of script, salutations to His Most Gracious Messenger who has raised his noble traditions and set them above the unreliable word and unfounded expression; and to his companions who related his traditions and struggled to keep alive his Customs.

Almighty God has ordained that the upright scholars among the community of His Beloved [Prophet] should succeed in their utmost endeavours to understand the content and meaning of His word and to penetrate the essence and spirit of the traditions of His noble Prophet. To order the affairs and decrees necessary for the community, they founded the bases of knowledge and established their proofs and they began to classify knowledge into its branches, to discover their difficulties, to build the foundations of belief and raise its structure and to fortify its walls. Thereafter they consigned knowledge to paper to establish it among the people lest it be lost. They therefore wrote books of beauty and value and produced works of simplicity and concision on every branch of the sciences of the Holy Law with its commentary, tradition and the principles and ramifications of jurisprudence, and on the branches of the Arabic literary sciences on which these are based. Following in their path, their successors completed the Palace of Knowledge on all four sides and cultivated and tended all corners of the garden of books. And thus will they continue till doomsday.

It has therefore become necessary for us to attend to the works of knowledge and to look after them, to discover them wherever they may be and to gather them, not to ignore them lest they be lost, and to endeavour always to ensure that they are read and cared for. Because this endeavour is nothing less than the preservation of Religion, it is extremely meritorious and its rewards are countless. All the faithful should desire to perform good deeds to achieve this good work and thus gain merit. Of those who are aware of the importance of this work, and are of intelligence, understanding and possessed of a brilliant mind and pure heart, one is the auspicious and martyr sultan, the

sultan son of a sultan, the son of Sultan Murad Han, Sultan
Mehmed Han – *may God bathe him in the rains of His mercy, and
place him in the Garden of Paradise.* Sultan Mehmed Han—*for
whom we pray that he may attain His mercy and that his life in the
Hereafter may be even more glorious than in this transient world –*
had great respect for the requisites of religion and boundless zeal
in the preservation of the principles of the way of our Prophet—
*salutations to him and to his family and companions who adhered
to the Holy Koran.*

Thus did he collect many rare works and valuable books, in a
way that few are privileged to do, and placed them in the library
of the mosque which he built in Istanbul, and endowed them to
the Semaniye College which he had also built, and the likes of
which had not been seen up to that time. And some beneficent
persons who were desirous of following in the path of the sultan,
the deeds of whom are meritorious and praiseworthy, placed, in
order to share the merit in the next world, their books in this
library.

Thus did the number of the books become greater, and thus
was the benefit to the people increased. The books were given
into the care of officials who were charged by order of the sultan
to preserve, inspect and supervise them within the confines of
the library, in return for a stipend. Each of these officials spent
a portion of their life in this duty until it devolved to a certain
Molla Arab called Hacı Mehmed.[17] He too spent time in this
duty. Later when he had to abandon this work and enter the
hereafter, the duty of inspection and examination of the books
was entrusted to me by the order of the sultan whose word is law.
I accepted this duty, and coming to the library I began to inspect
the books, each one individually, even their chapter headings
and subsections. To the best of my ability, I established the titles

---

17 About Hacı Mehmed (Molla Arab) we have incidental information in the biography of his
son Sabri, a poet, whose career is summarized in Aşık Çelebi's work the *Meşa'irü'ş-şu'ara*, a
compendium of biographies of Ottoman poets. There it is mentioned "Sabri, son of Molla
Arab, the librarian of the Fatih Mosque, worked as an accountant in Baghdad for twenty years,
went to Istanbul, but not receiving the due that he felt he deserved, sold all his belongings and
returned once more to Baghdad, taking his father with him." Aşık Çelebi, *Meşa'irü'ş-şu'ara*, ed.
G. M. Owens (London: E. J. W. Gibb Memorial, 1971), 217. Here we have one of the earliest
references to a librarian within the Ottoman educational system. Unfortunately, his catalogue
has not survived.

and authors and made the necessary corrections. Thus they were rearranged in perfect order.

Two catalogues, the one compiled by one known as Şah Çelebi ibnü'l-Fenari[18] who was assigned to the inspection of the books, the other prepared by the above-mentioned librarian of the books, in order that the books may more easily be preserved, were collated with the books in the library and in the hands of the readers, and they were all found to tally. Thus the librarian had done his duty and acquitted himself.

I was, for my part, now ordered to prepare a new catalogue which would represent the books as they are to be found in the library, that it too may be placed in his library. In preparing this catalogue I preferred and followed the system of Hacı Mehmed, where the arrangement was more satisfactory and more accessible than the system employed in the first catalogue.

Aid and success is from God alone. Only He can direct us in the true way and in the path of righteousness.

Mehmed bin Hızır bin el-hac Hasan, a teacher in one of the Semaniye Colleges, entrusted with the inspection of these books.

In the first part of the catalogue, we find bibliographical descriptions of the 839 books endowed by Fatih Sultan Mehmed. In the second part are listed the books donated by various individuals.[19] The third part is devoted to those collections endowed by Şeyhzade and Halebizade. The total number of books in the catalogue is 1,770.

In each of these three parts, the books are classified under separate subject headings. In the first part, they are: Koranic commentary, prophetic tradition, jurisprudence, principles of jurisprudence, Arabic works, logic, miscellaneous works, medicine. In the second part, two new headings, mysticism and philosophy, are added, while in the third part, there are more headings introduced to cover the larger variety of subjects which include history, poetry, Persian and Turkish books, and so forth. When classifying

---

18 Taşköprizade, *eş-Şeka'ikü'n-Nu'maniyye*, 382–383.
19 The names of individuals who endowed books to Fatih library are: Kabilizade; Kadızade; Hatibzade; Alaiyelü Muhyiddin; Tuzlahoğlu; Silahdarbaşı; Hasan Pasha; Sultan Hatun; Bezirganzade; Musannifek; Mişeved Acem; Kırk Kiliselüoğlu; Mahbub Çelebi; Hüsam b. İbrahim; Güngörmez Acem; Baba Ali; Hatib-i Antalya; Fazlullah Pasha; el-Hac Hasanzade; Ahmed Kabili; Aşık Nureddin.

the book, Hacı Hasanzade adopted the policy of introducing a subject only if there were enough books on that subject to warrant a separate heading. In the first part, for example, the books on history, mysticism, astronomy, literature, and geometry are lumped together as miscellaneous (38b–39b). However, in the third part, as Halebizade's endowment was rich in history and poetry, he introduces separate subject headings for those books (81b–82a), but even in this part there are books under the heading of "miscellaneous" or "Turkish and Persian," to cover books which did not fit under the established headings.

This catalogue is written in both Arabic and Turkish. The introduction is in Arabic, but the entries are either in Arabic or Turkish. This is certainly the best catalogue surviving from the sixteenth and seventeenth centuries. The books are described in detail and the author is careful to correct any error that has crept into previous catalogues, as for example, in the following entry:

> The second volume of the *Koranic Commentary of Ayasuliği*. But in the old catalogue it is described as an unknown commentary. However a note inscribed on the flyleaf names it as the *Commentary of Ayasuliği*. (7b)

After the title and author, the physical characteristics of the book are described in great detail. In general, he notes the type of paper and its color, the description of the binding, the type of calligraphy, the color of the inks, and ornamentation and illustrations. He also gives the name of the calligrapher or scribe, when known, sometimes the date, time and/or place of copying if known. Also noted is the original or other manuscript from which it was copied or with which it was checked, as well as the number of folios and the name of the donor. The following entry is not unusual:

> *The Koranic Commentary of Beyzavi*: all Damascene [paper] bound in full red leather, decorated with ornamentation. The following sentence is in white lead: "Opening chapter of the book, of seven verses [revealed in] Mecca." The noble *Besmele* (i.e., the formula "In the Name of God most Gracious most Merciful") in gold. The first two pages with gold margins. Also, a *tezhib* (ornamentation) at the top of Maryam chapter. The first half of the Koran in *celi* calligraphy. Ink sometimes red sometimes black, but in second half all red. At the end of the book: imperial seal. Imperial endowment. 510 folios (5a).

We can see from the entries that he did not rely on previous catalogues for the number of folios, preferring to count the folios himself:

> The book of commentary, the *Miftah* of Seyyid Şerif: In the old catalogue it is described as having 179 folios but it is found to have 144. After the first folio three and a half fascicles are missing. (34a)

When describing calligraphy, he uses the following phrases: "written in a good hand," "in a large hand," "in *kufi* script," "written in *sülüs* [script]," "written in *nesh* [script]."

Hacı Hasanzade sometimes quotes notes on the flyleaf or in the colophon, or information on the endowment when he thinks it is of interest. When describing a book entitled *Muğni* he quotes a couplet on the flyleaf. When describing a commentary entitled *Keşşaf* he quotes the collation notice thus "it is written at the end, it is collated and corrected, from beginning to end, with the autograph copy by Şemseddin bin Ahmed" (14a).

He sometimes quotes colophons as in the case of work copied by the famous scholar Musannifek in Herat, where he gives the whole lengthy colophon verbatim (61a).

Sometimes interesting endowment records are described at length, as for example in the following excerpt from the entry for Beyzavi's commentary:

> The date of the endowment is the beginning of Zilhicce of 940 (June 1534). Librarian Mehmed noted in his catalogue that this book reached him through Kara Mehmed Çelebi, a scholar, on 24 Rebiülevvel 952 (May 1545). (66a)

In his description of the *Divan of Mütenebbi*, he notes that it had been endowed by the famous scholar Sa'deddin Teftazani and he quotes the endowment seal "Endowed by Ahmed bin Yahya bin Sa'deddin Teftazani for the use of the students in the hope of their intercession with the Master of the Prophets." Hacı Hasanzade adds that "as the book was able to reach an endowment library, it must have been endowed with a pure heart" (82a).

When describing missing portions from the beginning of a work he gives the first sentence of the remaining folios. When dealing with biographical encyclopedias in more than one volume he gives the breakdown of the contents of each volume alphabetically: "The second volume of Ibn Hallikan's *History* begins at the letter '*ayn* and ends with the beginning of letter *mim,* the last entry being Malik bin Enes."

With collections of treatises, he gives the title and author. Hacı Hasanzade, realizing that this catalogue would be used to draw up inventories in the future adds notes about books which have been lost, the name of the person responsible for the loss and the books accepted in their place.[20]

The main difference in the entries between the catalogues of the library of the mosque of Mehmed II and the catalogue of the palace library is that in the catalogues of the mosque library attention is given to physically describing the book while in that of the palace library it is the contents of the book which is of foremost interest. This is because the mosque library was a lending library dealing exclusively in manuscripts. In order to establish that a book which was lent out was not replaced by an inferior copy, physical description was essential. There was no such danger in the palace library as access to it was very much restricted to palace personnel.

These three catalogues are of great importance in the history of Ottoman libraries. We can observe librarians in the mid-sixteenth century attempting to make some theoretical sense of the corpus of knowledge in their care. Knowledge is classified, but when books do not easily fit into these categories pragmatic solutions are applied and formulated into rules. In these catalogues, the raison d'être for libraries is formulated, an attempt at cataloguing rules and a uniformity of catalogue entries was made. These would become the established form for successive centuries.

From the second half of the sixteenth century onwards, there is an improvement in the quality of the bibliographical descriptions and classification of the books listed as appendices to the endowment deeds. Thus we see in the list of books endowed by İsmihan Sultan, the daughter of Sultan Selim II, a Koran which is described as follows: "Holy Koran: Large size. 15 lines. First 2 lines written in *reyhani* [script] in gold, remainder in *nesh*. Paper is *devlet-abadi*. Binding: black and ornamented."[21]

When Sultan Selim II endowed a library to his complex in Edirne, he ordered the preparation of a catalogue of the books which were to be taken from the palace treasury and which would form the founder collection of his endowment. At the beginning of this catalogue, the list is referred to by the word *defter*, which is, in the context of the Ottoman libraries, the conventional term for the catalogue.[22] In terms of subject headings, we see an interesting development; a subheading is introduced within the main heading of jurisprudence to cover

---

20 TSA, D. 9559, 15b, 19a, 23a, 38b, 39b, 50a, 51a, 54a.
21 VGMA, No. 572, 147.
22 VGMA, No. 1395, 91.

fetvas (collections of legal opinions).[23] However, in the description of the works, this catalogue follows the practice adopted by the Fatih and İsmihan Sultan catalogues.

In all three of the above catalogues, considerable emphasis is placed on the outward appearance of books. This is precisely to avoid fraudulent substitution, as we discover from some endowment deeds; for example, İsmihan Sultan's deed stipulates that should a binding require repair or renewal, the new binding is to be exactly as the old, in order to prevent deception.[24]

We see a preoccupation with the physical characteristics of the works in the catalogue for Pertev Pasha's library in İzmit. A typical entry in the catalogue reads thus:

> Koranic Commentary: *Tefsir-i Kebir.* 2 volumes. Large size. Calligraphy: small Arab *nesh.* Margins in gold. Written in black ink. Bindings: red decorated with large golden rosette embossed, edges bearing small rosettes.[25]

Although there is no development in the method of describing books in the list appended to the foundation deeds in the seventeenth century, there is a general tendency to proliferate headings and introduce subheadings as the collections grew larger. In the catalogue of Feyzullah Efendi's library in Istanbul, for example, we see subheadings under Koranic commentary and prophetic tradition to separate the supercommentaries (*şerh*) and glosses (*haşiye*). In the heading for history and biographies of the Prophet (*tarih ve siyer*), there is a subheading for the "[Biographical Dictionaries of] the Names of Men [which occur] in prophetic tradition" (*esami-i rical-i hadis*).[26] Another device introduced by this catalogue is a subheading entitled "What is appropriate to it" (*ve-ma yünasibuha*) to include books which are on subjects similar to the subject of the main heading when it is not certain that they should be included under that heading.[27] Books which did not easily fit under a particular heading are lumped together at the end as "miscellaneous."

In the eighteenth century, it is common to find a separate catalogue apart from the list appended to the foundation deeds. The description of the books is no better, if not worse, than their counterpart in previous centuries, but there is

---

23 VGMA, No. 1395, 101.
24 VGMA, No. 572, 147.
25 Beyazıt Umumi Library, No. 5157, 65a.
26 Millet Library, Feyzullah Efendi Section, No. 2196, 11b, 25b, 32b.
27 Millet Library, Feyzullah Efendi Section, No. 2196, 75b, 84b.

a further proliferation of headings and subheadings. However, while previously there may have been a certain consensus as to what the basic headings should be, with the expansion of the collections, librarians were often at a loss to find appropriate headings for books, and we see the arbitrary introduction of new headings which were peculiar to a particular library. For example, in Turhan Valide Sultan's library in Istanbul the catalogue separates history and biographies of the Prophet into separate subjects, which are otherwise conventionally kept under the same heading. Likewise a separate heading is made for Eulogies where one would normally expect to find them under literature.[28] In Sultan Ahmed III's library in Yeni Cami in Istanbul, there is a separate heading for accounting.[29]

The catalogues drawn up for the endowments made by Sultan Mahmud I to Ayasofya, the Fatih Mosque and Galata Palace bear a marked degree of uniformity, not only in their physical appearance, but more importantly in the method of describing the books and to some extent in the establishment of subjects headings. However, in the assignment of books to their subjects there are many discrepancies, which would suggest that the librarians were often at a loss to decide the appropriate heading for certain books. In Ayasofya Library, for example, the *Nefehatü'l-Üns*, a work of hagiography is under the heading mysticism while the *Tezkiretü'l-Evliya*, the lives of the saints, is placed under history.[30] All works on geography are also placed under history, as there was no separate heading for these books. In the Fatih catalogue, there is a subheading for Koranic recital under the main heading for Koranic commentary. Also some Turkish works of literature and some works, such as the *Kavaninü's-Sultaniyye* (a collection of imperial decrees) and the *Keşfü'z-Zünun* (a bibliographical dictionary), which do not easily fit under the established headings, are placed under a new heading "*Muhazarat*" (literary anecdotes).

In as far as the subject headings employed by the three libraries are concerned, they are more or less similar, with, however, exceptions which reflect the strengths and weaknesses of the individual collections. Galata Palace Library, for example, being established for the education of the Palace and the administrative personnel of the empire, was strong in the certain subjects, such as grammar and its commentaries, books of poetry, and histories. As we will see below, the library of this school was rather unusual in that the school did not teach the standard classical curriculum taught in the numerous colleges of the city, nor did it house works which were predominantly on mysticism, as

---

28 Türk-Islam Eserleri Museum, No. 2218.
29 Süleymaniye Library, Yazma Bağışlar Section, No. 2742.
30 Süleymaniye Library, Ayasofya Section, No. 1.

did the dervish convent libraries; rather it was a library intended for students who would serve the palace, and as such had to be familiar with all branches of knowledge. This library therefore became the repository for books which would not easily fit within the confines of a classical college library, and we consequently see that the cataloguers often found difficulty in placing certain books under appropriate headings. Thus we see *Usulu'l-Hikem*, a book on statecraft, the *Acayibü'l-Mahlukat*, a book of cosmogony, and a *Kanunname*, a codification of law, placed in the section on literature, while we see classical literary works of a narrative nature placed in the history section. We also see the *Kesfü'z-Zünun* and *Mevzuatü'l-Ulum*, both books of bibliography, placed under history, probably for lack of any better heading.

According to notes written on these three catalogues, they were drawn up when the libraries were endowed. A summary catalogue belonging to Ayasofya Library, refers to these catalogues as the "base catalogue."[31] The "tally signs" which can be found at the end of each entry would suggest that they were indeed used as an inventory at the subsequent inspections.

Mahmud I also endowed a fourth library in Istanbul, but due to his death it became his brother Osman III's endowment, and was consequently named Nuruosmaniye. The cataloguer of this collection was particularly careful in his descriptions. He invariably noted the calligraphic style of the books, sometimes the language of the text and with multivolume books not only noted the number of volumes, but included the last and first lines of each volume.[32] He also introduced a new subject heading entitled "Aspects" (*Vücuh*) which included books dealing with the various manners of reciting the Koran. However, in some areas this catalogue is deficient, as, for instance, when dealing with collections of treatises which are lumped together under one heading (Collections of Treatises) rather than according to their appropriate subject heading. Furthermore, when describing a collection, he often names only the first and last treatise, and in some cases only the first. Sometimes multiple copies are not placed together as we see in the case of İdris Bidlisi's Ottoman history, the *Heşt Bihişt*, four copies of which are together, with a further copy entitled *Kitabu Tarih-i İdris-i Bidlisi* placed separately. It would appear that the major difficulty facing this cataloguer too, was assigning books to their appropriate headings, especially books on history, literature and mysticism which often acted as catch-all for books which should have had a separate heading. Geography books, we find under History, books on ethics are placed under mysticism, and, books on

31 TSA, D. 3312, 16a.
32 Nuruosmaniye Library, No. 1.

music under astronomy.[33] We again see two famous bibliographical works, the *Keşfü'z-Zünun* and *Mevzuatü'l-'ulum* placed under History, which would suggest that the cataloguer was relying on a precedent set by Galata Palace Library.

In the libraries founded in the second half of the eighteenth century, we see some developments in the establishment of headings and their order. In Ragıb Pasha's library in Istanbul, Koranic commentary has three subheadings, the first devoted to the famous commentary by Zemahşeri, the *Keşşaf* and its supercommentaries, the second to the commentary of Beyzavi and its supercommentaries, and a further subheading devoted to aspects of methodology of commentary.[34] Having thus created three new subheadings the cataloguer then lumps the following headings together: logic, philosophy, astronomy, geometry, and arithmetic. It seems quite clear that a classification system was not imposed on the collection, rather the nature of collection itself, and sometimes the cataloguer's own particular interest, determined the subject headings. In the Bostancılar Ocağı Library catalogue, we see many idiosyncrasies in the subject headings as for example, a separate heading for *Divan*s (collections of a poets' works) to accommodate the numerous works of this nature.[35] The Çelebi Abdullah Library collection had subject headings for prosody, doctrine, litanies, and so on, which appear in no other catalogue.[36] The compiler of this catalogue found an ingenious device for placing difficult works: he established a heading entitled "Important Books" (*kütüb-i mu'tebere*) under which he listed all his *miscellanea*.

As we have seen, apart from the catalogues drawn up at the time of the endowment, further catalogues were made after inspections. We have inspection catalogues for many libraries. These catalogues generally reflect the organization and descriptions of the foundation catalogue and it is only in the counting of folios and lines to a folio that we see particular care taken. In an inspection catalogue made for Damad İbrahim Pasha's college library in 1820, we observe that the books are divided into two separate sections. The first includes the valuable books endowed, while the second is entitled "Books for the Use of Students." In an inspection catalogue of 1830 for the Fatih Library,[37]

---

33 The classification of music under astronomy is not as strange as it may seem to the Western reader. In the Islamic world of science, music was treated under mathematics which includes astronomy. See: Nesrin Feyzioğlu, "Müzik Malzemesinin Oluşum ve Biçimlenmesinde Matematiğin Rolü," *Güzel Sanatlar Enstitüsü Dergisi*, no. 13 (2004): 95–104.

34 TSA, D. 3307.

35 TSA, D. 3305.

36 Süleymaniye Library, Yazma Bağışlar Section, No. 2277.

37 Süleymaniye Library, Yazma Bağışlar Section, No. 243.

there are numbers placed after each entry, the purpose of which was probably to indicate the location of books on the shelf. Although it is not certain when these numbers were assigned to the books – possibly at a later date—it is clear that this catalogue was used by the librarian to locate books.

Inspection catalogues were invariably drawn up when a collection was moved from one library to another, as, for example when the books endowed by Rabia Hatun to Ayasofya were taken to Beşir Ağa's college in Eyüp,[38] when the Galata Palace collection was split up and sent to the Ayasofya and Fatih Libraries,[39] when Sultan Mustafa III's collection in Bostancılar Ocağı Library was sent to his college in Laleli,[40] and when Taşköprüzade İbrahim Efendi's books, together with some small collections were taken from the Fatih Mosque and sent to Veliyüddin Efendi's library.[41]

The catalogue prepared during the transfer of Sultan Mustafa III's books from Bostancılar Ocağı to Laleli College is one of the less well-organized catalogues to survive. It bears all the hallmarks of a rushed job. The same subject headings are repeated as for example at the beginning of the catalogue we have Koranic commentary (*Tefsir*) and some folios later continuation of Koranic commentary (*Zeyl-i Tefsir*). Although many subject headings are employed, the cataloguer still has difficulty in assigning books to their appropriate heading, and we observe for the first time the heading entitled "Books of the Various Sciences" and "Books which may be Assigned to Several Branches of Science." The three entries under this heading are the *Mevzu'atu'l-Ulum*, the *Keşfü'z-Zünun* and the *Netayicü'l-Fünun*, which would seem to indicate that works of a bibliographical or encyclopaedic in nature were still without an appropriate heading. At the end of the catalogue, we have a work about the mystical order of *Hurufi*s, entitled *Cavidanname*, which had a heading all to itself; this heading is entitled "Books of which their Branch of Science is Not Known."[42]

At the beginning of the nineteenth century we find catalogues drawn up as a summary, with title and sometimes author.[43] These were often described as a "Handbook" (*El defteri*) and under each entry was a location number. It is clear that they were intended to be consulted by the reader.

By the time we reach the end of the eighteenth and beginning of the nineteenth century we find some extremely well-prepared catalogues. Although great pains

---

38 VGMA, No. 638, 187.
39 Süleymaniye Library, Ayasofya Section, No. 6.
40 VGMA, No. 642, 103–145.
41 Beyazıt Umumi Library, Veliyüddin Efendi Section, No. 3291.
42 VGMA, No. 642, 136–138; 144.
43 Süleymaniye Library, Yazma Bağışlar Section, No. 252, 2721, 2740, 2744.

were taken to make the entries consistent and informative, the subject headings and classification of the books are still deficient. In Halet Efendi's library, for example, the geographical works are still classified under History, book on mathematics and astronomy are assigned to philosophy, and the bibliographic *Keşfü'z-Zünun* is again placed under literature.[44] In the Nakşibendi convent library in Selimiye, the catalogue is similar to others except in one regard: the books of collected treatises are classified under the heading "Collections" and thereafter each book is given its entry and each treatise within the book is given an independent entry.[45]

All the catalogues prepared for Ottoman libraries were subject catalogues, which adhered to a basic pattern with variations. Exceptions to this general rule are the catalogues of some private libraries of the sixteenth century, one of which classified according to language,[46] another according to authors[47] and some specialized collections which have unusual systems of classifications.[48] These exceptions apart, all library catalogues had subject headings for Koranic commentary, prophetic tradition, jurisprudence, and theology. Other subject headings were added according to the strengths and weaknesses of the particular collection or, indeed, according to the cataloguer's own interest or background. Although there was a general increase in subject headings from the beginning of the eighteenth century, they remained inadequate to cover all works and the cataloguers were constantly at a loss to assign all their books appropriately.

However, the deficiencies in the catalogues do not stem solely from an inadequate number of headings, for we can often observe copies of the same work under different headings. The reason lies in the background of most cataloguers who had received a classical Islamic education which more than adequately prepared them for handling college textbooks in commentary, prophetic tradition, theology, and Islamic law, but often left them unable to recognize works of history, bibliography, literature, and so on. The librarian also wanted duplicate copies to be under as many headings as possible to allow it to be found more easily. However badly classified the collections may have been, the reader was probably able to have access to all the books without difficulty. As few libraries had more than two to three thousand books it is more than likely that the librarian was able to remember all the titles in his collection. The function of the catalogue was to serve as a basis for taking inventories. It is only

---

44 Süleymaniye Library, Halet Efendi Section, No. 838.
45 Süleymaniye Library, Yazma Bağışlar Section, No. 2431
46 TSA, D. 9710.
47 TSA, D. 9940.
48 TSA, D. 9710.

as collections grew larger that catalogues were prepared so that librarian and indeed perhaps even the reader, could check the availability of a particular title.

The catalogue prepared at the time of endowment was usually drawn up by a scholar at the behest of the founder.[49] By the middle of the eighteenth century the job of drawing up a catalogue, when required, usually went to the assistant librarian, but it is probable that the librarian would have helped him in this duty. The supervisor, the administer, the inspector, and the secretary of the foundation were also involved in compiling an inspection catalogue.

In the middle of the nineteenth century, the Ottoman Empire witnessed a process of reform and restructuring which pervaded all areas of life, not least of all education. As Istanbul was already well furnished with books covering all sorts of subjects, it was natural that an attempt would be made to make these works more accessible to the readers. The most important single facility was a union catalogue of the Istanbul libraries.[50] The first attempt to list all the Istanbul library books in one catalogue was made by Ali Fethi Bey. Between 1850 and 1854, he put together a classified list of all works in forty-six foundation libraries in Istanbul, under fourteen subject headings.[51] His two-volume work *el-Asarü'l-Aliyye fi Haza'ini'l-Kütübi'l-Osmaniyye* took four and half years to compile, at the end of which he submitted his work to the sultan. However, for whatever reason, it was never published and remains in manuscript form in two copies.[52] Although this first attempt at compiling a union catalogue of works in the Istanbul libraries has been deemed praiseworthy by several scholars, in

---

49 VGMA, No. 188, 388; No. 731, 750; No. 759, 90; No. 730, 86; No. 742, 66; No. 630, 889–891; No. 629, 37–40; No. 743, 80–92; No. 624, 4–5.

50 For a survey of the work of cataloguing in this period see: R. Tuba Çavdar, "Tanzimat'tan Cumhuriyete Kadar Osmanlı Kütüphanelerinin Gelişimi" (PhD diss., Istanbul University, 1995), 93–100 and Necmettin Sefercioğlu, "Union Catalogs in Turkey in the Nineteenth Century," in *Ankara Üniversitesi, Dil ve Tarih-Coğrafya Fakültesi Kütüphanecilik Bölümü XXV. Yıl Anı Kitabı (1954–55/1979–1980)* (Ankara: Ankara Üniversitesi Basımevi, 1981), 91–93.

51 Ali Fethi Bey provides an introduction in which he gives the classification of subject headings and instructs the reader on how to find a given work. This introduction has been transcribed by Özer Soysal in his habilitation thesis: "Cumhuriyet Öncesi Dönem Türk Kütüphaneciliği: Sosyo-Ekonomik Yapı Üzerine Bir Araştırma" (Ankara University, 1973), 114–118.

52 For documents on the subject, see İsmail E. Erünsal, *Kütüphanecilikle İlgili Osmanlıca Metinler ve Belgeler*, vol. 1 (İstanbul: Edebiyat Fakültesi Matbaası, 1983), 382–386, *Kütüphanecilikle İlgili Osmanlıca Metinler ve Belgeler*, vol. 2 (İstanbul: Edebiyat Fakültesi Matbaası, 1990), 371–372. As Tuba Çavdar points out, the two volumes do not contain the whole work; from the above documents we learn that the two volumes were presented as an indication of what the larger finished work would be like. However, some scholars refer to the work as having been completed, see: Tekin Aybaş, *Toplu Kataloglar ve Türkiye Uygulaması* (Ankara: TÜRDOK, 1979), 35–37. For the location of copies of this work, see Ali Birinci, "Abdurrahman Nacim," *Müteferrika*, no. 8–9 (1996): 114.

fact the work was flawed in several respects: firstly the alphabetical listing of books came within each subject heading, so that to find a book one had to know under what subject heading it was placed. Secondly, Ali Fethi Bey indicates in which library a book was to be found, but does not give the location number of the book. Thirdly, the bibliographical references have little consistency, and the author's name is sometimes not given, and finally, there are inconsistencies in establishing headings and subheadings in the classification.

A second attempt was made, probably a quarter of a century later. This time the work was published in 552 pages. However, the catalogue bears no date and no mention of an author. One suggestion is that the author was Abdurrahman Nacim Efendi, who was the inspector of Istanbul libraries between 1861 and 1870 and was responsible for drawing up catalogues for the Ragıb Pasha and Damad İbrahim Pasha Libraries. Curiously enough, only one copy of this printed work has survived to this day.[53] The main improvement in this catalogue was that it provided the location number of the books in the libraries. However, once again the books are listed alphabetically under each subject heading, and for some reason this work included books from only twenty-four of the Istanbul libraries.

During the reign of Abdülhamid II (1876–1908), under the minister of education, Münif Pasha, an attempt was made to publish catalogues for all the Istanbul libraries. In a twelve-year period starting from 1884, the catalogues of sixty-seven libraries in Istanbul were published in 40 volumes. While it was worthwhile having printed catalogues to increase access to these libraries, the catalogues are quite disappointing in their organization. Apart from providing the location number of the books, the printed catalogue makes no improvement on the previous manuscript catalogues and in respect of the physical description of the works is a good deal inferior to the first independent catalogue, drawn up 370 years before. However, for lack of anything better, they continued to be used in manuscript libraries until card catalogues were introduced in the 1940s.

It is evident that these printed catalogues and the organization of Istanbul libraries were perceived as inadequate; the Grand Vizier Hüseyin Hilmi Pasha invited Ahmed Zeki Pasha from Egypt to evaluate and report on the state of the Istanbul libraries. Ahmed Zeki Pasha was known to be a specialist in bibliography and had played a part in organizing the Egyptian libraries. In 1909, he submitted a twenty-seven-page report in which he noted the many deficiencies in the way

---

53 Osman Ergin claims to have the only copy of this work and scholars use a microfilm of Osman Ergin's copy which is kept in the Süleymaniye Library.

the libraries were run.[54] He also remarked on the inadequacy of the existing printed catalogues and the desperate need for a comprehensive union catalogue with proper indexes.[55] Probably in response to this report, Hayri Efendi, the minister of endowments, and Muhtar Bey, the inspector of the libraries, instructed Ebu'l-Hayr Efendi to begin the work of drawing up a union catalogue in the style of that which had been done for the Egyptian libraries. He began this huge task, and in 1915 he was able to present the first fascicle in printed form to the Ministry of Endowments. This catalogue was to be prepared in alphabetical order according to the title of the work, with information on both the work and the author and the location number of all copies in the libraries and discrepancies between copies in terms of title and attribution of authorship. From the one fascicle available, it is apparent that it would have been a very useful and user-friendly work of reference. However, with the departure of Hayri Efendi from the Ministry of Endowments interest in the project probably waned and the outbreak of the First World War put an end to what would have been a very laudable project.

While the bulk of the books in the Ottoman Empire were in Istanbul, there were, however, many provinces with a concentration of libraries, such as Bursa and Konya. In the 1874 almanac for Konya, there is in the form of an appendix, a list of the contents of the twenty libraries in the city. In the 1887 almanac for Bursa, there is also a list of contents of all the libraries. Both lists are set out very much in the same style that was adopted by Ali Fethi Bey, making them of some limited use.

After this, no attempts were made to compile a union catalogue. This was because the traditional libraries were becoming increasingly irrelevant in the face of the modern libraries. The need for a union catalogue became increasingly less pressing with the passage of time.

---

54 In fact, Ahmad Faris al-Shidyaq (d. 1887), a Lebanese writer, journalist and intellectual, having had difficulties in using Istanbul libraries, made the same sort of criticisms. See: Geoffrey Roper's excellent article "Ahmad Faris al-Shidyaq and the Libraries of Europe and the Ottoman Empire," *Libraries & Culture* 33, no. 3 (Summer 1998): 233–248.

55 For the text of this report see: İsmail E. Erünsal, *Kütüphanecilikle İlgili Osmanlıca Metinler ve Belgeler* (İstanbul: Edebiyat Fakültesi Matbaası, 1982), 323–352.

Chapter Nine

Services Offered

Days and Times of Opening

Before the emergence of the independent library in the seventeenth century, Ottoman libraries, which were founded in colleges and mosques usually lent books to their reader, as established in previous chapters. However, from the beginning of the seventeenth century, there was a general trend against the practice of lending books. It became more usual to require the reader to consult the book within the library or building in which the library was situated. Thus, we find that in the earlier foundation deeds little, if any, mention is made of the times of opening while later on, when lending was usually more restricted, it became common for the founder to specify the hours and days during which the library should remain open.

In the library founded by the Chief Mufti Zekeriyya Efendi in 1594, the endowment deed specified that the library should be open two days a week, to allow students to borrow and return books.[1] In the deed for the library endowed to his college (1670), Abbas Ağa required the librarians to keep the library open on Fridays and Tuesdays.[2] These were usually the days on which college students

---

1   VGMA, No. 571, 165.
2   Istanbul Court Registers, Evkaf-ı Hümayun Müfettişliği No. 63, 18.

had no classes, and it was presumably the founder's intention that the students should spend these days in the library, which did not provide lending facilities.

The Köprülü, the first of the independent Ottoman libraries, founded in 1678 had a policy of restricted lending, and was open three days a week. The hours of opening were from sunrise to just before the mid-afternoon prayer.[3] From the end of the seventeenth century to the beginning of the eighteenth century, libraries generally were open on two or three days a week. Towards the middle of the eighteenth century, however, there was a trend to increase the days of opening. While Nevşehirli Damad İbrahim Pasha's and Sultan Mahmud I's libraries remained open three days, the library of Şerif Halil Pasha opened four days,[4] and Ahmed Pasha's college library in Urfa[5] and Hüseyin Ağa's mosque library in Bursa opened five days a week. The latter founder was rather specific in his requirements on opening, stipulating in the deed that the library should be open five days a week from sunrise till mid-afternoon "even if not one reader was to come to request a book in the space of a year."[6] This particular emphasis was to obviate any excuse on the part of the librarian for closing the library due to lack of demand.

Hacı Beşir Ağa, when he founded his college library in Eyüp in 1735, stipulated that books should not be taken out of the reading room, but that the library should be open throughout the whole week. The problem of staffing the library and allowing for the librarians' holidays[7] was met by requiring that the second and third librarian should be students of the college where they also resided.[8] Arpa Emini Ali Ağa also provided for his library to be open seven days a week and stipulated that the two librarians should be in attendance on alternate days.[9]

In the eighteenth century, the founders not only specified days of opening, but were careful to stipulate hours of opening as well. Generally, opening hours were regulated by the sun, so that the libraries were generally open longer in summer than in winter. They usually opened one hour after the sunrise and closed either before the mid-afternoon prayer or one hour before sunset. In one library in Bursa, an attempt was made to even out to some degree the discrepancy between summer and winter opening times by having the library open its doors

---

3 Köprülü Library No. 4, 42.
4 VGMA, No. 38, 90, Kasa 47, 15, No. 737, 117.
5 VGMA, No. 737, 213.
6 VGMA, No. 579, 41–42.
7 VGMA, No. 579, 42.
8 VGMA, No. 736, 4.
9 İstanbul Court Registers, Evkaf-ı Hümayun Müfettişliği No. 171, f. 10a.

two hours after sunrise in summer and only one hour after sunrise in winter.[10] No particular reason is suggested for the practice of opening libraries at these times, but it is clear that the requirements of natural lighting must have been pre-eminent. Although in some libraries the provision of lamps is specified it was probably felt that they were undesirable as the lamp soot from the oil could have damaged the books.

Libraries founded at the end of the eighteenth and throughout the nineteenth centuries generally opened five or six days a week from one hour after sunrise to one hour before sunset. Libraries founded by Ragıb Pasha (1763), Veliyüddin Efendi (1769), Rodosi Ahmed Ağa (1793), Yusuf Ağa (1794), Kılıç Ali Pasha (1801) Vahid Pasha (1811), and Saffeti Pasha's Library in the Nakşibendi convent in Cağaloğlu (1845)[11] were closed on Friday.[12] On the other hand the libraries founded by Raşid Efendi (1797), Aşir Efendi (1800), and Kavalalı Mehmed Ali Pasha (1813) were closed on Tuesdays and Fridays.[13] Some founders included unusual provisions for the opening times of their libraries: Ahmed Efendi, when founding his library (1775) in the Yakup Bey Mosque in İzmir, specified that his library should be open every day in the month of Ramazan, which was not only the holy month during which Muslims fast, but was often a month in which many people did not carry on their normal occupations, and thus had time to read.[14] Hasan Efendi founded a library (1825) in the Cedide Mehmed Efendi College in Istanbul and specified Fridays and Tuesdays as the days on which the library should be kept open. However, he also included a clause which provided for the library to be opened on other days should there be a demand for it.[15] In the library of Hafız Mustafa Pasha in Arapgir (1774), it was the librarian who determined which days of the week it should close.[16]

It is always difficult to determine to what extent the wishes of the founder as expressed in the foundation deed were being carried out in respect of opening hours. However, in the absence of complaints or any other evidence it is fair to assume that the librarians kept the libraries open for the period stipulated

---

10 VGMA, No. 579, 41.

11 VGMA, No. 581/2, 277–278.

12 VGMA, No. 82, 6, No. 745; 80, No. 743, 93; Müjgan Cunbur, "Yusuf Ağa Kütüphanesi ve Kütüphane Vakfiyesi," TAD 1, no. 1 (1963): 214; Süleymaniye Library, Kılıç Ali Paşa No. 1049/l, 10; VGMA, No. 579, 702 respectively.

13 VGMA, No. 579, 67; No. 580, 275; Süleymaniye Library, Aşir Efendi No. 473, 9.

14 VGMA, No. 744, 59.

15 Istanbul Court Registers, Davud Paşa Mahkemesi No. 95, 85.

16 TSA, E. 137/44.

in the foundation deeds,[17] though from the middle of the nineteenth century complaints about libraries not opening regularly began to increase rising to a crescendo just before the First World War.

The Reading Room

As the libraries ceased to lend books and functioned as independent institutions which remained open for most of the day, provisions were made for the conduct of the readers, the performance of prayers and in some cases even for teaching to be carried out on the premises. The description of the library building will be dealt with in a later chapter, but it is perhaps appropriate to describe here a typical reading room, before going on to discuss those activities which were carried on in it. Typically, the reading room would be a single large room devoid of tables and chairs. The floor would be covered in rush mats, carpets, or both, and cushions would be placed along the sides of each wall. At intervals, book stands (rahle) would be placed around the room, and the readers would use these to hold their books while they leant against the cushioned wall for support. If they were copying a book, they would rest their paper on a board which was supported by their knee. As there is usually no mention of libraries providing ink, paper, and pens, we must presume that writing materials were furnished by the readers themselves.

As we would expect in a tradition where most, if not all, books were in manuscript form, copying was a major activity in the Ottoman libraries. While most foundation deeds refer to this practice, it is rare to find any specific instruction as to how copying should be carried out, though some founders specifically forbid the binding of a book to be broken to distribute the fascicles among a number of readers allowing multiple students to copy one book. Readers are often asked to take care not to spill ink on the books and not to fold the pages. But in some libraries, especially college libraries, multiple copies of some textbooks were kept to facilitate copying. The historian Hoca Sa'deddin reports that in the Fatih College Library most textbooks could be found in several copies.[18]

---

17 A North African traveler visited Istanbul at the end of eighteenth century and reported that there were a large number of libraries open to the public in which it was permitted to copy books, but not to borrow. This suggests that at least until the end of the eighteenth century opening hours were being observed. (Muhammed bin Abdülvehhâb el-Miknâsî, *Rıhletü'l-Miknâsî 1785* (Abu Dhabi: n.p, 2003), 92.

18 *Tâcü't-Tevârih*, vol. 1 (İstanbul: Matbaa-i Amire, 1279H), 580.

According to Antoine Galland, who worked in the French Embassy in Istanbul in 1672–1673, there were seven copies each of Sudi's commentary on Sa'di's *Gülistan* and *Bostan* and the *Divan of Hafiz* in Hadım Hafız Ahmed Pasha's library in the Fatih district of Istanbul. These books were lent out for copying against a deposit of two piastres.[19]

We have very little information governing the conduct of the readers in the libraries. When lending was allowed, there were usually fairly detailed instructions on how the books were to be issued and returned, but in cases where lending was not allowed the foundation deeds usually state that books should be read in the reading room. It is only occasionally that we find specific rulings on how books were to be treated while being used. Köprülü Hafız Ahmed Pasha, when endowing some books to the library founded by his grandfather, specified that the head bands holding the fascicles together were not to be removed to facilitate copying. In an endowment to his father's college in Crete, he made the same stipulation.[20] Other founders were particular to demand that their librarians be careful to ensure that the readers did not cut out pages from a book,[21] and some asked the readers to be careful not to splash ink on the books.[22]

The only reference to the number of books allowed to a reader at any one time is in the catalogue of the books endowed by Bafralı es-Seyyid Ahmed Revnaki to the Fatih Mosque, in which is recorded the following condition: "In the library one book should be given to one person, not two books. This is a condition which should be made known."[23]

Up to the seventeenth century, before the establishment of independent libraries, books were endowed to colleges, mosques, and dervish convents and were issued to readers who would consult them in those buildings. We cannot therefore talk about activities in the library, as there was no particular area which functioned purely as a reading room. From the beginning of the eighteenth century, with the foundation of the larger independent libraries, we find that some founders made provisions for prayers to be said at the required times and for teaching to be carried out. The library in Topkapı Palace also served as a classroom for the palace trainees, and the Hekimoğlu Ali Pasha Library (1735) had teachers on its staff.[24] In the Ayasofya Library (1740) endowed by Mahmud

---

19 Antoine Galland, *İstanbul'a Ait Günlük Hatıralar (1672–1673)*, trans. N. S. Örik, vol. 1 (Ankara: Türk Tarih Kurumu Basımevi, 1949), 204.
20 VGMA, No. 76, 43; BOA, Süleymaniye Section, 2918, 13.
21 M. Cunbur, "Yusuf Ağa Kütüphanesi ve Kütüphane Vakfiyesi," *TAD* 1, no. 1 (1963): 215.
22 VGMA, No. 579, 67.
23 Süleymaniye Library, Yazma Bağışlar No. 251, 1.
24 TSA, Y. 75, 16; Millet library, Feyzullah Efendi No. 2197, respectively.

I, teaching was done on a regular basis as we see from a clause in the endowment deed:

> In the said library one person who can teach Koranic Commentary and subjects related to it should act as head-teacher and offer lessons twice a week for a daily stipend of 50 aspers. And a person qualified in tradition should teach it one day a week for a daily stipend of 40 aspers. And a person competent in Recital should teach the Holy Koran one day a week, for a daily stipend of 25 aspers.[25]

In an additional endowment deed of 1741, we find that students who attended those classes were given a stipend of ten aspers a day.[26]

In the library of the palace at Galata (1754), the teaching staff included a teacher of Commentary, a teacher of Koranic Recital and three teachers, each for the three grades of palace servants. These last three teachers were referred to in some documents as the "library teachers."[27]

At the end of the eighteenth and beginning of the nineteenth centuries, provisions were also made for teaching in some libraries. Hacı Selim Ağa and Ahmed Ağa of Rhodes required their librarians to provide classes,[28] but in Aşir Efendi's library (1800) separate teachers were appointed.[29] Dervish Mehmed Pasha made it a condition of his endowment deed that *Buhari*, the famous book of Prophetic tradition, should be taught every day in his library.[30] Halet Efendi required that a person knowledgeable in Arabic, Persian, and mysticism should offer lessons on the *Mesnevi*, a thirteenth-century mystical work by Mevlana Celaleddin-i Rumi, and any other subject demanded by the library users.[31]

During the hours in which the libraries were open, the noon and sometimes the afternoon prayers were said. In the libraries situated within mosques or colleges, the readers would have said their prayers within the same building. With the emergence of the independent libraries the readers would probably have left the reading room to say their prayers in the nearest mosque. However, by the mid-eighteenth century, some founders required the librarians to lead the

---

25 VGMA, Kasa 47, 12–13.
26 VGMA, No. 638, 8.
27 VGMA, Defter No. 87, 9; BOA, Cevdet-Maarif No. 8474.
28 VGMA, No. 579, 122 and No. 743, 93.
29 VGMA, No. 738, 142; Süleymaniye Library, Aşir Efendi No. 473, 6–8.
30 Istanbul Court Registers, İstanbul Kadılığı No. 122, 37.
31 Süleymaniye Library, Halet Efendi No. 837/2, 31.

readers in the noon and afternoon prayers. Atıf Efendi and Ragıb Pasha asked their first and second librarians to act as imam and muezzin respectively.[32]

Other religious ceremonies were carried out in the library, as for example the ceremonies surrounding the relics of the Beard of the Prophet, which were performed on some special nights in the Abdullah Münzevi Library (1787) in Bursa, in the Ahmed III Library (1719) in Topkapı Palace, and the Galata Palace Library (1754).[33] In the Yusuf Ağa and Kılıç Ali Pasha Libraries, librarians had to say prayers for the soul of the founder when the library was opened in the morning, and read portions of the Koran silently every day.[34]

Hafid Efendi, son of Aşir Efendi, endowed income to his father's library to provide for the performance of religious activities: the Koran was to be read in portions by the librarians throughout the year ending on the tenth of Muharrem. On this day a special prayer was offered and all those in attendance were given a plate of sweetmeats. Also, on the twenty-sixth of the month of Şaban, the Koran was read by all in attendance and the *Mevlid*, a Turkish poem about the birth and life of the Prophet, was recited, after which a meal and sherbet was offered to all in attendance.[35]

Dervish Mehmed Pasha required that in his library (1818) in Burdur on certain nights and following the noon and afternoon prayers on Sundays and Thursdays, all in attendance should perform a silent ritual in the Nakşibendi dervish tradition, and that twice a year, in the months of Rebiü'l-evvel and Rebiü'l-ahir, *Mevlid* should be recited. The cost of sweetmeats which were to be offered to all in attendance on these occasions was to be paid from the surplus funds of the foundation.[36]

Book Lending

There was no uniform policy towards lending books in Ottoman libraries. While some founders took great pains to encourage the librarians to lend books, others forbade the practice entirely. The question of whether books should be lent out or consulted in the reading room was not merely a matter of library policy, it was governed by principles enshrined in the holy law of Islam, one of the tenets

32 VGMA, No. 735, 257 and No. 82, 6.
33 Bursa Eski Eserler Library, Abdullah Münzevi's Foundation deed, 17–26; TSA E. 11,924; Süleymaniye Library, Ayasofya No. 5, 53 and VGMA, Kasa 175, 46–48, respectively.
34 Eski Eserler Library, the *Vakfiye* of Abdullah Münzevi.
35 Süleymaniye Library, Hafid Efendi No. 487, 6–7, 10–12.
36 Istanbul Court Registers, İstanbul Kadılığı No. 122, 37.

of which was that knowledge should not be withheld. Whatever misgivings a founder had about his valuable collection being lent out to the public, he was often unable to express them, lest he be found in violation of this religious principle.[37] However, as time passed, some founders introduced restrictions on lending, in order to prevent losses which libraries had previously suffered. No matter how specific the restrictions or injunctions against lending may have been in the libraries of the Islamic world, we cannot be sure that they were not overruled by this religious principle which encouraged the spread of knowledge.

For instance, we observe a case in which the provisions of a foundation deed forbidding the borrowing of books were overruled under certain conditions. This particular case occurred in Cairo in the sixteenth century, when the famous scholar Es-Suyuti observed two of his teachers borrowing books from the Mahmudiye College Library, the deed of which forbade lending. Suyuti, having a high regard for the religious integrity of his teachers, had recourse to the law books to determine the legitimacy of their action, and found that under certain conditions it was allowed. In a short treatise which he wrote on the subject, he determined that no matter what the deed of the library stipulated, books may be borrowed provided that copies of the book were readily available in other libraries and that the reader did not keep the book longer than absolutely necessary.[38]

It is not surprising, therefore, that the founders of Ottoman libraries were in some difficulty when dealing with provisions for lending. While their instincts may have led them to restrict borrowing, the prevalent religious ethos demanded that books be made as available as possible. Up to the seventeenth century most libraries allowed borrowing, but restrictions were increasingly introduced from the beginning of the seventeenth century onwards. In the libraries founded in the eighteenth and nineteenth centuries, the practice of lending books was virtually abandoned.

Information about lending in the early period of Ottoman libraries is scant. We have, for example, a foundation deed of Murad II which makes provisions for the replacement of missing books, which would suggest that lending, at least within the confines of the college complex, was the practice in that library.[39] In Umur Bey's libraries in Bergama and Bursa, some deeds dated 1440 specifically forbade books to be taken out of the college or mosque.[40] However, nine

---

37 Youssef Eché, *Les Bibliotheques Arabes* (Damascus: n.p., 1967), 383–386.
38 Süleymaniye Library, Fatih No. 5294/6, 43a–44a. I am grateful to the late Professor Nihat Çetin for drawing my attention to the existence of a copy of this treatise.
39 TSA, D. 7081.
40 VGMA, No. 591, 181.

years later we find him donating a book to the library, and when writing the endowment conditions on the flyleaf he demands that the book should not be lent unless a pledge be taken to cover its value.[41] In a further deed in 1453, he expanded the conditions covering borrowing:

> All students, Koranic scholars and others who are resident in the complex around the mosque may use the books freely and other students may not use the books unless they find some trusted persons to act as guarantors.[42]

In 1457, a further endowment deed was drawn up by Umur Bey in Arabic. It is specified that the administrator of the foundation was to issue and collect books.[43] However, when the same deed was drawn up in Turkish at a later date, it was specified that books should not leave the mosque.[44]

From the time of the conquest of Istanbul onwards, most of the foundation deeds for the libraries seem to have made provision for lending, or at least did not forbid the practice. In the Fatih Complex, lending was organized by the assistant librarian, and in a catalogue from 1552 we have records of books missing as a result of lending.[45] There were two small libraries in Edirne, founded by Mesud Halife and Ali Fakih, which seem to have been established as lending libraries in the time of Mehmed II, and about a century later most of the books had gone missing.[46] In another library founded in Mehmed II's reign, by Şeyh Vefa in his dervish convent in Istanbul, the deed was quite specific about lending. He classified the readers into three categories, the higher class, middle class, and lower class, distinctions which are not described, but were probably based on education and cultural attainment. The members of the upper-class need give no surety if they be known to be trustworthy and reliable, but the members of the middle and lower classes were to give a pledge and provide a guarantor. All three classes were to be residents of Istanbul.[47] Molla Yegan's deed, from the same period, specifies that books were to be lent to deserving readers, on the condition that a pledge be given and a guarantor furnished; but to nonresidents

---

41 Bursa Eski Eserler Library, Ulu Cami No. 435, 1.
42 Bursa Eski Eserler Library, Ulu Cami No. 436, 329.
43 Belediye Library (İstanbul), Mc. No. 38.
44 Ekrem Hakkı Ayverdi, *Osmanlı Mimarisinde Çelebi Mehmed ve II. Sultan Murad Devri* (İstanbul: İstanbul Fetih Cemiyeti, 1972), 339.
45 *Fatih Mehmed II Vakfiyeleri* (Ankara: Vakıflar Umum Müdürlüğü Neşriyatı, 1938), facsimile 269; TSA, D. 9559, 15, 39, 50, 51, 54.
46 BOA, Tapu-Tahrir Defteri, No. 1070, 19, 220.
47 Istanbul Court Registers, Evkaf-ı Hümayun Muhasibliği No. 102, 151.

of Bursa they were to be lent for no more than a year and on the condition that they did not take the books out of Bursa.[48]

While there is no indication from the foundation deed of the imperial endowment at Eyüb that books were to be lent, we find on the flyleaf of two books which were endowed by the Grand Vizier Mehmed Pasha in 1480 that the books could be taken out for up to three months;[49] this would imply that the library had adopted the practice of lending.

One further example from the same period should be given because of an interesting condition contained in the foundation deed. When Abdurrahim Karahisari founded a library in Afyon in 1483, he specified that books could be lent out for up to a year. At the end of each year, the books were to be brought back and the value of the pledge which had been given was to be reassessed and the pledge be changed if necessary.[50] This was presumably to allow for an increase in the pledge in cases where the value of the book had increased over the year.

There are so few documents from the reign of Mehmed II that it is hard to make any categorical statement about the practice of lending books. Whatever few documents we do have would suggest that the founders of libraries were disposed to lending books.

For the period of Bayezid II's reign (1481–1512) we have only a limited number of references, one being a provision made in the deed for his own endowment in Edirne where it is stipulated:

> Books should not be lent outside the college. Those who need to consult them should come and read them there. They [the librarians] should not allow them to be taken out [of the college].[51]

There are further conditions which required the librarian to check all the folios and illustrations in a book before issuing and after recall. Although the books were only lent out within the college, two witnesses were required when a book was issued and on its return.

Kıssahan Hacı Muslihiddin Mustafa, the founder of a library in Çavlı, in Kandıra, allowed books to be lent, but only to scholars and students.[52] The

---

48 Bursa Court Registers, A. 156/208, 25–26.
49 Süleymaniye Library, Hz. Halid No. 178, 111.
50 Edip Ali Baki, *Mısırlıoğlu Abdurrahim Karahisari* (Afyon: Yeni Matbaa, 1953), 103.
51 Belediye Library Mc. 0. 61, 44.
52 VGMA, No. 579, 227.

practice of lending books was carried on to the end of the sixteenth century with only a few exceptions.[53] Two developments are observable in this period: the depositing of pledges to guarantee the return of the books was becoming the norm throughout all libraries, and attempts to restrict the period of loans were made with increasing regularity.

Kasım b. Abdullah, in his endowment in Edirne, allowed books to be lent, but demanded that the librarian should take a pledge;[54] while Hacı Hasan b. Ali, in a foundation, also in the same city, stipulated that the books should not be taken out of the district of the town in which the library was situated.[55]

While previously there were no restrictions on the period of loans, with the one exception of the Molla Yegan Library in Bursa, the library founders in this period began to be uneasy about the idea of lending for long periods. Thus we see a teacher in the Darü'l-Hadis in Edirne, Emir Hüseyin, stipulating that the books in his endowment should be lent on the following condition:

> A book should not be left with a reader for a prolonged period; on the contrary as soon as he has finished with it the librarian should recall it and give it to someone else. This is lest the books become unavailable for use.[56]

Stipulations about pledges were generally vague, merely stating that a pledge should be taken in return for the loan of a book. However, in an exceptional case, we see that the deed for Sinan Bey's foundation in Bursa lists the books endowed with a record of their value, and states that either sums of money as recorded or a pledge to their value should be deposited as guarantee of their return.[57]

In other libraries founded in this period, the practice of demanding pledges and guarantors is stipulated without further conditions, as in Bedreddin Mahmud's library in Kayseri, Alaaddin b. Abdurrahman's library in Istanbul, Pertev Pasha's library in İzmit, Şeyh Mehmed Çelebi's library in Bursa, and Molla Çelebi's library in Istanbul. However, in the deed of Ali Çelebi b. Receb's library in Yiannitsá, it is demanded that the reader should deposit a pledge of

---

53 Feridun Bey and Hayreddin Pasha both opposed the practice of lending books in their endowments: VGMA, No. 570, 198 and No. 571, 185, respectively.

54 BOA, Tapu-Tahrir Defteri, No. 1070, 211.

55 BOA, Tapu-Tahrir Defteri, No. 1070, 239–241.

56 BOA, MAD, 557, 12.

57 VGMA, No. 578, 318.

twice the value of the book, and that books should not be given to nonresidents of Yiannitsá or to villagers or to people who were likely to lose them.[58]

In the extant fragments of an endowment deed for some books donated to the Cami-i Atik Mosque in Bursa, the donor allows books to be freely lent to the future generations of scholars and students or his family if they obtain the permission of the judge of the city, and to other deserving borrowers provided they deposit a pledge. Books are to be returned when the reader has finished with them or before he leaves the confines of the city of Bursa. Rather curiously, the donor prohibited his books being lent to the teachers of Arslaniye College in the city.[59] Thus we see that besides the conditions governing pledges, the most common restriction on borrowing is that governing residential status. There was a general tendency to deny nonresidents the loan of a book, or at least to demand that they should not leave the town or city with the books they borrowed. This restriction takes the form of an imperial decree regulating the loan of books endowed by Murad III to his college in Manisa:

> To the teacher of Manisa
> The books endowed for the use of scholars by the late Sultan Murad Han should not be given to strangers. You should act as supervisors and take care lest the books be lost.[60]

There are also other more exceptional conditions attached to certain libraries by the decree of the reigning sultan. In the library of the Selimiye Mosque in Edirne, a decree of Murad III allowed that the preacher of the mosque should be lent books freely:

> To the administrator of the endowment of my late father, Sultan Selim Han—*may God have mercy on his soul.*
> Should the preacher of the mosque, Mevlana Valihi Mehmed, the pride of the scholars—*may God increase his piety*—require any book from the endowment of my father, it is commanded that it should be given. Therefore, it is required that when the above preacher requests a book it should be given to him without delay or hindrance.[61]

---

58 Istanbul Court Registers, Rumeli Sadareti No. 3, 38.
59 Bursa Court Registers, A. 180/406, 132.
60 BOA, Fekete No. 1694.
61 BOA, Mühimme No. 51, 79.

Towards the end of the sixteenth century, clauses governing the lending of books began to appear in the foundation deeds with greater regularity. Şeyhülislam Hamid Efendi provided for the lending of the books he endowed to the Süleymaniye Complex in 1584 thus:

> In order that all may benefit from the books, no one should keep a book. No book may be left with a reader for more than a year, nor should books be taken outside the city, nor should they be lent without a pledge, with the exception of Abdullah Çelebi, a teacher, who may borrow whatever he requires without a pledge. When books are copied, they should not be broken up into fascicles.[62]

When Mahmud Bey gave books to the Cihangir Mosque in Istanbul, in 1593, he limited the period of loan to a month:

> The librarian having taken a pledge, should issue books to those who read them, he should record the title of the book, the name of the borrower with his description, the nature of the pledge, the date of issue, and should not allow the book to remain out for more than a month.[63]

The period of a month is unusually short, but can be explained by the nature of the collection which was made up of story books, mystical narratives, folk tales, and the like. These books were intended to be taken home and read, rather than studied and copied.[64]

From the beginning of the seventeenth century, we see attempts by founders to prohibit borrowing. The main reason is probably to prevent losses which some libraries had suffered on account of liberal lending policies. As one would expect it was not the college or mosque libraries that were the most prone to

---

62 VGMA, No. 572, 13.

63 Istanbul Court Registers, Galata Mahkemesi No. 17, 187.

64 There seems to have been a great demand for story books of this type. So much were these books sought after that there arose the practice of lending books out for a charge. In a copy of the *1001 Arabian Nights* which in Turkish is known as the *1001 Nights* there is a record on the flyleaf of every borrower and how much he paid to borrow the book. For example, one entry reads: Two volumes of this book rented out by Hüseyin Ağa for sixteen aspers in advance on 25 Reb. I, 1068 [April 28, 1658].
Şinasi Tekin, "Binbir Gece'nin İlk Türkçe Tercümeleri ve Hikayelerdeki Gazeller Üzerine," *Türk Dilleri Araştırmaları*, no. 3 (1993): 242–244.

losses, but the smaller local libraries established in the districts of the cities and intended for the use of students and the public. We discover in an endowment register for Edirne, carried out during the reign of Selim II (1566–1574), that these types of local libraries had suffered great losses almost to the point where some collections had disappeared.[65]

Mustafa Dede, in his foundation (1602) in the island of Lesbos required that his books be read in the building and that the reader "should not commit the crime of taking a book out of the dervish convent."[66] Mehmed Ağa insisted that the books which he had endowed to the Şehzade Mosque in 1634 should be read in the mosque.[67] Abbas Ağa b. Abdüsselam, realizing that there was a demand for copies of the basic textbooks, provided a number of books in fascicle form which could be borrowed fascicle by fascicle on the deposit of a pledge. Should a fascicle be lost, the deposit was to be used to copy out the missing portion of the book. Other books were not to be taken out of the building.[68] Here we have an extremely practical remedy to the problem of lending.

While the above libraries attempted to restrict borrowing other libraries founded in the seventeenth century continued to allow books to be borrowed as we can observe in the deeds or records of the following libraries: Ahmed I's library (1617) in Sultan Ahmed Mosque, Turhan Valide Sultan's library (1663) in Yeni Cami, Chief Mufti Zekeriyya Efendi's library in his college in Istanbul, Şeyh Husameddin Efendi's library (1612) in his dervish convent in Bursa, İsmail b. Mehmed's library (1617) in his father's convent in Istanbul, Mustafa Efendi's library (1667) in the Üsküplü Mosque in Istanbul, and Mehmed Efendi's library (1673) in the İplikçi Mosque in Konya.[69]

However, all loans were made conditional on the deposit of a pledge, and in the case of Turhan Valide Sultan the conditions were quite onerous. She stated that a pledge to a value of twice that of the book should be deposited and the assistant librarian should record the title, subject, and the number of fascicles and folios in his ledger, along with the nature and value of the pledge. No book

65 BOA, Tapu-Tahrir Defteri, No. 1070. Typical of entries describing collections are the following: "Most of the books recorded in the abovementioned person's deed are lost ... but most have disappeared" (19). In another register (MAD, 557), it is recorded that "most of Emir Hüseyin's books are lost."
66 Istanbul Court Registers, Evkaf-ı Hümayun Müfettişliği No. 8, 106.
67 VGMA, No. 730.
68 Istanbul Court Registers, Evkaf-ı Hümayun Müfettişliği No. 63, 18, 21.
69 Istanbul Court Registers, Evkaf-ı Hümayun Müfettişliği No. 57, 49; Süleymaniye Library, Yeni Cami No. 150, 45; Bursa Court Registers, B. 63/259, 97 and B. 41/235, 160; Istanbul Court Registers, Evkaf-ı Hümayun Müfettişliği No. 27, 37, Ahi Çelebi Mahkemesi No. 19, 36 and No. 29, 23.

was to be lent in the absence of either the librarian or the assistant librarian. Before lending a book, they should investigate the reputation and status of the would-be borrower.[70]

Thus, we see that in the seventeenth century the policy of the founders of libraries towards lending is best characterized as one of confusion and disarray, with no uniform trend discernable. Throughout the period some libraries allowed lending while others prohibited the practice. It is almost as if the founders themselves were in two minds about whether books should be lent, the conflict being between their natural desire that the books should be read and their fear that their collections might be diminished by losses. In fact, we have evidence to suggest the existence of conflict in the mind of the founders. When Mustafa Efendi b. Abdülvehhab endowed his books to a college he founded in Istanbul in 1676 he first drew up a deed in which he states that he had hoped to allow everyone of upright and honest appearance to borrow freely, but had realized that some borrowers who had the appearance of honest scholars were not, and he therefore insisted on the deposit of pledges and strict scrutiny of books on issue.[71]

In the Köprülü Library (1678), this hesitant attitude to lending is clearly illustrated in the deed. It is first established that books "may not be taken out," but then this rule is qualified by so many broad exceptions, as to render it virtually meaningless. The founder noted that lending was a necessity, in that students required texts to copy and, also, that it was the practice of other libraries to lend. Books could therefore be borrowed by trustworthy people on deposit of a pledge, the provision of a guarantor, and with the permission of the administrator. Students could borrow on provision of a pledge and guarantor only.[72]

When Şeyh Ali Efendi donated his books to the Ayasofya Mosque in 1681 he forbade the lending of books to people who may lose them.[73] When Mehmed b. Süleyman left his books to the Süleymaniye Mosque in 1688, he allowed his books to be borrowed only by poverty-stricken scholars who were disciples of the strict zealot preacher Kadızade, and then without pledge or guarantor.[74]

From the beginning of the eighteenth century, a more consistent policy towards lending is observable. The larger libraries founded in this period, with

---

70 VGMA, No. 744, 28.
71 Istanbul Court Registers, Bab Mahkemesi No. 29, 130.
72 Köprülü Library No. 4, 42, 52.
73 Istanbul Court Registers, Rumeli Sadareti No. 129, 81.
74 Istanbul Court Registers, Ahi Çelebi No. 64, 46.

one or two exceptions,[75] prohibited lending books, while some of the smaller collections in many mosques continued to provide a borrowing service. In the college libraries of el-Hac Mehmed Efendi, Mehmed Efendi b. Veliyüddin, Nevşehirli İbrahim Pasha, and Çorlulu Ali Pasha, the prohibition is strongly expressed.[76] The foundation deeds for the last of these libraries stipulates that if the librarian is found to have lent even a single folio he is to be dismissed.[77] On the endowment seals of the books donated by Abdullah Pasha, Köprülü-zade Hafız Ahmed Pasha, and Carullah Veliyüddin, it is inscribed that the books may not leave the building. Hacı Beşir Ağa prohibited the circulation of his books within the college he built in Istanbul and insisted that they be read in the reading room.[78]

Throughout the eighteenth century and the beginning of nineteenth century, the trend against the practice of lending books gathered momentum, so that by the end of this period it was exceptional to find a library lending books. Indeed, in the documents related to the libraries the clauses prohibiting this practice are worded in increasingly stricter terms. Mahmud I issued an imperial decree (dated August 1743) for his library in Belgrade to strengthen the prohibition against lending: "Governors, judges and other men of influence should not take a book out in order to read it. No book should be lent out."[79]

Other libraries in this period are also governed by similar clauses, obviously to allow librarians to refuse books to highly influential readers who would have sought exceptional treatment in view of their exalted position. Hüseyin Ağa, who founded a library in a dervish convent and mosque complex in Bursa in 1760 stated categorically that the supervisor of the endowment, a post to be held by the spiritual master of the dervish convent, was not to take the books from the library to his room in the complex.[80] Ali Ağa, in the deed to his library in Tırnova (1763), expressed his feeling that the conditions prohibiting borrowing were the most important stipulations of the deed, and for good measure he invokes the curse of God on all who broke, or helped or allowed a person to violate these conditions.[81] Vahid Pasha also, in the deed for his library in Kütahya (1811), forbade lending to anyone, and he invokes the curse of God

---

75 The most notable exceptions are Ahmed III's endowments to Topkapı Palace and Yeni Cami Mosque, where borrowing was allowed under certain conditions. See TSK, Y. 75, 15 and Süleymaniye Library, Yeni Cami No. 1200, 22–23.

76 VGMA, No. 571, 92; No. 734, 43; No. 38, 90; No. 188, 389.

77 VGMA, No. 188, 389; BOA, Cevdet-Maarif No. 2044.

78 VGMA, No. 736, 4.

79 BOA, Cevdet-Maarif No. 7730.

80 VGMA, No. 578, 41.

81 Istanbul Court Registers, Evkaf-ı Hümayun Müfettişliği No. 171, 10.

on anyone who borrows a book by putting pressure on the librarians through influential people.[82]

On the other hand, in the smaller townships in the provinces we find a slightly more relaxed attitude to lending, since books were not so easily obtained, and the needs of the students could not be satisfied unless some lending was allowed. Yusuf Ziya Pasha, for example, endowed a library to his college in Keban in 1797, for which the deed prohibited lending as a general rule. He qualifies the prohibition by recognizing that some students may need to read books throughout the day and night and that they should be given them in return for a pledge two or three times the value of the book.[83] Gedosi Mehmed Efendi, in his library in the province of Kastamonu (1834), divided his books into two sections, the first being college textbooks which could be borrowed for copying on the provision of a guarantor. Other books had to be read in the library.[84]

When foundation libraries came under the jurisdiction of the Ministry of Education, lending was entirely prohibited in all foundation libraries, even in those where the founder had provided for lending. While the wish of the founder was generally regarded as sacrosanct, on the question of lending the ministry seems to have treated the preservation of collections as the paramount consideration.

However strict the conditions laid down by the founders, there is evidence to suggest that the librarians broke the rules and lent books out. According to a document from 1784, librarians of Hacı Beşir Ağa Library in Cağaloğlu in Istanbul had lent books for five days on deposit of a pledge.[85] When the first librarian of the Nuruosmaniye Library died in 1776, an inventory of the books was made and it was discovered that some books were lost through lending. In the entry for one of the books which had gone missing, it is noted that the book was lost having been lent to the former Vizier Yusuf Ziya Pasha, whose signed receipt was to be found in the receipt box.[86] Indeed, it would seem that the librarians were often unable to resist the pressure of important officials who wished to borrow books. Thus we see the supervisor of the Nuruosmaniye Foundation writing to the first librarian a letter in which he notes that in the past books had been lent out at the behest of the administrator of the library or some influential officials, and warns him that in future only an imperial decree would be a valid reason to lend a book, and that an infringement of this ruling would

---

82 VGMA, No. 579, 702.
83 VGMA, No. 579, 50–51.
84 VGMA, No. 491, 491.
85 VGMA, No. 639, 129.
86 Nuruosmaniye Library No. 6, 111 and 106.

entail not only dismissal, but further punishment.[87] When Ragıb Pasha died (1763), books from his own endowed collection were found in his room and were returned to the library. Even though he was the founder of the library, it was not permitted, by the terms of his foundation deed, even for him to borrow a book.[88]

In a catalogue for the Galata Palace Library, we see notes which would suggest that books were being lent in violation of the terms of the deed. We note that in 1786 three books had been lent to the library teacher, Halil Efendi. In a further note from 1810, three books are named as having been lent to another library teacher. It is afterwards added that this loan is in breach of regulations and contrary to the practice which had been observed previously, but that they were lent on the orders of the Ağa of the palace.[89]

Besides these isolated examples of the rules being broken, there is also other evidence to suggest that the injunctions against lending were not always observed. This evidence exists in the numerous, repeated, and increasingly more explicit prohibitions of lending to be found in the foundations deeds themselves. There are also imperial decrees which reflect the seriousness with which the rule against lending was treated. In an imperial decree, Mustafa III forbade the supervisor to lend books to anyone, even palace officials or other men of influence. Any infringement of this decree would be punished by the sultan.[90]

It would thus appear that while in the earlier period lending was allowed, and to some extent encouraged, in the later period a change of opinion took place until eventually lending was forbidden in most libraries. The reason for the change was due to several factors. Besides the loss of valuable books, there was also the fact that as libraries proliferated in the eighteenth century, so that almost all educational institutions had their own library, copies of books which could easily be consulted became increasingly more available to all classes of readers. Another factor to be considered is that by the nineteenth century, a viable market in books had been established. Istanbul had become by far the leading center for the sale and exchange of Islamic manuscripts. When Carlyle visited Istanbul at the beginning of the nineteenth century, he estimated that at the time he bought his books there were at least four thousand manuscripts on the market.[91] Thus

---

87 Nuruosmaniye Library No. 2, 51.

88 VGMA, No. 82, 5.

89 Süleymaniye Library, Ayasofya No. 5, 1.

90 TSA, D. 3305.

91 Robert Walpole, *Memoirs Relating to European and Asiatic Turkey, edited from manuscript journals by Robert Walpole* (London: Longman & Co., 1817), 176.

we can see that it had become comparatively easy for students to obtain copies of books they needed for their studies. With the greater availability of books on the market, and the proliferation of library collections throughout the empire and particularly in Istanbul, the library founders no longer felt themselves bound by the religious injunction against restricting the spread of knowledge.

In the period in which borrowing was allowed, the procedure to be followed when lending out books was often described in the endowment deeds in some detail. In the deed for Fatih Library, the procedure is left to the assistant librarian who is merely required to record the book and the borrower in his register, in order, presumably, that the book could be recalled when necessary.[92] However, when Bedreddin Mahmud founded a library in Kayseri, in 1559, he was much more specific and described the procedure thus:

> The librarian should record all borrowers in his register by name, family name, description and by epithet. Nothing should be lent without a pledge. The acceptance of the pledge should also be recorded in the register with its description, nature, special features and date of acceptance, and his pledge should be deposited in the book depot. On issue or return of a book the supervisor and librarian should check the book from beginning to end to determine whether there are any missing folios. The librarian should keep two identical registers, one of which he should hold himself, the other to be placed in the book depot.[93]

The same procedure was stipulated in the deeds for Mahmud's library in the Cihangir Mosque (1594) and İsmail b. Mehmed's endowment to his father's dervish convent near the Gül Cami.[94] In the library of Turhan Valide Sultan in the Yeni Cami, it was the assistant librarian who was responsible for supervising the lending of books.[95] In the library founded by Ahmed III attached to Yeni Cami, the assistant librarian issued and recalled books, but in the presence of the librarian and with the permission of the endowment supervisor.[96]

---

92 *Fatih Mehmed II Vakfiyeleri* (Ankara: Vakıflar Umum Müdürlüğü Neşriyatı, 1938), facsimile 269.

93 VGMA, No. 581/1, 33.

94 Istanbul Court Registers, Galata Mahkemesi No. 17, 187; Evkaf-ı Hümayun Müfettişliği No. 27, 37.

95 Süleymaniye Library, Yeni Cami No. 150, 45.

96 Süleymaniye Library, Yeni Cami No. 1200, 22–23.

The records of books given out on loan were often treated as outdated records by later generations of librarians who often threw out these registers to make shelf space for new accessions. As a result, we have only three registers of loans which have survived. The following extracts are taken from the register belonging to the Mevlevi dervish convent at Yenikapı in Istanbul:[97]

> Two copies of the *Pend-i Attar* taken from the library and handed over to Şeyh Osman for him to read in [the month of] Rebiülevvel, 1248 [July 1832].
> One volume of the *Sevakıb* given to Eyyübî Mehmed Dede in [the month of] Muharrem 1250 [May 1834].
> To Mehmed Dede one volume of the commentary on the *Mesnevi*, 15 Muharrem 1252 [2 May 1836].
> To Mehmed Dede of Amid [Diyarbakır] a *Mushaf-ı Şerif* and a *Menakıb-ı Şerif* given in Rebiülevvel, 1252 [June 1836].

We can observe that in a period of six years a mere four loans were made and then only to the Sufi masters or to the *dede*s, that is, elders in a dervish convent. It would seem that lending books was exceptional and only sanctioned for the senior member of the convent.

The second of these three registers belongs to a foundation library in Samakov in present-day Bulgaria, which records 103 loans over a period of some thirteen years.[98] As lending books was more widespread in this library, the record is more detailed and includes the name of the borrower, his position in whatever institution or the name of the quarter in which he resided, the name of the book and the date of the loan. The following are three examples:

> To the müezzin of the New Mosque, Mehmed Efendi, one volume of the commentary on *Talim-i Müteallim* in *nesh* hand, two volumes of the *Metn-i Talim-i Müteallim,* one volume in *nesh* hand, one in *talik* and one volume in which there are the following works: *Menakib-i Mevlana, Dibace, Talim-i Müteallim, Kavaid-i Farisiyye* in *nesh* hand all on the nineteenth Rebiülahir 1257 [9 June 1841].

---

97 M. Erdoğan, "İstanbul'da Kütahyalı Bir Şeyh Ailesi Seyyid Ebu Bekir Dede ve Ahfadı," *İstanbul Araştırmaları*, no. 7 (1998): 138 and 169.

98 Stoyanka Kenderova and Zorka Ivanova, *From the Collections of Ottoman Libraries in Bulgaria During the Eighteenth–Nineteenth Centuries* (Sofia: n.p., 1999), 30 and 97.

To a certain person by the name of Kara Salih b. Osman, living in the Şeyh quarter of Samakov, and originally coming from the village of Kıranlar in the district of İhtiman, a copy of the *Holy Koran* on the nineteenth Rebiülahir 1257 [9 June 1841].

To his excellency Mehmed Aşir Efendi, one volume of *Lugat-ı Ahteri*, in *nesh* hand, one volume of *Fetava-yı Kadıhan*, in *nesh* hand.

In the third register belonging to the same library, there are forty-seven instances of lending books which are similarly recorded.[99]

The period for which books may be taken out on loan varied considerably. Many deeds do not specify a limit while others stipulate that the books should not be lent longer than necessary. Other deeds stipulate maximum periods of one month, three months, six months and twelve months.

---

99 Stoyanka Kenderova, "Les lecteurs de Samakov au XIXe siècle," *Revue des mondes musulmans et de la Méditerranée*, no. 87–88 (1999): 61–75.

Chapter Ten

Budgets and Audits

Library founders typically set aside properties which would render an income for the maintenance and running of the library, various aspects of which were described in the foundation deeds. As we would expect, all foundations were required to render accounts and balance sheets at fixed intervals.

Most library founders had in fact made large endowments of which the library was only a part. It was customary to endow properties and other sources of income to the endowment as a whole, but to list expenditure in detail. Consequently, while we may have some idea of how much money was allocated to the library in any year, we cannot determine its original sources, except to say that it came out of the general income received by the foundation at large. Annual expenditures, on the other hand, were specified in the deeds.

At regular intervals, an audit was carried out and a detailed account of expenditures was made by the administrator with the help of the clerks of the foundation. This account was subject to the control of the inspectors of foundations. The audit was then summarized and sent to the office of the trustee of the endowment. The detailed accounts remained with the administrator of the foundation and, for the greater part, have not survived. The summary accounts which were deposited in the state archives still exist, but they are drawn up in a form which gives us very little information relevant to the libraries themselves. Usually, the figures are merely totals of incomes and expenses for the foundation as a whole.

The usual source of income was the rents of houses, shops, and other buildings. Imperial foundations and the foundations endowed by high-ranking statesmen also included tracts of cultivated land and enterprises, such as mines and workshops, which produced profits.[1] Some founders preferred to endow a sum of money which was to be invested by the administrator for the benefit of the foundations.[2] Some benefactors donated books and buildings and requested the state to provide the endowment with an income; thus Veliyüddin Efendi (1769),[3] Yusuf Ağa (1794),[4] and Necip Pasha (1827)[5] endowed libraries which were allocated sources of income by the state.

The largest element of expenditure in the libraries was the salaries of the librarians and other library personnel. When Veliyüddin Efendi founded his library (1182/1768–1769) the state allocated a yearly sum of 1,150 piastres from the excess revenues of the foundations of Sultan Bayezid II. The following is a statement of how the money was to be spent:

> The administrator is to receive 1,150 piastres from the endowment of the above-mentioned Sultan Bayezid II, at the beginning of March every year. 960 piastres is to be expended for the stipends of the librarians, the guards, the sweeper and the doorkeeper. 150 piastres to feed the residents of the dervish convent of Şeyh Murad ... and, yearly, 40 piastres for the expenses of drawing up an inventory.[6]

In some deeds, money is allocated for repairs to the building and renewal of bindings. In the Istanbul court registers from 1718 we find an entry which shows that 2,400 aspers were spent on repairs to the Mahmud Pasha Library in Istanbul.[7] In the deeds of the Chief Mufti Aşir Efendi (1800),[8] and Ahmed Ağa

1 Bursa Court Registers, B. 89/294, 75b; BOA, Cevdet-Evkaf 29,601; BOA, İbnülemin-Hatt-ı Hümayun 503.
2 Süleymaniye Library, Hafid Efendi Section 487, 6b–7a; Istanbul Court Registers, Galata Mahkemesi 584, 63b.
3 VGMA, No. 745, 81.
4 Istanbul Court Registers, Evkaf-ı Hümayun Müfettişliği No. 261, 57–58; BOA, Cevdet-Maarif No. 355.
5 BOA, Cevdet-Maarif No. 2301.
6 VGMA, No. 745, 81.
7 Istanbul Court Registers, Evkaf-ı Hümayun Müfettişliği No. 109, 16–18.
8 Süleymaniye Library, Aşir Efendi Section No. 473, 10b.

of Rhodes (1793),[9] the maintenance of the fabric of the library building was to be met by the surplus revenues of the foundation. In the libraries founded by Abbas Ağa (1670),[10] Merzifonlu Kara Mustafa Pasha (1681),[11] Hacı Beşir Ağa (Baghdad, 1734),[12] Arpa Emini Ali Ağa (1762),[13] Hüseyin Ağa (1760),[14] Raşid Efendi (1797),[15] Edremidli Mehmed Emin Efendi (1801),[16] Zeynüddinzade Hacı Ali Efendi (1804),[17] Abdülkadir Bey (1808),[18] Kavalalı Mehmed Ali Pasha (1813),[19] Halet Efendi (1820),[20] and Pertev Pasha (1836)[21] the deeds provide for the bindings of the books to be repaired from the general funds of the foundation.

In some foundations, the administrator was allowed to buy books when they were needed. Sultan Murad II (1435),[22] İsmihan Sultan (1568),[23] Sokollu Mehmed Pasha (1575)[24] and Mahmud Bey (1593)[25] all provided for the purchase of necessary books from the general income of the foundation. Mustafa b. Ahmed (1798),[26] Mehmed Asım Bey (1805),[27] and Vahid Pasha (1811),[28] however, only allowed the purchase of books in years in which there was a surplus.

Although the cleaning of the books was part of the duties of the library personnel, some founders made special provision to ensure that cleaning was properly carried out and in some deeds a fixed allocation was set aside for drawing up an inventory, for cleaning, for the maintenance of the books and for the purchase of cleaning materials.[29] Chief Mufti Feyzullah Efendi (1699) made a special allocation of three aspers daily to his librarians so that they would

---

9 VGMA, No. 743, 94.
10 Istanbul Court Registers, Evkaf-ı Hümayun Müfettişliği No. 63, 18.
11 VGMA, No. 641, 94.
12 VGMA, No. 735, 94.
13 Istanbul Court Registers, Evkaf-ı Hümayun Müfettişliği No. 171, 10b.
14 VGMA, No. 578, 75.
15 VGMA, No. 579, 67–68.
16 VGMA, No. 629, 311.
17 VGMA, Kasa 8.
18 Istanbul Court Registers, Galata Mahkemesi No. 584, 63b.
19 VGMA, No. 580, 275.
20 Süleymaniye Library, Halet Efendi Section No. 837, 9b.
21 VGMA, Kasa 108, 12.
22 TSA, D. 7080.
23 VGMA, No. 572, 147.
24 VGMA, Kasa 103, 3.
25 Istanbul Court Registers, Galata Mahkemesi No. 17, 187.
26 VGMA, No. 579, 95.
27 VGMA, No. 580, 14.
28 VGMA, No. 579, 704.
29 VGMA, No. 82, 3; No. 745, 81; No. 579, 122; TSA, D. 8594.

carry out the task of cleaning each book thoroughly every four months.[30] Sultan Ahmed III's library in the Topkapı Palace (1719) was allocated three thousand aspers a year for the purchase of brushes for sweeping and sponges for dusting the books.[31] In Ragıb Pasha's library, money was set aside for the purchase of sweeping brushes and for repairs to the carpets and rush mats.[32]

Fixed sums of money were often set aside for heating and lighting, as for example in Aşir Efendi's library (1800) where the sum of fifteen piastres a year was allocated for coal,[33] or in Ragıb Pasha's library (1762) where a daily allowance of three aspers was made for candles and lamp oil.[34] In some libraries, a certain amount of money was set aside to pay for sherbet and sweetmeats, which were offered to all those who attended certain religious ceremonies.[35]

Although it was rare, we sometimes find a founder using a library foundation as a trust for his family, so that in Feyzullah Efendi's library (1699) part of the budget was a daily allowance of twenty aspers for each of his daughters until they were married,[36] Debbağzade İbrahim Efendi used his library foundation (1801) to provide twenty aspers daily for his wife.[37]

Detailed lists of expenses are so rare that the following budget drawn up in 1722 for the library of Şehid Ali Pasha is given below in full:[38]

First librarian	daily	15 aspers
Second librarian	daily	10 aspers
Binder of endowed books	daily	10 aspers
Sweeper in the library	daily	8 aspers
Doorman in the library	daily	4 aspers
Plumber of the library	daily	2 aspers
Salaries of clerks and cost of necessary stationary	yearly	780 piastres
Repairs of binding and their cases (27 at 60 piastres)	total	1,620 piastres

30 VGMA, No. 571, 119.
31 TSA, Y. 75, 18a.
32 VGMA, No. 82, 8.
33 Süleymaniye Library, Aşir Efendi Section No. 473, 10b. 35 VGMA, No. 82, 8.
34 VGMA, No. 82, 8
35 Süleymaniye Library, Hafid Efendi Section No. 487, 6b–7a.; Kılıç Ali Paşa Section No. 1049/1, 11b; Istanbul Court Registers, İstanbul Kadılığı No. 122, 37b.
36 VGMA, No. 571, 119.
37 Süleymaniye Library, Kılıç Ali Paşa Section No. 1049/1, 11b.
38 Süleymaniye Library, Şehid Ali Paşa File No. 1

Thirty-one years later in a budget for the year 1753, we note that there is no longer a binder employed in the library and the staff has acquired the further position of a supervisor of books. We also note that in this year repairs of books, care of garden and the repair of water pump cost 7,740 piastres.[39]

Another list of expenses of interest is that for Sultan Mahmud I's foundations which was drawn up for the period March 1773 to April 1774 on in preparation for his visit to the library of Fatih:[40]

For flowers and fruit	50 piastres
For aloe wood [incense]	15 piastres
For amber	6 piastres
The expenses of amber and aloe wood during the reading of *Buhari* in Ayasofya and Fatih	27 piastres
Repairs and renewals of bindings to books in the Fatih Library	130 piastres
Repairs to lock and sundries	130 piastres
To transport of books	55 piastres
To the Süleymaniye caretakers for guarding the books	25 piastres
For repair of glass of the library and sundries	10 piastres
[blank]	12 piastres
Total	232 piastres
Expenses for cushions in the Fatih and Ayasofya Libraries:	129 piastres

In the section above dealing with repairs and binding renewals, there is no mention of the actual cost of binding. This must have been accounted for in some other list. The above costs are incidentals for sending the books away for binding.

In the expenses lists which span the 30 years during which Mehmed Sadık Efendi was administrator of Mahmud I's imperial endowment, there are only two entries directly related to the Ayasofya Library:[41]

---

39 Süleymaniye Library, Şehid Ali Paşa File No. 2
40 VGMA, No. 639, 118.
41 TSA, E. 174/105.

Cost of sponges: 25 piastres

Cost of brushes and sponges for a year in Ayasofya: 25 piastres.

Another undated document for the same foundation notes the costs of framing, glass, cushioning, and so on.[42]

In folio 1b in the yearly budget of Raşid Efendi Library in Kayseri, for the year 1798[43] it is stated that the yearly income amounted to 1,536 piastres, and the sources of the income are given. On folios 2b–3a the stipends for personnel is listed thus:

Salary of first librarian	360 piastres
Salary of second librarian	300 piastres
Salary of third librarian	240 piastres
Salary of sweeper	30 piastres
Salary of supervisor of library	30 piastres
Salary of deputy administrator	90 piastres
Salary of administrator of the endowment	120 piastres
[Subtotal]	1,170 piastres
For the expenses of auditing and the inspection	15 piastres
[Total]	1,185 piastres

After subtracting the salaries from the annual income, the library is left with an operating surplus of 351 piastres. However, there were other expenses to be met, as we can see in the following balance sheet for the last quarter of this year. We observe that most of 1,536 piastres income came in this quarter. The expenses for salaries are, as one would expect, about a quarter of the annual cost, but the incidental expenses are extraordinarily high in this quarter:

The income of the foundation	1,084 piastres
Expenses of the foundation	

42 BOA, Sultan Mahmud I's file.
43 Marmara Üniversitesi, Fen-Edebiyat Fakültesi Library, Raşid Efendi file.

For expenses of repairing and renewal of bindings of books sent to Kayseri, and for guarding them.	380 piastres
For transporting above books and for making packing cases for them	50 piastres
For other expenses of the library	477.50 piastres
Salaries	292.50 piastres
[subtotal]	1,200 piastres
Cost of auditing and inspection	15 piastres
[Total]	1,215 piastres

Balance

Expenses of the foundation	1,215 piastres
Income of the foundation	1,084 piastres
Deficit	131 piastres
Additional expenses	15 piastres
Total deficit	146 piastres

As we can see from the above balance, there is a deficit of 146 piastres for that quarter, but as it was the first year of its existence, we may presume that it had incurred extraordinary expenses. However, we note that in a three-yearly account submitted several years later the foundation was still in deficit, despite the fact that the rents from its workshops in Istanbul had increased and that the salaries had remained stable.

Another example of an extant yearly account is that for Vahid Pasha's flour mill which was endowed to his library in Kütahya. It can be noted that the mill produced a yearly income of 320 piastres, which was spent on the library, for which we have a list of expenses.[44]

There are also extant expense lists for the years 1835–1838 for the Köprülü Library. The expenses include the cost of purchasing books, coal, ink and subscribing to a newspaper.[45]

Documents concerning the finance of libraries are so rare that we cannot build any overall view. As we have noted, the documents cited above are all that we have at present. However, if more documents come to light in the future, we may arrive at a more complete picture of this aspect of the financials of Ottoman libraries.

---

44 BOA, Cevdet-Maarif 2343.
45 Köprülü Library, No. 2491/16, 2a.

Chapter Eleven

Library Buildings
and Furnishing

Much has already been written about library buildings and their architecture.[1] It is not the purpose of this chapter to reproduce this material in detail, but we will supplement existing knowledge with information from foundation deeds concerning not only the buildings, but also the furnishings. Until the establishment of the independent library, the Ottoman library pursued a precarious existence. As we noted in the introduction, the Ottoman word for library, *"kütübhane,"* could cover any collection of books from a single shelf to a building with several rooms. The library was, conceptually, the books, rather than the building which housed them, so that we see in the early period that it was often a cabinet in a mosque or

1   Semavi Eyice, "Eski Kütüphane Binaları Hakkında," *Türk Yurdu*, no. 267 (1957), 728–732; Behçet Ünsal, "Türk-Vakfı İstanbul Kütüphanelerinin Mimari Yöntemi," *VD*. XVIII (1984), 95–124; Ahmet Küçükkalfa, "İstanbul Vakıf Kütüphaneleri," *Vakıflar* (n.d.): 51–70; Bahtiyar Eroğlu, "Bazı Örnekleri ile Anadolu'da Tarihî Türk Kütüphane Mimarlığı" (MA thesis, Selçuk Üniversitesi, 1990); Alime Şahin, "İstanbul'daki Osmanlı Dönemi Kütüphane Yapıları Üzerine Bir Araştırma ve Hacı Beşir Ağa Kütüphanesi" (MA thesis, Yıldız Teknik Üniversitesi, 1997); Ayşe Yetişkin Kubilay, "18 ve 19. Yüzyıl İstanbul Vakıf Kütüphaneleri Üzerine Tipolojik Bir Değerlendirme," *Osmanlı Mimarlığının 7 Yüzyılı: Uluslarüstü Bir Miras Uluslararası Kongresi* (İstanbul: YEM Yayın, 1999): 149–153; M. Sami Bayraktar, "Türk Kütüphane Mimarisi," *Türkler* 15 (2002): 388–394; H. Sibel Çetinkaya, "Anadolu'daki Türk Kütüphaneleri (İstanbul Dışındaki), Anadolu Selçuklu Döneminden Cumhuriyet Dönemine Kadar" (PhD diss., Ege Üniversitesi, 2006); Özer Soysal, *Türk Kütüphaneciliği*, vols. 1–6 (Ankara: T.C. Kültür Bakanlığı, Kütüphaneler Genel Müdürlüğü, 1998–1999).

college. Often a space in a mosque was grilled off with iron railings to secure the library. In large mosque complexes, typically, one or two rooms were allocated specifically to the library. The earliest example of rooms being specifically allocated and probably built for the specific purpose of serving as a library is at the Çoban Mustafa Pasha Complex at Gebze (1526). Here, two rooms joined by a passage situated over the main archway are set aside for books.[2]

Among several complexes built in the early eighteenth century, each specified that a single room be set aside to be used as a library. In Amcazade Hüseyin Pasha's complex (1700), the library room is specially constructed to have eight windows to allow as much light as possible for the benefit of the readers.[3] Another complex built in 1724, Hekimoğlu Ali Pasha Complex, specified that a room above the main archway be set aside as a library. As in Çoban Mustafa Pasha's library, two hundred years earlier, the idea of situating the library over the archway was to provide as much circulation of air around the building as possible and thus prevent humidity damaging the books.[4]

In some of the complex libraries, the rooms set aside as libraries were solely for storing the books. The books themselves were to be read in other parts of the complex. However, in Damad İbrahim Pasha's complex (1720) in Istanbul, a larger room, the size of a classroom, is set aside as the library.[5] This seems to suggest, as in the case of Amcazade Hüseyin Pasha's complex, that the library room was intended not only to store books, but also as a reading room. This would seem to fit in with general trend of the period towards restrictions being placed on lending books. As lending books became restricted the tendency seems to have confined their reading not only to the complex, but to the library room itself, hence the provision of space for readers in the library.

With the arrival of the independent library we are able to observe purpose-built libraries unrestricted by the needs of the larger complex. The first of these is the Köprülü library which is the simplest possible construction. It consists of a single room roofed with a single dome. The single-room library became the standard model although a two-roomed format was also common. The square,

---

2 Tülay Reyhanlı, "Osmanlılarda Külliye Mimarisinin Gelişmesi" (PhD diss., İÜ, Edebiyat Fakültesi, 1974), 275. "... and the two upper rooms [over the main entrance] to be a library," İstanbul Ahkam Defterleri 1 (1998): 236.

3 Erdem Yücel, "Amcazade Hüseyin Paşa Külliyesi," VD 8 (1969): 259–260.

4 Semavi Eyice, "İstanbul, İstanbul'un Tarihî Eserleri," İA 5, no. 2 (1997): 111–114.

5 Godfrey Goodwin, History of Ottoman Architecture (London: Thames and Hudson, 1971), 368–369; Metin Sözen, Türk Mimarisinin Gelişimi ve Mimar Sinan (İstanbul: [Türkiye İş Bankası], 1975), 268.

domed, single room was not the only shape; some rooms have rectangular and octagonal floorplans. Later on, some of the independent libraries would be built on three levels, counting the basement as its own floor.

Library founders went to great lengths to describe how their libraries were to function: cataloguing, lending, opening times, personnel and salaries are often specified in minute detail, but very little is said about the actual building. This may be surprising when we consider that the major initial cost was the building itself. However, there are some exceptions and in some of the foundation deeds specifications are made to the building. In the foundation deed of the Atıf Efendi Library (1741), the size of the building is specified.[6] In his foundation deed, Veliyüddin Efendi specifies that his library should be built of stone, have a basement and two domes.[7] In Yusuf Ağa's foundation deed, it is specified that the library building should be of stone and have one dome.[8]

As for the furnishing, there is absolutely no mention made in foundation deeds. This is a little less surprising when we consider the spartan furnishings of a library. Like the inside of a mosque, the Ottoman library consisted of carpeted flooring uncluttered by furnishing. There were no tables or chairs, the readers sitting cross-legged on the cushioned floor reading on their laps. Occasionally reading stands (*rahle*) were provided. Apart from the shelves of cabinets for storing the books, the only furnishing would be rush mats on the floor sometimes covered by carpets and cushions. Usually, the libraries were open during daylight hours to avoid having to use lamps which produced soot that would harm the books. Where additional light was required, lamps were suspended from the domes, as in mosques.[9] It is almost as if the furnishings were considered an integral part of the library building and therefore not worthy of any particular mention.

An American woman who worked in Istanbul as president of Women's College at the end of the nineteenth and beginning of the twentieth century describes the typical foundation library thus:

> The library buildings were very different from modern ones. They were simply built, with fine lines, often of stone, with a dome—or several domes arranged in a circle—over the reading room. Through picturesque irregular windows in these domes the light fell directly upon those who were reading, below. Under the

6 VGMA, 735, 256.
7 VGMA, 745, 79.
8 Istanbul Court Registers, Evkaf-ı Hümayun Müfettişliği 261, 54.
9 Ahmet Küçükkalfa, "Kütüphanelerde Aydınlatma, Kandiller ve Tavana Asılı Diğer Semboller," *Folklor, Halkbilim Dergisi* 4, nos. 2–3 (1984): 47–50.

domes were cushions, both round and square, to sit upon, and low inlaid stools upon which to rest the books. One could even recline on a cushion and, with his manuscript on a stool in the light under a dome, pursue his education comfortably. The floors were always covered with valuable, and sometimes almost priceless, rugs. Shoes must be removed at the door. The books were usually manuscripts, and each one kept in a case to protect it from dust.[10]

In the Ayasofya Library (1740), Mahmud I specified that among the personnel there should be a repairman specialized in mother-of-pearl which would indicate that he intended that the cupboard doors should be inlaid with mother-of-pearl and that they would require regular replacing as they fell out, but there is no provision made for their installation in the foundation deed.

Any reference to furnishing is to be found not in the foundation deeds, but in account books from later periods. In an account book covering both the Ayasofya and Fatih Libraries, there are references to the cost of providing cushions and rush mats. During the building of Ayasofya Library an account book details some of the furniture:

> Pair of grills in walnut frames for the library cabinets
> Lock for the library cabinets
> Walnut cabinet doors
> Gilded furnishing for the cabinet
> Cypress wood shelves
>
> Linden wood drawer[11]

Ayasofya seems to have been particularly well fitted out. Subhi, the contemporary chronicler, noted that when it was opened it was furnished with low divans which had cushions embroidered in gold and silver thread.[12] We must bear in mind that Ayasofya Library is a special case: it is the endowment of Mahmud I, a sultan who was particularly interested in libraries.

When Raşid Efendi built his library in Kayseri in 1797, he wanted to ensure that it was properly furnished. In an account book of the time, we note that curtains, coverings and cushions for the divans and a stove was bought for the

---

10 Mary Mills Patrick, *Under Five Sultans* (London: Williams and Norgate, 1930), 94.
11 TSA, D. 3153.
12 Subhi, *Tarih*, 174b.

library. He also made sure that there was writing materials for the students. In a letter to the deputy administrator, he wrote:

> Students who visit the library to study, in improving their knowledge may wish to make notes in their notebooks and may be without reed pen and pen cases. Pens, pen knives, scissors, pen cases and three writing platforms made in Edirne style have been sent to you.[13]

Although it was not the practice for libraries to provide writing equipment for readers to make notes and students normally carried pen cases in their girdle, Raşid Efendi wanted to cater for those students who arrived unprepared.

We can see from a set of accounts for the building of the Vahid Pasha Library in Kütahya (1811) just how little expenditure was made on the furnishings. After spending over 20,000 piastres on the library itself a mere 383 piastres are spent on furnishing the reading room:[14]

Bilecik-make wall cushions	140 piastres
3 kilims for the floor	87 piastres
1 central carpet	40 piastres
Wool for the floor cushions	43 piastres
Covering for the floor cushions	47 piastres
Covering for the wall cushions	21 piastres
Rush matting	5 piastres
Total	383 piastres

In Yusuf Ağa's Library in Konya (1794), we discover that the total cost of the library building came to 2,281,098 paras [57,027 piastres] and 21,342 paras [538 piastres] for furnishings which consisted of nineteen carpets, cushions and their covers, some rush matting and one prayer rug.[15]

From contemporary descriptions and more recent research we have piecemeal descriptions of how some libraries stored their collections. In the Topkapı Palace Library, the bookcases were placed against the wall and had grills to secure

---

13 Ali Rıza Karabulut, *Kayseri Râşid Efendi Kütüphanesindeki Türkçe Arapça Farsca Yazmalar Katalogu* (Kayseri: İl Halk Kütüphanesi Müdürlüğü, 1982), 17.
14 BOA, DBŞM, No. 7965.
15 BOA, Kepeci No. 806.

them.[16] In Bostancılar Ocağı Library, again in Topkapı Palace, the bookcases were also secured with grills.[17] In Ayasofya Library, some books were stored in niches in the wall of the reading room and were secured with grills, while other books which were kept in the book-store were placed in bookcases which were in the middle of the room.[18] In the Köprülü and Ragıb Pasha libraries, the books were in bookcases in the reading room. According to Ubicini the bookcases in the Köprülü Library had grills.[19] In the Ragıb Pasha Library, the bookcases, which were placed in the middle of reading room, were secured in an iron cage.[20] In the Nuruosmaniye and Atıf Efendi Libraries, each consisted of two rooms, where one was used as a reading room and the other as a book store.

FIGURE 13. The Quranic verse *Fiha kutubun qayyimatun* (Quran 98:3), "In which are true writings," was sometimes used to indicate a library. Ragıb Pasha Library, Istanbul, est. 1763.

16 Şükrü Yenal, "Topkapı Sarayı Müzesi Enderun Kitaplığı," *Güzel Sanatlar* 6 (1949): 87.

17 Robert Walpole, *Memoirs relating to European and Asiatic Turkey, edited from manuscript Journals by Robert Walpole* (London: Longman & Co., 1817), 172.

18 Ahmet Küçükkalfa, "Ayasofya Kütüphanesi," *İlgi* 17, no. 37 (1983): 16; Sabahattin Türkoğlu, *Ayasofya'nın Öyküsü* (İzmir: Yazıcı Basım, 2002), 134.

19 M. A. Ubicini, *Letters on Turkey, translated from the French by Lady Easthope* (London: W. Clowes and Sons, 1856), 100.

20 B. Ünsal, "Türk-Vakfı İstanbul Kütüphanelerinin Mimari Yöntemi," *VD* 18 (1984): 100.

Behçet Ünsal, an art historian, has, in a study of foundation library buildings, noted the following characteristics: Ottoman library buildings were usually surrounded by high walls on all four sides to cut out as much sound as possible from the surrounding streets and buildings. The buildings usually had one wall without windows which faced the southeast to avoid the direct morning sun which would have damaged the books. Lighting was provided by a double row of windows on the remaining three walls and sometimes more windows at the base of the dome. The floor of the building was usually built some height from the ground to ensure that there was ventilation under the library. Access was by a staircase to the door of the library. The walls were made up of two separate layers of stone to ensure insulation both from heat and noise. Storeroom doors were usually made of iron to preserve the collection from fires. All of the windows in the library had iron bars to protect it from burglary; inside, iron shutters served as a protection against fire.[21]

Other sources allow us to identify other general characteristics; Ottoman libraries were usually very plain inside, and the walls were either painted white or were tiled. The floors were covered in rush mats, woven kilims or carpets topped with cushions. Occasionally divans were set against the walls and these too were covered with cushions. Reading stands and writing platforms were often provided for the readers.

---

21 B. Ünsal, "Türk-Vakfı İstanbul Kütüphanelerinin Mimari Yöntemi," *VD* 18 (1984): 104–105.

Conclusion

Knowledge was prized as one of the greatest virtues in the Ottoman society. In order to spread it, the foundation of mosques, colleges, and libraries as charitable endowments were so common that it was virtually the sole means of establishing an infrastructure of educational and religious institutions. By the end of the Ottoman period, Istanbul alone had several thousand institutions built as charitable foundations. Typically, founders would build a building and set aside properties, the rent of which would go towards the upkeeping of this endowment. Thereafter, less wealthy benefactors often endowed the institution with gifts of all types. It was by these means that the Ottoman Empire established a system of higher education which consisted of colleges not only in the capital, but in every province. It was partly to facilitate the teaching activities that the first libraries were founded, that is, in order to allow the common people access to knowledge.

The word *kütübhane* (library) in Turkish has a wide range of meanings. It denotes a library, in the present sense of the word, but equally refers to any collection of books, be they stored in a cabinet in a series of bookcases, in a single bookcase, or even on a single shelf. The earliest Ottoman libraries were often small collections of books which were kept in a cabinet or room. Although some college complexes had a room which was used as the library, the primary function of the room was to store books which were lent to the reader to take away. This room was not a reading room. With the appearance of the independent library (1678), we can talk about Ottoman libraries in the modern sense of the word: a building with provision for storing and reading books with space for the librarians to work.

Although the first college established in the Ottoman Empire was founded by Orhan Gazi in İznik in 1331, we have no record of when and by whom the first library was established. There are indications, from archival material, that libraries existed in some colleges in the reign of Bayezid I (1389–1402). The earliest libraries for which we have foundation deeds are Murad II's college library in Edirne (1435), Umur Bey's mosque library in Bursa (1440), and İshak Bey's college library in Skopje. These early libraries, with one exception, were made up of small collections, donated to colleges and mosques and serviced by the staff of the institution to which they had been endowed. Librarians chosen from the existing staff of the college or mosque and fulfilled the role on a part-time basis, and nowhere do we find more than one librarian appointed.

After the conquest of Istanbul in 1453, there was an increase in the number and size of libraries founded, and by the end of the sixteenth century it became the norm for Istanbul colleges to be endowed with libraries. We find that the small libraries established in the districts of Edirne and Istanbul were gradually replaced by larger college libraries. The seventeenth century witnessed the proliferation of libraries not only in Istanbul, but in the provinces of the empire as well, and library collections everywhere benefited from numerous endowments by individuals, so that by the end of the seventeenth century most colleges had a library.

Up to the mid-seventeenth century most libraries had collections of two hundred to four hundred books, except for one or two larger college complexes. However, after the foundation of the Köprülü, the first independent Ottoman library (1678), many libraries began to have collections exceeding one thousand volumes, and library staff grew significantly.

During the first half of the eighteenth century, several large libraries were founded with an establishment of several librarians and other personnel. The reign of the bibliophile Sultan Mahmud I (1730–1754) can be considered the golden age of Ottoman libraries, a period which saw the establishment of libraries in every part of the empire, even in the border fortresses. In the last quarter of the eighteenth century, large independent libraries were founded also in the provinces, mainly by high-ranking government officials who wished to benefit their birthplace or the province which they had governed. In this period, the government attempted to regulate and control the libraries through the office of the trustees and some smaller libraries were consolidated into larger, more manageable, collections.

Mahmud II (1808–1839) attempted to rationalize the control of all charitable foundations, including libraries, by bringing their supervision under the single jurisdiction of a Ministry of Endowments, but it was not until the period of reforms, known as the *Tanzimat*, that this goal was realized. However, in Mahmud II's reign there was an intensive program of inspections in which inventories were made for most libraries.

The organization of Ottoman libraries also developed throughout the centuries of its existence. Although there was no uniform pattern for employing staff in the Ottoman libraries, there was a general trend to increase the number of librarians as the collections became larger. In the early period, it was usual to have a single librarian, but after the conquest of Istanbul many libraries established the post of assistant librarian, who was usually charged with organizing the lending service and the preparation of catalogues. As the practice of lending books gradually died out in the eighteenth century, the assistant librarian was employed in drawing up catalogues and inventories and the post finally disappeared by the end of the century. At the beginning of the seventeenth century, there began a trend to employ binders in the larger libraries. With the emergence of the independent library building, it was necessary to employ maintenance and cleaning personnel.

While in the early period it was the practice for the libraries to lend books, there was a general trend among library founders to restrict borrowing. By the end of the eighteenth century, this practice was virtually abolished altogether. As a result, the opening days and hours of the libraries were extended to give the reader reasonable access to the collections.

The smaller libraries, which were endowed to mosques or even kept in private houses, tended to suffer losses often through the practice of lending. Lack of funds to pay personnel exacerbated the problem. As the books disappeared, the supervisors responsible for the endowment, realizing that they lacked the power to maintain the collection, often transferred the books to a larger institution where there were facilities for the reader to consult without borrowing and necessary staff and income to look after the books. This move allowed such collections to survive to the present day. The larger institutions to which they were moved, either independent libraries or the libraries of the larger colleges, had both a reading room as well as a secure and lockable place for storing books. Mausoleums, which were usually kept locked, were sometimes used to store books, giving rise to the expression mausoleum libraries.

Some scholars in the past have classified libraries according to the location where the books were stored. This is misleading, as it is the nature of the collection which is paramount; the mausoleums in the college complex were used as a store place merely because they were secure. A collection of Arabic works intended for college students is still a college library no matter where the books are stored, be it a mosque, a mausoleum, or even a room in the bazaar.

By insisting that the books be read in the library, facilities for reading the books were provided in a reading room. The books were sometimes stored in the reading room and sometimes in an adjacent storeroom. The floors were covered in carpets and rush mats and the reader would sit on the floor and read his book often with the aid of a bookstand.

The classical Ottoman library ceased to have a monopoly over access to knowledge with the introduction of the Westernization movement in the nineteenth century. Although they continued to operate to the end of the

Ottoman period, and their collections could still be consulted, they became increasingly irrelevant in the last eighty years of the empire's existence as new, Western-style libraries with printed books began to appear. By their very nature and the way that they were established, the foundation libraries could not meet the sudden demand for a new type of knowledge, and it was left to the state to provide for the new generation of libraries. Their death knell was sounded in 1928 when the script that their books were written in was banned in a modern Turkey that had little regard for what it considered obsolete to the immediate needs of a modern society. Their collections have now become of antiquarian value, a source for Islamic studies and the study of Ottoman intellectual life.

Bibliography

Abbreviations

BOA	Başbakanlık Osmanlı Arşivi (Ottoman Archives)
DİFM	*Darülfunun İlahiyat Fakültesi Mecmuası* (İstanbul)
DTCF	Dil ve Tarih-Coğrafya Fakültesi
İA	*İslam Ansiklopedisi*
İFM	*İktisat Fakültesi Mecmuası* (İstanbul)
İVTD	Ömer Lütfi Barkan-Ekrem Hakkı Ayverdi. *İstanbul Vakıfları Tahrir Defteri, 953 (1546) Tarihli*. İstanbul: Baha Matbaası, 1970
MAD	Maliyeden Müdevver
Şaka'ik	Taşköprîzâde. *Eş-Şakâ'ikü'n-Nu'maniyye fi Ulemâi'd-Devleti'l-Osmaniyye*. Edited by Ahmed Subhi Furat. İstanbul: Edebiyat Fakültesi Basımevi, 1985
ŞSA	Şer'i Siciller Arşivi: Archives of Court Registers
TAD	*Tarih Araştırmaları Dergisi* (Ankara)
TD	*Tarih Dergisi* (İstanbul)
TDED	*Türk Dili ve Edebiyat Dergisi* (İstanbul)
TED	*Tarih Enstitüsü Dergisi* (İstanbul)
TKDB	*Türk Kütüphaneciler Derneği Bülteni* (Ankara)
TKT	İsmail E. Erünsal. *Türk Kütüphaneleri Tarihi II: Kuruluştan Tanzimat'a Kadar Osmanlı Vakıf Kütüphaneleri*. Ankara: Türk Tarih Kurumu Basımevi, 1988
TM	*Türkiyat Mecmuası* (İstanbul)
TOEM	*Tarih-i Osmani Encümeni Mecmuası* (İstanbul)
TSA	Topkapı Sarayı Arşivi (Topkapı Palace Archives)
TTEM	*Türk Tarih Encümeni Mecmuası* (İstanbul)
VD	*Vakıflar Dergisi* (Ankara)
VGMA	Vakıflar Genel Müdürlüğü Arşivi (Archives of the Directorate of Endowments [Ankara])

1. Archive Materials

A. **Başbakanlık Osmanlı Arşivi (Ottoman Archives)**

a. Mühimme Defterleri (Mühimme Registers). 6; 14; 16; 27; 35; 49; 51; 55; 64; 152. Mühimme-i Mısır 13.

b. Maliyeden Müdevver Defterler: MAD, (Treasury Account Books). 22; 626; 557; 994; 1018; 2056; 4792; 4973; 5019; 5070; 5102; 5103; 5170; 5179; 5305; 5455; 5761; 6483; 6888; 7706; 9771; 19 342; 19 432.

c. Tapu-Tahrir Defterleri (Land Registers). BOA Tapu-Tahrir Defterleri, 386, 398; 495; 1070. Belediye Library (now Atatürk Library) Tapu-Tahrir Defterleri, Mc. 0. 61; Mc. O. 70; Mc. O. 91; Mc. O. 116/1.

d. Kamil Kepeci Tasnifi, Kepeci-Ruus 217; Kepeci No. 806; Kepeci 7 500; Kepeci Mâliye Ahkâm Defteri, 67.

e. BOA, Divan Ruus Defterleri, 1; 9; 13; 16; 25; 29; 30; 32; 33; 35; 42; 43; 55; 63; 64; 66; 78; 80; 82; 84; 85; 89; 91; 92; 92 Mükerrer; 93; 94.

f. BOA, EV, HMH, 746, 2663, 5928; 7392; 8264, 8289; 8322; 8346.

g. BOA, DBŞM, 7965.

h. DBŞM, MHF, 13 242.

i. BOA, Hatt-ı Hümayun. 16 161; 18 713; 26 913

j. BOA, Cevdet Tasnifi, Cevdet-Evkaf: 711; 10 344; 13 507; 24 290; 29 601. Cevdet-Maârif: 100; 101; 103; 141; 355; 360; 404; 410; 557; 580; 583; 1870; 2044; 2301; 2342; 2343; 2821; 5043; 5465; 5825; 5850; 6581; 6585; 7730; 7991; 8093; 8213; 8474; 8613. Cevdet-Dahiliye: 6615; 8797. Cevdet-belediye: 4479. Cevdet-Maliye: 24 548.

k. BOA, İbnülemin Tasnifi, İbnülemin-Evkaf: 97; 718; 2989; 3109; 3194; 5990; 6486. İbnülemin-Hatt-ı Hümayun: 388; 503; 586. İbnülemin-Muharrerât-ı Hususiye: 76; 98. İbnül-emin-Tevcihat: 890; 1691; 2531.

l. BOA, Other Classifications
BOA, Ali Emiri Tasnifi, Fâtih Devri No. 70; BOA, Ayniyat Defteri No. 421; BOA, Fekete Tasnifi No. 1694; BOA, D. HMH, SFTH, No. 21 941/B; BOA, H. HMD, 1322 (9.1); BOA, Haremeyn, Dosya I; BOA, Müteferrik 89.
BOA, Sül, 26; BOA, Sül, 2861; BOA, Sül, 2864; BOA, Sül, 2874; BOA, Sül, 2918; BOA, Sül, 3261, s. 3b; BOA, Sül, Sultan I, Mahmud Dosyası; BOA, Sül, Haremeyn Dosyası I.
BOA, Şura-yı Devlet Evkaf 126/4;
BOA, Şura-yı Devlet 568; BOA, Şura-yı Devlet 209/9.

BOA, Y.E., 14/2045/126/10.

BOA, MF, KTU 1/19, 39, 51, 52, 87, 89; BOA, MF, KTU 2/49, 63, 95; BOA, MF, KTU 3/22, 90, 91; BOA, MF, KTU 4/44, 120, 119; BOA, MF, KTU 5/15, 35, 37, 57, 78, 94, 100; BOA, MF, KTU 6/31, Lef 2; 35, 51, 64, 96; BOA, MF, KTU 7/11 lef 3, 41, 71, 75, 77, 85, 87, 100 Lef 1; BOA, MF, KTU 8/15, 90, 104, 150, 153, 157; BOA, MF, KTU 9/2, 27.

B. *Topkapı Sarayı Arşivi (Topkapı Palace Archives)*

a. Defterler-Codices. TSA, D: 12; 21; 23; 305; 486; 500; 1067; 1767; 2002; 2362/2; 2184; 2184; 2211/1; 2362/10, 12; 2362/9; 2363/8,10, 12; 2993; 3153; 3228/4 ve 8; 3305; 3306; 3307; 3310; 3311; 3312; 4057; 4155; 4801; 6090; 7003; 7080; 7081; 8228; 8555; 8594; 9101; 9291; 9559; 9710; 9940; 10 294; 10 524; 11 510; 11 924.

b. Evraklar-Documents. TSA, E: 137/44, 45, 46; 174/58, 63, 70, 105; 463/2; 474/7; 861/1, 5, 11, 12; 1767; 2803/1; 2885/17, 19, 30; 5596; 6345; 8101.

C. *Şer'i Siciller (Court Registers)*

a. İstanbul Müftülüğü Şer'i Siciller Arşivi (Istanbul Court Registers), Ahi Çelebi Mahkemesi, 19; 29; 64; 78; 163; 210; 480. Bab Mahkemesi, 14; 26; 29; 57; 61; 70; 82; 98; 99; 238; 431; 446; 488; 518. Balat Mahkemesi, 2; 44; 76. Beşiktaş Mahkemesi, 158; 162; 197. Davud Paşa Mahkemesi, 95; 129. Evkaf-ı Hümayun Muhasibliği, 7; 102. Evkaf-ı Hümayun Müfettişliği, 8; 25; 27; 46; 50; 57; 63; 107; 109; 110; 130; 149; 164; 171; 213; 233; 261; 418; 647. Eyüp Mahkemesi, 212; 287; 426. Galata Mahkemesi, 17; 485; 584; 705. İstanbul Kadılığı, 79; 122. Kasımpaşa Mahkemesi, 107. Kısmet-i Askeriyye, 8; 12; 533; 1598; 1623. Rumeli Sadareti, 3; 8; 129; 131; 161; 188; 189; 196; 197; 250; 323; 337; 448; 491; 531. Üsküdar Mahkemesi, 148; 383; 564; 673. Mahmud Paşa Mahkemesi, 43; 62.

b. Ankara Milli Kütüphane Şer'i Siciller, Afyon Court Registers, 504; 514; 548 (A-51); 555 (A-57); 591. Bursa Court Registers, A. 82/96; A. 83/97; A. 107/126; A.94/110; A. 124/146; A. 143/170; A. 156/208; A. 180/406; A.91/107; A.81; B. 107; B. 135; B. 26/217; B. 41/235; B. 63/259; B.208; B. 89/294; B. 352/736. Kastamonu Court Registers. 17, 20, 81, 85, 121, 133. Manisa Court Registers, 113.

D. *Vakıflar Genel Müdürlüğü Arşivi (The Archives of the Directorate of Endowments)*
6; 19; 20; 29; 38; 39; 47; 52; 64; 67; 71; 74; 75; 76; 79; 82; 86; 87; 87; 90; 93; 98; 187; 188; 583/3; 502; 570; 571; 572; 574; 578; 579; 580; 580;

581/1; 582/1; 582/1; 585; 591; 623; 624; 625; 626; 628; 628; 629; 630; 631; 632; 632/8; 633; 634; 638; 639; 641; 642; 642; 720; 730; 731; 732; 733; 734; 735; 736; 737; 738; 739; 740; 741; 742; 743; 743; 744; 745; 746; 747; 987; 988; 1395; 1395; Dolap 1628.; Dolap 49; Haremeyn 14; Haremeyn X; Kasa 103; Kasa 108; Kasa 157; Kasa 159; Kasa 169; Kasa 175; Kasa 175; Kasa 187; Kasa 188; Kasa 188; Kasa 47; Kasa 47; Kasa 47; Kasa 8; Kasa 8; Kasa l59; Kuyudat-ı Evâmir-i âlişân Tabi-i Kalem-i Muhasebe-i Haremeyn No. 316.

Sultan Ahmed câmiinin Vazife Defteri, VGMA, 71; Vâlide Sultan evkafının Hazine Defteri, VGMA, 67; Köprülü Kütüphanesinin Vazife Defteri VGMA, 75; 76; Nevşehirli İbrahim Paşa evkafının Hazine Defteri, VGMA, 64; Hacı Beşir Ağa evkafının Hazine Defteri, VGMA, 19; Hekimzâde Ali Paşa evkafının Hazine Defteri, VGMA, 74, 79; Galata Sarayı Kütüphanesinin Vazife Defteri, VGMA, 87; Sultan Osman evkafının Hazine Defteri, VGMA, 52, 98; Mehmed Ragıb Paşa evkafının Hazine Defteri, VGMA, 82; Laleli Sultan Mustafa'nın Bostancılar Ocağında kurduğu Kütüphanenin Hazine Defteri, VGMA, 93; Abdülhamid evkafının Hazine Defteri, VGMA, 86; Laleli medresesindeki Kütüphanenin Hazine Defteri, VGMA, 93; Defter-i irad u mesârifât-ı evkaf-ı şerif-i merhum Sa'id Halet Efendi, tevkii-i sâbık, VGMA, 746, 113–114; Hazine-i Evkaf-ı Sultan Ahmed Hân-ı sâlis: VGMA,, Defter 90.

E. *İzmir Vakıflar Müdürlüğü Arşivi*
   II. Vakfiye Defteri, 40–45.

2. Library Catalogues

BOA, Ali Emiri Tasnifi, Fâtih Devri No. 70; TSA, D. 9559.; Süleymaniye ktp, Yazma Bağışlar 244; Süleymaniye ktp, Yazma Bağışlar 241, 242, 243; Türk— İslâm Eserleri Müzesi 2216; TSA, D. 3310; El Defteri: TSK, EH. 3003; Defter-i Kütüb (The Catalogue of the Palace Library): Magyar Todomanyos Akademia Künyvtara Keleti Gyüjtement, Török F. 39; VGMA, 1395, 91–114; Süleymaniye ktp, Yazma Bağışlar 2740; Süleymaniye Ktp, Yazma Bağışlar 2274; Süleymaniye Ktp, Yazma Bağışlar 2730.; Köprülü Kütüphânesi 2462, 2463; Beyazıt Umumi ktp, 21 346; Millet Kütüphânesi, Feyzullah Efendi 2196; Süleymaniye Ktp, Yazma Bağışlar2876, 2878; Süleymaniye ktp, Yazma Bağışlar 2269; Süleymaniye ktp, Yazma Bağışlar 2742, 2743, 2745, 2746; El Defteri: Yazma Bağışlar 2744;

Süleymaniye ktp, Ayasofya, Fihrist l, 2, 3; Türk - İslâm Eserleri Müzesi 2215;
TSA, D. 3312; Süleymaniye Ktp, Yazma Bağışlar 2278; VGMA, 731, 49–54;
Süleymaniye ktp, Aya-sofya, Fihrist 4, 5; Süleymaniye ktp, Ayasofya, Fihrist 6;
Nuruosmaniye Kütüphânesi, Fihrist l, 2, 3, 6; TSA, D. 3307; Ragıb Paşa ktp.
4111; TSA D. 3305; VGMA, Defter 642, 103–14; Süleymaniye ktp, Laleli 3792;
Süleymaniye Ktp, Yazma Bağışlar 2732; Beyazıt Umumi ktp, Veliyüddin Efendi
3290; Âtıf Efendi 2860; Süleymaniye ktp, Yazma Bağışlar 2277; Süleymaniye
Ktp, Yazma Bağışlar 2720, 2722, 2725. El Defteri: Süleymaniye ktp, Yazma
Bağışlar 2721; Süleymaniye ktp, Halet Efendi 838; BOA, EV, HMH, 7392;
Süleymaniye ktp, Yazma Bağışlar 243; Süleymaniye Ktp, Yazma Bağışlar 245,
246; Süleymaniye Ktp, Yazma Bağışlar, No. 251; Süleymaniye Ktp, Yazma
Bağışlar 249; BOA, EV, 32 721).

3. Books and Articles

Abdurrahman Hibrî. *Enîsü'l-Müsâmirîn.* Edited by Ratip Kazancıgil. Edirne:
   Türk Kütüphaneciler Derneği Edirne Şubesi, 1996.

Adıvar, Adnan. *Osmanlı Türklerinde İlim.* İstanbul: Maarif Matbaası, 1943.

Afşar, İrec. "Fihrist-i Kitâbhâne-i Sadrüddin-i Konevî." *Tahkikât-ı İslâmî* 10, no.
   1–2 (1374/1996): 477–502.

Ahmed Refik. "Damad Ibrahim Paşa Zamanında Ürgüp ve Nevşehir." *TTEM,*
   no. 80 (1340H): 156–185.

———. *Onuncu Asr-ı Hicride İstanbul Hayatı.* İstanbul: Matbaa-i Orhaniye,
   1333H.

———. *Alimler ve Sanatkarlar.* İstanbul: Kütübhane-i Hilmi, 1924.

———. "Fatih Devrine Âit Vesikalar." *TOEM,* no. 49–62 (1337H): 49–62.

———. *Onaltıncı Asırda İstanbul Hayatı: 1553–1591.* İstanbul: İstanbul Devlet
   Basımevi, 1935.

Akar, Azade. "Ayasofya'da Bulunan Türk Eserleri ve Süslemelerine Dair Bir
   Araştırma." *VD* 8 (1969): 284–286.

Aksan, Virginia. *An Ottoman Statesman in War and Peace: Ahmed Resmi Efendi
   1700–1783.* Leiden: E. J. Brill, 1995.

Aksu, Fehmi. "Yazma Kitaplar." *Ün* 3, no. 28 (1936): 394.

Aktepe, Münir. "Nevşehirli Damad Ibrahim Paşa'ya Aid İki Vakfiye." *TD* 11
   (1960): 149–160.

———. "İzmir Şehri Osmanlı Devri Medreseleri Hakkında Ön Bilgi." *TD* 26
   (1972): 114–117.

Aldoğan, Ayşen. "Şehit Ali Paşa Kütüphanesi." *Türkiyemiz*, no. 35 (1982): 1–7.

Ali Haydar. *Tertîbü's-Sunûf fî Ahkâmi'l-Vukûf.* İstanbul: Şirket-i Mürettebiyye Matbaası, 1337H.

Altan, Mustafa Haşim. "Die Bibliotheken im türkisch-zypriotischen Bundesstaat." *Biblos* 28 (1979): 306–309.

Aşık Çelebi. *Meşa'irü'ş-şu'ara.* Edited by G. M. Owens. London: E. J. W. Gibb Memorial, 1971.

Atâ'î. *Hadaikü'l-Haka'ik.* Vol 1. İstanbul: n.p., 1268H.

Ateş, İbrahim. "Mescid-i Nebevî'nin Yapıldığı Günden Bu Yana Geçirdiği Genişletme Girişimleri." *VD* 24 (1994): 5–50.

Aybaş, Tekin. *Toplu Kataloglar ve Türkiye Uygulaması.* Ankara: TÜRDOK, 1979.

Ayverdi. Ekrem Hakkı, *Osmanlı Mimarisinin İlk Devri.* İstanbul: İstanbul Fetih Cemiyeti, 1966.

———. *Osmanlı Mimarisinde Çelebi Mehmed ve II. Sultan Murad Devri.* İstanbul: İstanbul Fetih Cemiyeti, 1972.

———. *Avrupa'da Osmanlı Mimari Eserleri, Yugoslavya.* Vol. 3.3. İstanbul: İstanbul Fetih Cemiyeti, 1981.

———. *Avrupa'da Osmanlı Mimari Eserleri: Bulgaristan, Yunanistan, Arnavutluk.* İstanbul: İstanbul Fetih Cemiyeti, 1982.

Baki, Edip Ali. *Mısırlıoğlu Abdurrahim Karahisari.* Afyon: Yeni Matbaa, 1953.

Baltacı, Cahid. *XV., XVI. Asırlarda Osmanlı Medreseleri.* İstanbul: İrfan Matbaası, 1976.

Barkan, Ömer Lütfi. "Edirne ve Civarındaki Bazı İmaret Te'sislerinin Yıllık Muhasebe Bilançoları." *Belgeler* 1, no. 2 (1965): 235–377.

———. "Fatih Camii ve İmareti Tesislerinin 1489–1490 Yıllarına Ait Muhasebe Bilançoları." *İktisat Fakültesi Mecmuası* 23, nos. 1–2 (1962): 297–341.

———. "Ayasofya Camii ve Eyüp Türbesinin 1489–1491 Yıllarına ait Muhasebe Bilançoları." *İktisat Fakültesi Mecmuası* 23, nos. 1–2 (1963): 342–379.

———. "XVI. Asrın İkinci Yarısında Türkiye'de Fiat Hareketleri." *Belleten* 34, no. 136 (1970): 557–607.

———. "H. 933–934 (M. 1527–1528) Mali Yılına Ait Bir Bütçe Örneği." *İktisat Fakültesi Mecmuası* 15 (1954): 251–329.

———. "Süleymaniye Camii ve İmareti Tesislerine ait Bir Yıllık Bir Muhasebe Bilançosu 993/994 (1585/1586)." *VD* 9 (1971): 109–161.

Baudier, Michel. *Histoire Generalle du Serrail et de la Cour du Grand Seigneur Empereur des Turcs.* Paris: Chez Claude Caramoisy, 1626.

Baykal, İsmail. " Topkapı Sarayı Müzesi Kitaplıkları." *Güzel Sanatlar* 6 (1949): 75–84.

———. "Fatih Sultan Mehmed'in Hususi Kütüphanesi ve Kitapları." *VD* 4 (1958): 77–79.

Baykal, Kazım. *Bursa Anıtları*. Bursa: Aysan Matbaası, 1950.

Bayraktar, M. Sami, "Türk Kütüphane Mimarisi." In *Türkler*, vol. 15, edited by Hasan Celal Güzel-Kemal Çiçek, 388–394. Ankara: Yeni Türkiye, 2002.

Bayraktar, N. "İstanbul'daki Vakıf Kütüphaneler ve Süleymaniye Kütüphanesi." *TKDB* 15. No. 3 (1966): 134–138.

Bayraktar, S. Nail "Amcazâde Hüseyin Paşa Kütüphanesi." *İstanbul Ansiklopedisi* 2 (1959): 799.

Baysal, Jale. "Turkish Publishing Activities Before and After the New Alphabet." *Anatolica* 8 (1981): 115–131.

Behçet Ünsal. "Türk-Vakfı İstanbul Kütüphanelerinin Mimari Yöntemi." *VD* 18 (1984): 95–124.

Berker, Aziz. "Mora İhtilali Tarihçesi veya Penah Efendi Mecmuası." *Tarih Vesikaları* 2, no. 12 (1943): 473–480.

Beydilli, Kemal. *Türk bilim ve matbaacılık tarihinde Mühendishane. Mühendishane Matbaası ve Kütüphanesi (1776–1826)*. İstanbul: Eren, 1995.

Bilge, Mustafa. *İlk Osmanlı Medreseleri*. İstanbul: Edebiyat Fakültesi Basımevi, 1984.

Birinci, Ali. "Abdurrahman Nâcim." *Müteferrika*, no. 8–9 (1996): 109–116.

Birnbaum, E. "The Ottomans and Chagatay Literature." *Central Asian Journal* 20 (1976): 157–190.

Burton, Richard F. *Personal Narrative of a Pilgrimage to el-Medinah and Meccah*. Vol. 2. London: Longman, Brown, Green, Longmans, and Roberts, 1855.

Cerasi, Maurice. *The Istanbul Divanyolu*. Würzburg: Ergon-Verlag in Kommission, 2004.

Cichocki, Nina. "The Life Story of the Çemberlitaş Hamam: From Bath to Tourist Attraction." PhD diss., University of Minnesota, 2005.

Crecelius, Hamza Abd al-Aziz Badr-Daniel. "The Awqaf of al-Hajj Bashir Agha in Cairo." *Annales Islamologiques* 27 (1993): 291–308.

Cunbur, Müjgan. "Fatih Devri Kütüphaneleri ve Kütüphaneciliği,." *TKDB* 6 (1957): 1–16.

———. "I. Abdülhamid'in Vakfiyesi ve Hamidiye Kütüphanesi." *Dil ve Tarih-Coğrafya Fakültesi Dergisi* 22 (1964): 17–69.

———. "Kanuni Devrinde Kitap Sanatı, Kütüphaneleri ve Süleymaniye Kütüphanesi." *TKDB* 17, no. 3 (1968): 134–142.

———. "Kayseri'de Raşit Efendi kütüphanesi ve Vakfiyesi." *VD* 7 (1969): 185–195.

———. "Lâle Devrinde İstanbul Kütüphaneleri." *Türk Kültürü* 9 (1971): 363–368.

———. "Münif Paşa Lâyihâsı ve Değerlendirilmesi." *TAD* 2, nos. 2–3 (1964): 223–231.

———. "Osmanlı Çağı Türk Vakıf Kütüphanelerinde Personel Düzenini Geliştirme Çabaları." In *VII. Türk Tarih Kongresi*, 675–688. Ankara: Türk Tarih Kurumu Basımevi, 1973.

———. "Tarihimizde Anadolu'da kütüphane Kurma Çabaları." *TKDB* 15, no. 3 (1966): 129–133.

———. "Türk Kütüphaneciliğinin Tarihî Kökenleri." *TKDB* 12, nos. 3–4 (1963): 105–116.

———. "Vakfiyelerine Göre Eski Türk Kütüphanelerinin Yönetimi," in *TKDB* 11, nos. 1–2 (1962): 3–21.

———. "Yusuf Ağa Kütüphanesi ve Kütüphane Vakfiyesi," *TAD* 1, no. 1 (1963): 203–217.

Çavdar. Tuba R. "Tanzimat'tan Cumhuriyet'e Kadar Osmanlı Kütüphanelerinin Gelişimi." PhD diss., Istanbul University, 1995.

Çetinalp, Özden. "Âtıf Efendi Library in Vefa." *Rölöve* 1 (1968).

Dağlı, Muhtar Yahya. *İstanbul Mahalle Bekçilerinin Destan ve Mani Katarları*. İstanbul: Türk Neşriyat Yurdu, 1948.

Defterdar Sarı Mehmed Paşa. *Zübde-i Vekayi'ât*. Edited by Abdülkadir Özcan. Ankara: Türk Tarih Kurumu Basımevi, 1995.

De Kay, James E. *Sketches of Turkey in 1831 and 1832 by an American*. New York: J. & J. Harper, 1833.

Della Valle Pietro. *Viaggi*. Venice: Baglioni, 1667.

Dener, Halit. *Süleymaniye Umumi Kütüphanesi*. İstanbul: İstanbul Maarif Basımevi, 1957.

Dobrača, Kasim. *Katalog arapskih, turskih i perzijskih rukopisa*. Sarajevo: Starješinstvo islamske vjerske zajednice za SR Bosnu i Hercegovinu, 1963.

Düstûr, Tertib-i sânî. Vol. 6. İstanbul: Matbaa-i Amire, 1331H.

Dwight, H. G. *Constantinople Old and New*. London: C. Scribner's Sons, 1915.

Eché, Youssef. *Les Bibliotheques Arabes*. Damascus: n.p., 1967.

Elezovic, Glisa. *Turski Spomenici* 1, no. 2 (1952).

Emecen, Feridun. "Korkut, Şehzâde." *DİA* 26 (2002): 205–207.

Emsen, Şemim. "Osmanlı İmparatorluğu Devrinde Türkiye Kütüphanelerinin Tarihçesi." *TKDB* 9, no. 1–2 (1960): 14–35.

Erdoğan, Abdülkadir. "Kanuni Süleyman Devri Vezirlerinden Pertev Paşa ve Eserleri." *VD* 2 (1942): 233–243.

———. *Şeyh Vefa, Hayatı ve Eserleri.* İstanbul: Ahmed İhsan Basımevi, 1941.

Erdoğan, M. "İstanbul'da Kütahyalı Bir Şeyh Ailesi Seyyid Ebu Bekir Dede ve Ahfâdı." *İstanbul Araştırmaları*, no. 7 (1998): 125–169.

Ergin, Osman. *Fatih İmareti Vakfiyesi.* İstanbul: Belediye Matbaası, 1945.

Eroğlu, Bahtiyar. "Bazı Örnekleri ile Anadolu'da Tarihî Türk Kütüphane Mimarlığı." MA thesis, Selçuk Üniversitesi, Konya 1990.

Erten, S., Fikri. *Tekelioğulları.* İstanbul: Hüsnütabiat Basımevi, 1955.

Erünsal, İsmail E. "Türk Edebiyatı Tarihine Kaynak Olarak Arşivlerin Değeri." *TM* 19 (1980): 213–222.

———. "Fatih Devri Kütüphaneleri ve Molla Lütfi Hakkında Birkaç Not." *TD* 33 (1980–1981): 57–78.

———. " Türk Edebiyatı Tarihinin Arşiv Kaynakları I: II. Bayezid Devrine Ait Bir İn'âmât Defteri." *TAD* 10–11 (1981): 303–342.

———. *Kütüphanecilikle İlgili Metinler ve Belgeler.* Vols. 1–2. İstanbul: Edebiyat Fakültesi Matbaası, 1982–1990.

———. "Şehid Ali Paşa'nın İstanbul'da Kurduğu Kütüphaneler ve Müsadere Edilen Kitapları." *Kütüphanecilik Dergisi* 1 (1987): 79–88.

———. "Catalogues and Cataloguing in the Ottoman Libraries." *Libri* 37, no. 4 (1987): 333–349.

———. *Türk Kütüphâneleri Tarihi II; Kuruluştan Tanzimat'a Kadar Osmanlı Vakıf Kütüphâneleri.* Ankara: Türk Tarih Kurumu Basımevi, 1988.

———. "959/1552 Tarihli Defter-i Kütüb." *Erdem* 9, no. 10 (1988): 181–193.

———. "The Establishment and Maintenance of Collections in the Ottoman Libraries: 1400–1839." *Libri* 39, no. 1 (1989): 1–17.

———. "The Catalogue of Bayezid II's Palace Library." *Kütüphanecilik Dergisi, Belge Bilgi Kütüphane Araştırmaları*, no. 3 (1992): 55–66.

———. "The Oldest Extant Ottoman Library Catalogue." *61st IFLA General Conference*, booklet 7 (1995): 58–62.

———. "Yazma Eserlerin Kataloglanmasında Karşılaşılan Güçlükler I: Eser ve Müellif Adının Tesbiti." In *Hakkı Dursun Yıldız Armağanı*, 233–243. Ankara: Türk Tarih Kurumu Basımevi, 1995.

―――. "Fatih Camii Kütüphanesine Ait En Eski Müstakil Katalog." *Erdem* 9, no. 26 (1996): 659–664.

―――. "Şeyh Vefa ve Vakıfları Hakkında Yeni Bir Belge." *The Journal of Islamic Studies* 1 (1997): 47–64.

―――. "Evkaf Nâzırı Hammâde-zâde Halil Paşa'nın İstanbul'da mevcut Vakıf Kütüphânelerinin Islahı ve Bir Mekânda Toplanması Konusundaki Çalışmaları." In *Türk Kütüphâneciliğinden İzdüşümler: Nail Bayraktar'a Armağan I (Hatıra ve Bilimsel Makaleler).* Edited by İrfan Dağdelen, Hüseyin Türkmen, and Nergis Ulu, 90–98. İstanbul: Büyükşehir Belediye Başkanlığı, 2005.

―――. "Fetihten Sonra İstanbul'da Kurulan İlk Vakıf Kütüphânesi ve Vakfiyesi." In *Prof. Dr. Mübahat S. Kütükoğlu'na Armağan,* edited by Zeynep Tarım Ertuğ, 391–403. İstanbul: İstanbul Üniversitesi Edebiyat Fakültesi, 2006.

―――. "Tanzimat Sonrası Türk Kütüphaneciliği ile İlgili Belgeler." *The Journal of Ottoman Studies* 31 (2008): 229–339.

Evkaf Nâzırı Hammâdezâde Halil Hamdi Paşa Tarafından Evkaf Hakkında Sadarete Takdim Edilen Lâyiha Suretidir. İstanbul, n.d.

Evkaf-ı Hümâyun Nezâreti'nin Tarihçe-i Teşkilatı ve Nüzzârın Terâcim-i Ahvâli. İstanbul: Evkaf-ı İslâmiye Matbaası, 1335H.

Eyice, Semavi, "İstanbul, İstanbul'un Tarihî Eserleri." *İA* 5, no. 2 (1997): 111–114.

―――. "Eski Kütüphane Binaları Hakkında." *Türk Yurdu,* no. 267 (1957): 728–732.

Faroqhi, Suraiya. "Vakıf Administration in Sixteenth Century Konya: The Zaviye of Sadreddin-i Konevî." *JESHO* 17, no. 2 (1974): 145–172.

―――. *Subjects of the Sultan: Culture and Daily Life in the Ottoman Empire.* London: I. B. Tauris, 2000.

Fatih Mehmed II Vakfiyeleri. Ankara: Vakıflar Umum Müdürlüğü Neşriyatı, 1938.

Feridun Bey. *Münşe'ât-ı Selâtîn.* Vol. 1. İstanbul: Darü't-Tıbaati'l-Amire, 1274H.

Feyzioğlu, Nesrin. "Müzik Malzemesinin Oluşum ve Biçimlenmesinde Matematiğin Rolü." *Güzel Sanatlar Enstitüsü Dergisi,* no. 13 (2004): 95–104.

Fisher, Sydney Nettleton. *The Foreign Relations of Turkey 1481–1512.* Urbana, IL: University of Illinois Press, 1948.

Galland, Antoine. *İstanbul'a Ait Günlük Hatıralar (1672–1673).* Vol. 1. Translated by N. S. Örik. Ankara: Türk Tarih Kurumu Basımevi, 1949.

Goodwin, Godfrey. *History of Ottoman Architecture.* London: Thames and Hudson, 1971.

Göçek, Fatma Müge. *East Encounters West, France and the Ottoman Empire in the Eighteenth Century.* Oxford: Oxford University Press, 1987.

Gökbilgin, M. Tayyib. *XV-XVI. Asırlarda Edirne ve Paşa Livası.* İstanbul: Üçler Basımevi, 1952.

———. "Süleyman I." *İA* 11 (1940–1986): 149.

———. "Köprülüler." *İA* 6 (1940–1986): 902.

Gökçen, İbrahim. *Manisa Tarihinde Hayırlar ve Vakıflar.* İstanbul: Marif Basımevi, 1950.

Gökman, Muzaffer. *Kütüphanelerimizden Notlar.* İstanbul: Kardeşler Basımevi, 1952.

———. *Murat Molla. Hayatı, Kütüphanesi ve Eserleri.* İstanbul: Cumhuriyet Matbaası, 1943.

Gökoğlu, A. *Paphlagonia-Pagflagonya.* Kastamonu: Doğrusöz Matbaası, 1952.

Gökyay, Orhan Şaik. *Evliya Çelebi Seyahatnamesi.* Vol. 1. İstanbul: Yapı Kredi Yayınları, 1996.

Guyaş, Paul. *Halk Kütüphanelerinin Suret-i Te'sisi ve Usul-i İdaresi.* Translated by Hamit Zübeyir Koşar. İstanbul, 1925; reprinted in Erünsal's *Kütüphanecilikle İlgili Osmanlıca Metinler ve Belgeler.* Vol. 2. İstanbul: Edebiyat Fakültesi Matbaası, 1982.

Gültepe, Necati. "Vakıf Kütüphaneciliğinin Müesseseleşmesi." *Türk Yurdu* 8, no. 6 (1987): 22–32.

Güner, Hamza. *Kütahya Camileri.* Kütahya: n.p., 1964.

Hadika, no. 40, 320. İstanbul: n.p. 1286R.

Hadžiosmanović, Lamıja. *Biblioteke u Bosni i Hercegovini za vrijeme austrougarske vladavine.* Sarajevo: Veselin Masleša, 1980.

Hâfız-ı Kütüb Fâre. *Muallimler Mecmuası,* year 2, no. 22 (1924): 742.

Hasandedic, Hafzija. "Muslimanske Biblioteke u Mostaru." *Anali Gazi Hüsrev-begove biblioteke* 1 (1972): 107–112.

Hayat 2, no. 46 (1927): 2.

Heinz, Wilhelm. "Die Kultur der Tulpenzeit des Osmanischen Reiches." *WZKM* 61 (1967): 62–116.

Hızlı, Mefail. *Osmanlı Klasik Döneminde Bursa Medreseleri.* İstanbul: İz Yayıncılık, 1998.

Hicaz Vilayeti Salnamesi. Mekke-i Mükerreme: [Vilayet Matbaası?], 1309 [1891].

Hüsameddin, Hüseyin. *Amasya Tarihi.* Vol. 1. İstanbul: Hikmet Matbaası, 1327H.

Hüseyin Ayvansarayî. *Hadikatü'l-Cevâmî.* Vol. 1. İstanbul: Matbaa-i Amire, 1281H.

İnalcık, Halil. "The Policy of Mehmed II towards the Greek Population of Istanbul and Byzantine Buildings of the City." *Dumbarton Oaks Papers* 23–25 (1968–1969): 231- 249.

―――. *Osmanlı İmparatorluğu: Klâsik Çağ (1300–1600).* Translated by Ruşen Sezer. İstanbul: Yapı Kredi Yayınları, 2003.

―――. *The Ottoman Empire: The Classical Age 1300–1600.* Translated by Norman Itzkowitz and Colin Imber. London: Praeger Publishers, 1973.

İnciciyan, P. Ğ. *XVIII. Asırda İstanbul Tarihi.* Translated by Hrand D. Andreasyan. İstanbul: İstanbul Fethi Derneği, 1956.

İsfendiyaroğlu, Fethi. *Galatasaray Tarihi.* İstanbul: n.p., 1952.

Işkî Mustafa b. Ömer Kilisî. *Ta'tirü Ercâi'd-Devleti'l-Mecdiyye.* Istanbul University Manuscript Library, T. Y. 1490.

İzzi. *Tarih.* İstanbul: Mehmed Raşid ve Ahmed Vasıf [Matbaası], 1199H.

Jacobs, Emil. *Untersuchungen zur Geschichte der Bibliothek im Serai zu Konstantinopel.* Heidelberg: C. Winter, 1919.

Kaleşi, Hasan. "Yugoslavya'da İlk Türk Kütüphaneleri." *Türk Kültürü* 6, no. 38 (1965): 40–43.

―――. "Ishak Çelebi von Bitola und seine Stiftungen." *La Macedonia et les Macedoniens dans la Passe.* 149–162. Skopje: n.p., 1970.

―――. *Najstariji vakufski dokumenti u Jugoslaviji na arapskom jeziku.* Priština: Zajednica naučnih ustanova Kosova, 1972.

―――. "Oriental Culture in Yugoslav Countries from the Fifteenth Century until the Eend of the Seventeenth Century." In *Ottoman Rule in Middle Europe and the Balkans in Sixteenth and Seventeenth Centuries,* edited by Jaroslav Cesar, 359–404. Prague: Oriental Institute in Academia, 1978.

Kaleşi, Hasan-Mehmed Mehmedovski. *Tri vakufnami na kačanikli Mehmed-Paša.* Skopje: Nova Makedonija,1958.

Karabulut, Ali Rıza. *Kayseri Râşid Efendi Kütüphanesindeki Türkçe Arapça Farsca Yazmalar Katalogu.* Kayseri: İl Halk Kütüphanesi Müdürlüğü, 1982.

Karatay, Zafer. "Bahçesaray." *DİA* 4 (1991): 482–483.

Karaöz, Sadık. *Manisa İli Kütüphaneleri.* Ankara: Ayyıldız Matbaası, 1974.

el-Kebisî, Muhammed Abdullah. *Ahkâmu'l-Vakf fi'ş-Şeriati'l-İslamiyye.* Baghdad: Matbaatü'l-İrşad, 1977.

Kenderova, Stoyanka, and Zorka Ivanova. *From the Collections of Ottoman Libraries in Bulgaria During the Eighteenth–Nineteenth Centuries.* Sofia: n.p., 1999.

————. "Les lecteurs de Samakov au XIXe siècle," *Revue des mondes musulmans et de la Méditerranée*, nos. 87–88 (1999): 61–75.

Kepeci, Kamil. *Bursa Şer'iyye Sicilleri Kütüphaneler Defteri*. Manuscript in private collection.

Köprülü, Orhan. "Feyzullah Efendi." *İA* 4 (1940–1986): 599.

Kritovoulos. *History of Mehmed II*. Translated from the Greek by Charles T. Riggs. Princeton: Princeton University Press, 1954.

Kubilay, Ayşe Yetişkin. "18 ve 19. Yüzyıl İstanbul Vakıf Kütüphaneleri Üzerine Tipolojik Bir Değerlendirme." In *Osmanlı Mimarlığının 7 Yüzyılı: Uluslarüstü Bir Miras Uluslararası Kongresi*, 149–153. İstanbul: YEM Yayın, 1999.

Kuran, Abdullah. "Orta Anadolu'da Klasik Osmanlı Mimarisi Çağının Sonlarında Yapılan İki Külliye." *VD* 4, no. 5 (1971): 239–247.

Kut, Günay. "Sultan I, Mahmud Kütüphânesi (Ayasofya Kütüphânesi)." In *Osmanlı Devleti'nde Bilim Kültür ve Kütüphâneler*, edited by Özlem Bayram et al., 99–128. Ankara: Türk Kütüphaneciler Derneği, 1999.

————, Nimet Bayraktar. *Yazma Eserlerde Vakıf Mühürleri*. Ankara: Başbakanlık Basımevi, 1984.

Kuyulu, İnci. *Kara Osmanoğlu Ailesine Ait Mimarî Eserler*. Ankara: Kültür Bakanlığı, 1992.

Küçükkalfa, Ahmet. "Ayasofya Kütüphanesi." *İlgi* 17, no. 37 (1983): 13–17.

————. "İstanbul Vakıf Kütüphaneleri." *Vakıflar* 2 (1985): 51–70.

————. "Şehid Ali Paşa Kütüphanesi," *TKDB* 33 (1984): 132–148.

————. "Kütüphanelerde Aydınlatma, Kandiller ve Tavana Asılı Diğer Semboller." *Folklor, Halkbilim Dergisi* 4, nos. 2–3 (1984): 47–50.

Kürkçüoğlu, Kemal Edib. *Süleymaniye Vakfiyesi*. Ankara: Vakıflar Umum Müdürlüğü, 1962.

Kütükoğlu, Mübahat. "1869'da Faal İstanbul Medreseleri." *Tarih Enstitüsü Dergisi*, no. 7–8 (1977): 277–392.

Latîfî. *Tezkiretü'ş-Şu'arâ ve Tabsıratü'n-Nuzamâ*. Edited by Rıdvan Canım. Ankara: Atatürk Kültür Merkezi Başkanlığı, 2000.

Levend, Agah Sırrı. *Gazavatnameler*. Ankara: Türk Tarih Kurumu, 1956.

Lewis, Bernard. *The Muslim Discovery of Europe*. New York: W. W. Norton, 1982.

Lowry, Heath W. *Trabzon Şehrinin İslamlaşma ve Türkleşmesi*. Translated by Demet and Heath Lowry. 2nd ed. İstanbul: Boğaziçi Üniversitesi Matbaası, 1998.

Oral, M. Zeki. "Mevcut Vesikalara Göre Burdur Kütüphaneleri ve Kitap Vakfiyeleri." *Belleten* 24, no. 94 (1960): 233–261.

Mahmud Cevad İbnü'ş-Şeyh Nâfi. *Maarif-i Umumiye Nezareti, Tarihçe-i Teşkilatı ve İcraatı*. İstanbul: Matbaa-i Amire, 1338H.

Maróth, Miklós. "The Library of Sultan Bayezid II." In *Irano-Turkic Cultural Contacts*, edited by Eva M. Jeremiàs, 111–132. Piliscsaba: Avicenna Institute of Middle Eastern Studies, 2003.

Masry, Ahmed M. *Die Bauten von Hâdim Sulaimân Pascha (1468–1548)*. Berlin: Klaus Schwarz, 1991.

Meclis-i Meb'usân Zabıt Ceridesi. Devre 1, İctima Senesi 2, vol. 6. Ankara: TBMM Basımevi, 1986.

Meclis-i Meb'usanın Yüzsekizinci İctimâ Zabıtnamesi, Takvim-i Vekayi' Year 2, no. 544 (18 May 1326R).

Mehmed II Vakfiyeleri. Ankara: Vakıflar Umum Müdürlüğü Neşriyatı, 1938.

Mehmed Süreyya. *Sicill-i Osmanî*. 4 vols. İstanbul: Matbaa-i Amire, 1308–1315 H.

Meriç, R. Melül. "II. Sultan Bayezid Zamanı Binaları, Mimarları, Sanat Eserleri ve Sanatkarları." *Yıllık Araştırmalar Dergisi* 2 (1958): 5–76.

Meservey, Sabra F. "Feyzullah Efendi: An Ottoman Şeyhülislam." PhD diss., Princeton University, 1966.

Minorsky, V. *A Catalogue of the Turkish Manuscripts and Miniatures*. Dublin: Hodges Figgis, 1958.

Muallim Cevdet. *Zeyl ala fasli'l-ahiyyeti'-fityâni't-Türkiyye fi Rıhleti İbni Batuta*. İstanbul: Kurtuluş, 1932.

Muhammed bin Abdülvehhâb el-Miknâsî. *Rıhletü'l-Miknâsî 1785*. Abu Dhabi: n.p, 2003.

Müderrisoğlu. Mehmed Emin, *Akhisarlı Türk Büyükleri ve Eserleri*. İzmir: Piyasa Matbaası, 1956.

Nayır, Zeynep. "İstanbul Haseki'de Bayram Paşa Külliyesi." In *Ord. Prof. İsmail Hakkı Uzunçarşılı'ya Armağan*, 397–410. Ankara: Türk Tarih Kurumu, 1976.

Neşrî, *Kitâb-ı Cihânnümâ*. Vol. 1. Edited by Faik Reşit Unat and Mehmed A. Köymen. Ankara: Türk Tarih Kurumu Basımevi, 1949.

Numani, Şibli. *Anadolu, Suriye ve Mısır Seyahatnamesi*. Translated by Yusuf Karaca. İstanbul: Risale, 2002.

Okiç, M. Tayyib. "Saraybosna Gazi Hüsrev Beğ Kütüphanesi Yazma Eserler Kataloğu." *İlahiyat Fakültesi Dergisi* 12 (1964): 143–154.

Orhonlu, Cengiz. "Fındıklı Semtinin Tarihi Hakkında Bir Araştırma." *TD* 7, no. 10 (1954): 61–78.

Osmanzâde Tâ'ib. *Hadikatü'l-Vüzerâ*. İstanbul: n.p., 1271H.

Öcalan, Hasan Basri. *Bursa'da Tasavvuf Kültürü*. Bursa: Gaye Kitabevi, 2000.

Öz, T. *Zwei Stiftungsurkunden des Sultan Mehmed II, Fatih.* İstanbul: n.p., 1935.

Özalp, Tahsin. *Sivrihisar Tarihi.* Eskişehir: Tam-İş Matbaası, 1960.

Özcan, Abdülkadir. "Kanuni Devri Vezirlerinden Sofu Mehmed Paşa'ya ve Sofya'daki Külliyesine Dâir." In *Balkanlar'da İslam Medeniyeti Milletlerarası Sempozyumu Tebliğleri, Sofya 21–23 Nisan 2000,* edited by Ali Çaksu; Ekmeleddin İhsanoğlu, 267–276. İstanbul: IRCICA, 2002).

Özdoğan, Kazım. *Kayseri Tarihi.* Kayseri: Kayseri Erciyes Matbaası, 1948.

Özkaya, Yücel. "Anadoludaki Büyük Hanedanlıklar." *Belleten* 56, no. 217 (1992): 809–845.

Özoran, Beria Remzi. "Kıbrıs'ta Sultan Mahmut Kütüphanesi." *Türk Kültürü* 8, no. 92 (1970): 513–515.

Öztürk, Nazif. *Türk Yenileşme Tarihi Çerçevesinde Vakıf Müessesesi.* Ankara: Türkiye Diyanet Vakfı, 1995.

Pamuk, Ş. *A Monetary History of the Ottoman Empire*: Cambridge: Cambridge University Press, 2000.

Parmaksızoğlu, İsmet. *Kıbrıs Sultan İkinci Mahmud Kütüphanesi.* Ankara: Türk Kütüphaneciler Derneği, 1964.

———. "Manisa Kütüphaneleri." *TKDB* 8, no. 1 (1959): 17–22.

———. "Türk Kütüphanelerinde Gelişmeler." *TKDB* 22, no. 2 (1974): 87–93.

Patrick, Mary Mills. *Under Five Sultans.* London: Williams and Norgate, 1930.

Peremeci, Osman Nuri. *Tuna Boyu Tarihi.* İstanbul: Resimli Ay Matbaası, 1942.

Polat, İlhan. "Osmanlı İmparatorluğu Devrinde Yugoslavya'da Kurulan Türk Kütüphaneleri." Graduate thesis, Dil ve Tarih-Coğrafya Fakültesi, Kütüphanecilik Bölümü, University of Ankara, 1969.

———. "Saray-Bosna'da Gazi Hüsrev Bey Kütüphanesi." *TKDB* 18, no. 4 (1969): 244–248.

Rahimov, Ebulfez. "Safevîlerin Türkiye'ye Hediye Gönderdiği Kitaplar." *Türk Kültürü* 33, no. 386 (1995): 344–352.

Râşid Tarihi. Vol. IV. İstanbul: Matbaa-i Amire, 1282H.

Reyhanlı, Tülay. "Osmanlılarda Külliye Mimarisinin Gelişmesi." PhD diss., Istanbul University, 1974.

Roper, Geoffrey. "Ahmad Fâris al-Shidyaq and the Libraries of Europe and the Ottoman Empire." *Libraries & Culture* 33, no. 3 (Summer, 1998): 233–248.

Sarıcaoğlu, Fikret. *Kendi Kaleminden Bir Padişahın Portresi, Sultan I, Abdülhamid (1774–1789).* İstanbul: Tatav, Tarih ve Tabiat Vakfı, 2001.

Sayılı, Aydın. "Alauddin Mansur'un İstanbul Rasathanesi Hakkındaki Şiirleri." *Belleten* 20, no. 79 (1956): 411- 428.

Sefercioğlu, Necmettin. "Union Catalogs in Turkey in the Nineteenth Century." In *Ankara Üniversitesi, Dil ve Tarih-Coğrafya Fakültesi Kütüphanecilik Bölümü XXV. Yıl Anı Kitabı (1954–55/1979–1980)*, 91–101. Ankara: Ankara Üniversitesi Basımevi, 1981.

Sehi Bey. *Heşt Behişt*. Edited by Günay Kut. Cambridge, MA: Harvard University Press, 1978.

Sevgi, Ahmet. "Nedim'in Nevşehir İle İlgili Tarihleri Üzerine." *Yedi İklim* 4, no. 36 (1993): 29.

Sezgin, Fuad. "Âtıf Efendi Vakfiyesi." *İ. Ü. Edebiyat Fakültesi, Türk Dili ve Edebiyatı Dergisi* 6 (1955): 132–144.

Shatzmiller, Maya. "Islamic Institutions and Property Rights: The Case of the Public Waqf." *JESHO* 44, no. 1 (2001): 44–74.

Shaw, Stanford J. *History of Ottoman Empire and Modern Turkey*. Vol. 1. Cambridge: Cambridge University Press, 1976.

Soysal, Özer. "Cumhuriyet Öncesi Dönemi Türk Kütüphaneciliği." Habilitation thesis, Ankara University, 1973.

———. *Türk Kütüphaneciliği: Geleneksel Yapıdan Yeniden Yapılanışa*. 6 vols. Ankara: T. C. Kültür Bakanlığı, Kütüphaneler Genel Müdürlüğü, 1998.

Sözen, Metin. *Türk Mimarisinin Gelişimi ve Mimar Sinan*. İstanbul: Türkiye İş Bankası, 1975.

Spies, O. "Die Bibliotheken des Hidschas." *ZDMG* 90 (1936): 96–98.

Stajnova, Mihaila. "Ottoman Libraries in Vidin." *Etudes Balkaniques*, no. 2 (1979): 54–69.

———. *Osmanskite biblioteki v bulgarskite zemi XV-XIX vek. Studii*. Sofia: NBKM, 1982.

Stanley, Tim. "The Books of Umur Bey." *Muqarnas* 21 (2004): 323–331.

Stavrides, Theoharis. *The Sultan of Vezirs: The Life and Time of the Ottoman Grand Vezir Mahmud Paşa Angeloviç (1453–1474)*. Leiden: E. J. Brill, 2001.

Subhi. *Tarih*. İstanbul: Raşid Mehmed Efendi Matbaası, 1198H.

Şahin, Alime. "İstanbul'daki Osmanlı Dönemi Kütüphane Yapıları Üzerine Bir Araştırma ve Hacı Beşir Ağa Kütüphanesi." MA thesis, Yıldız Teknik Üniversitesi, 1997.

Şehsuvaroğlu, B. N. *İstanbul'da 500 Yıllık Sağlık Hayatımız*. İstanbul: İstanbul Fethi Derneği Neşriyatı, 1953.

Şemdanîzâde Fındıklılı Süleyman Efendi Tarihi, Mür'i't-Tevârih. Vol 2a. Edited by M. Münir Aktepe. İstanbul: Edebiyat Fakültesi Matbaası, 1978.

Tâcü't-Tevârih. Vols. 1–2. İstanbul: Matbaa-i Amire, 1279H.

Tamer, Vehbi. "Fatih Devri Ricalinden Ishak Paşa'nın Vakfiyeleri ve Vakıfları." *VD* 4 (1958): 107–124.

Tanındı, Zeren. "Bibliophile Aghas (Eunuchs) at Topkapı Sarayı." *Muqarnas* 21 (2004): 333–343.

Tanman, M. Baha. "İstanbul'un Ortadan Kalkan Tarihî Eserlerinden Fındıklı'da Hatuniye Külliyesi." In *Prof. Dr. Yılmaz Önge Armağanı*, 139–161. Konya: Selçuk Üniversitesi, 1993.

Tarih-i Atâ. Vol. 1. İstanbul: Yahya Efendi Matbaası, 1291H.

Tarih-i Cevdet. vol. 2. İstanbul: Matbaa-i Osmaniye, 1309H.

Tarih-i İsmail Asım Efendi. İstanbul: Matbaa-i Amire, 1283H.

Tarih-i Peçevî. Vol. 1. İstanbul: Matbaa-i Amire, 1283H.

Taşköprîzâde. *eş-Şeka'ikü'n-Nu'maniyye.* Edited by Ahmed Subhi Furat. İstanbul: Edebiyat Fakültesi Basımevi, 1985.

Tayşi, Mehmed Serhan. "Şeyhülislam Seyyid Feyzullah Efendi ve Feyziye Medresesi." *Türk Dünyası Araştırmaları*, no. 23 (1983): 9–100.

Tekin, Şinasi. "1729 Yılında Vakfedilmiş Bir İstanbul Medresesinin Öğretim ve İdare Kadrosu Hakkında." *Türk Kültürü* 6, no. 71 (1968): 836–839.

———. "Binbir Gece'nin İlk Türkçe Tercümeleri ve Hikayelerdeki Gazeller Üzerine." *Türk Dilleri Araştırmaları*, no. 3 (1993): 239–255.

Tekindağ, Ş. "İstanbul; Şehrin İmar ve İskanı." *İA* 5, no. 2 (1993): 1205.

———. "Medrese Dönemi." *Cumhuriyetin 50. Yılında İstanbul Üniversitesi.* İstanbul: İstanbul Üniversitesi, 1979.

Tezkire-i Latifî. İstanbul: İkdam Matbaası, 1314H.

Tietze, A. *Mustafa Ali's Counsel for Sultans of 1581.* Vienna: Verlag der Oesterreichischen Akademie der Wissenschaften, 1979.

Toderini, G. *De la litterature des Turcs, traduit de l'Italien en Français par l'Abbe de Cournand.* Vol. 2. Paris: Chez Poinçot, 1789.

Treasures of Knowledge: An Inventory of the Ottoman Palace Library (1502/3-1503/4). Edited by Gülru Necipoğlu, Cemal Kafadar, and Cornell Fleischer. Leiden - Boston: Brill, 2019.

Truhelka, Ciro. "Dubrovnik Arşivinde Türk-İslâm Vesikaları." *İstanbul Enstitüsü Dergisi* 1 (1955): 39–68.

et-Tunisî, Hammadî Ali Muhammed. "el-Mektebâtü'l-âmme bi'l-Medineti'l-Münevvere, mâdihâ ve hâzirihâ." MA thesis, King Abdülaziz University, Jiddah 1981.

Turan, Şerafettin. "Sinan Paşa." *İA* 10 (1940–1986): 674.

Turgut Kut's Private Archive, Library Files.

Tüccarzâde İbrahim Hilmi. *Maarifimiz ve Servet-i Milliyemiz Felâketlerimizin Esbâbı.* İstanbul: Kitabhane-yi İslâm ve Askerî, 1329H.

Türek, Ahmed İhsan. "Ragıp Paşa Kütüphanesi Vakfiyesi." *Edebiyat Fakültesi Araştırma Dergisi* 1, no. 1 (1970): 65–78.

Türkay, Cevdet. "İstanbul Kütüphaneleri," *Belgelerle Türk Tarihi Dergisi* 13, nos. 74–76 (1974): 69–74.

———. "İstanbul Kütüphaneleri." *Belgelerle Türk Tarihi Dergisi* 12, no. 69 (1973): 30–35.

Türkoğlu, Sabahattin. *Ayasofya'nın Öyküsü,* İzmir: Yazıcı Basım, 2002.

Ubicini, M. A. *Letters on Turkey.* Translated from the French by Lady Easthope. London: W. Clowes and Sons, 1856.

Uluç, Lale. "Ottoman Book Collectors and Illustrated Sixteenth Century Shiraz Manuscripts." *Revue des Mondes Musulmans et de la Méditerranée,* no. 87–88 (1999): 85–107.

Uluçay, Çağatay. *Padişahların Kadınları ve Kızları.* Ankara: Türk Tarih Kurumu Basımevi, 1980.

Uzluk, Feridun Nafız. *Fatih Devrinde Karaman Eyaleti Vakıfları Fihristi.* Ankara: Doğuş Matbaası, 1958.

Uzunçarşılı, İsmail Hakkı. *Kitabeler.* İstanbul: Devlet Matbaası, 1929.

———. *Osmanlı Devletinin İlmiye Teşkilatı.* Ankara: Türk Tarih Kurumu Basımevi, 1965.

———. *Osmanlı Devletinin Merkez ve Bahriye Teşkilatı.* Ankara: Türk Tarih Kurumu Basımevi, 1948.

———. *Osmanlı Devletinin Saray Teşkilatı.* Ankara: Türk Tarih Kurumu Basımevi, 1945.

———. *Osmanlı Tarihi.* Vol. 1. Ankara: Türk Tarih Kurumu Basımevi, 1972.

———. *Osmanlı Tarihi.* Vol. 2. Ankara: Türk Tarih Kurumu Basımevi, 1972.

———. *Osmanlı Tarihi.* Vol. 4a. Ankara: Türk Tarih Kurumu Basımevi, 1978.

———. "Osmanlı Tarihinde Gizli Kalmış veya Şüphe ile Örtülü Bazı Olaylar ve Bu Hususa Dair Vesikalar." *Belleten* 91, no. 163 (1977): 507–554.

———. "Sultan Korkut." *T.T.K. Belleten* 30, no. 120 (1966): 539–601.

Uzunçarşılıoğlu, İsmail Hakkı. *Kütahya Şehri.* İstanbul: Devlet Matbaası, 1932.

Ünsal, B. "Türk-Vakfı İstanbul Kütüphanelerinin Mimari Yöntemi." *VD* 28 (1984): 95–124.

Ünver, S. *Fatih Külliyesi ve Zamanı İlim Hayatı.* İstanbul: [Kader Basımevi], 1946.

———. "Mahmud Paşa Vakıfları ve Ekleri." *VD* 4 (1958): 65–76.

———. Archive in the Süleymaniye library, Ayasofya File.

————. *Fatih Aşhanesi Tevzi'nâmesi.* İstanbul: İstanbul Fetih Derneği, 1953.

————. "Fatih'in Tuğrasıyla Bir Kitap Vakfı Hakkında," *TKDB* 9, nos. 1–2 (1960): 7–9.

————. "İkinci Selim'e Kadar Osmanlı Hükümdarlarının Hususi Kütüphaneleri Hakkında." *IV. Türk Tarih Kongresi* (1952): 294–312.

————. *İstanbul Rasathanesi.* Ankara: Türk Tarih Kurumu Basımevi, 1965.

————. "Sadrazam Karamanlı Mehmed Paşa'nın Eyüp Sultan Medresesi Kütüphanesine Vakfettiği Iki Kitaba Dair." *Konya*, no. 74–77 (1945): 3–4.

————. *Tıp Tarihimiz Yıllığı.* İstanbul: İstanbul Üniversitesi Tıp Fakültesi, 1966.

Vâsıf Tarihi. Vol. 1. Cairo: Bulak, 1246H.

Volney, C. *Travels Through Syria and Egypt, in the Years 1783, 1784 and 1785.* Vol. 2. London: G. G. J. and J. Robinson, 1788.

von Diez, Heinrich Friedrich. *Denkwürdigkeiten von Asien in Künsten und Wissenschaften, Sitten, Gebräuchen und Alterthümen, Religion und Regierungverfassung aus Handschriften und eigenen Erfahrungen.* Berlin: n.p., 1811.

Vryonis, Speros. "Byzantine Constantinople and Ottoman Istanbul." In *The Ottoman City and Its Parts: Urban Structure and Social Order*, edited by Irene A. Bierman and Rifa'at A. Abou-el-Haj, 13–52. New York: A. D. Caratzas, 1991.

Walpole, Robert. *Memoirs Relating to European and Asiatic Turkey, Edited from Manuscript Journals, by Robert Walpole.* London: Longman & Co., 1817.

Wittek, P. "Ankara Bozgunundan İstanbulun Zaptına" [trans. Halil İnalcık]. *Belleten* 7, no. 27 (1943): 557–589.

Yenal, Şükrü. "Topkapı Sarayı Müzesi Enderun Kitaplığı." *Güzel Sanatlar* 6 (1949): 85–90.

Yiğitbaşı, Süleyman Sükutî. *Eğridir-Felekâbâd Tarihi.* İstanbul: Çeltüt Matbaacılık, 1972.

Yücel, Erdem, "Amcazâde Hüseyin Paşa Külliyesi." *VD* 8 (1969): 249–266.

Yüksel, İ., Aydın. "Sadrazam Rüstem Paşa'nın Vakıfları." In *Ekrem Hakkı Ayverdi Hatıra Kitabı*, 219–281. İstanbul: İstanbul Fetih Cemiyeti, 1995.

Yüksel, Murat. "Kara Timurtaşoğlu Umur Bey'in Bursa'da Vakfettiği Kitaplar ve Vakıf Kayıtları." *Türk Dünyası Araştırmaları* 31 (1984): 134–147.

Zirozeviç, Olga. "Prizren Şehri," In *XI. Türk Tarih Kongresi, Kongreye Sunulan Bildiriler*, vol. 5, 2115–2123. Ankara: Türk Tarih Kurumu Basımevi, 1994.

Index

CPSIA information can be obtained
at www.ICGtesting.com
Printed in the USA
JSHW060802060822
28790JS00001B/17

9 781644 698624